JOHN *the* BAPTIST *and Jesus*

THE
JESUS
SEMINAR

PUBLISHED VOLUMES

Robert W. Funk, with Mahlon H. Smith. *The Gospel of Mark*: *Red Letter Edition*.
Robert W. Funk, et al. *The Parables of Jesus: Red Letter Edition*.
W. Barnes Tatum. *John the Baptist and Jesus. A Report of the Jesus Seminar*.

JOHN *the* BAPTIST *and Jesus*

A report of the Jesus Seminar

W. BARNES TATUM

Polebridge Press   *Sonoma, CA*

On the cover, close-up of the sarcophagus of Santa Maria Antiqua, with a view of the baptism of Jesus. Photograph courtesy of Graydon F. Synder.

Library of Congress Cataloging-in-Publication Data

Jesus Seminar (1991 Oct. 24-27 : Edmonton, Alta.)
    John the Baptist and Jesus : a report of the Jesus Seminar / W. Barnes Tatum.
        p.   cm.
    Results of the meetings of the Jesus Seminar held in Edmonton, Alta., Oct. 24-27, 1991, and in Santa Rosa, Calif., Feb. 27-Mar. 1, 1992.
    Includes bibliographical references (pp. 181–82) and index.
    ISBN 0-944344-42-9 : $17.95
    1. John, the Baptist, Saint–Congresses. 2. Jesus Christ–Words-
-Congresses. I. Tatum, W. Barnes. II. Jesus Seminar (1992 Feb.
27-Mar. 1 : Santa Rosa, Calif.) III. Title.
BS2456.J47   1991
232.9'.4—dc20   93-49378
                                                                                          CIP

Printed in the United States of America

10   9   8   7   6   5   4   3   2   1

Contents

Cameo Essays and Illustrations

ACKNOWLEDGEMENTS

This volume constitutes a report of the Jesus Seminar.

I am therefore indebted in varying ways to all participants in that ongoing forum, but especially to those who were active in the sessions dedicated to our collective study of the one who preceded Jesus—John the so-called Baptist or Baptizer.

Robert W. Funk, founder of the Jesus Seminar and Westar Institute its sponsoring organization, and Mahlon H. Smith of Rutgers University were instrumental in organizing the Seminar sessions. Several members of the Seminar prepared papers on John the Baptist for circulation, presentation, and discussion. Appendix B lists their names and the topics of their papers, as well as the roster of Fellows for the Jesus Seminar.

Two of those whose names and papers are included in Appendix B call for special comment: Walter Wink and Robert L. Webb. Both have published monographs on John the Baptist. Wink's book appeared as *John the Baptist in the Gospel Tradition* (SNTS MS, 7; Cambridge: University Press, 1968). Webb's work was published as *John the Baptizer and Prophet: A Socio-Historical Study* (JSNT SS 62; Sheffield: JSOT Press, 1991). Wink's volume remains the definitive redaction-critical study of the way the individual gospel writers have shaped their presentations of John. Webb acknowledges his indebtedness to Wink in his review of the portrayals of John in each gospel. His own volume represents the most recent comprehensive historical reconstruction of John's ministry in its social setting. One of the distinguishing marks of Webb's monograph is its judicious use not only of Christian sources but of the characterization of John in the writings of Flavius Josephus, the Jewish historian.

The contributions of Wink and Webb to the collaborative work of the Seminar were considerable. As the author of this work on John the Baptist, I have also been nurtured by their more extensive writings. My indebtedness herein to the work of Wink will be most evident in PART TWO where I summarize the portrayal of John in the individual gospels. My indebtedness to the work of Webb will appear at a number of points in PART THREE where I discuss issues related to John as a historical figure. Particularly helpful were his discussion of the agricultural image employed in the saying of John reported in Luke 3:17 and Matthew 3:12, and his analysis of the political threat posed by John to Herod Antipas.

My objective as the author of this volume on John the Baptist, however, has been to represent as accurately as possible the range of views about John which surfaced among *all* the members of the Seminar, although I too was an active participant. I have attempted to explain the reasons underlying the collective judgment of the Seminar about this item or that point. I hope the effort to communicate complex issues simply and understandably does not result in misrepresentation.

The texts of the gospels reproduced in this volume on John the Baptist represent the translation known as the Scholars Version (SV) published under the editorship of Robert J. Miller: *The Complete Gospels: Annotated Scholars Version* (Polebridge: Sonoma, CA, 1992). Most of the panel of translators and contributors have been active in the work of the Jesus Seminar. The texts from the Pseudo-Clementine and the Mandaean literature represent the translation work of F. Stanley Jones, also a member of the Jesus Seminar. The texts from Josephus were translated by Robert L. Webb and Robert W. Funk.

So far as I am aware, this is the *only* volume devoted to John the Baptist that makes available between the same book covers virtually all the principal early texts that provide information about John. The readers can conveniently examine these texts for themselves. This volume also sets John within broader cultural contexts, both ancient and modern, in a series of brief cameo essays.

I am indebted to Greensboro College, Greensboro, NC, for supporting both my ongoing involvement in the Jesus Seminar and my writing of this report. Annually since 1988, I have received grants for travel to, and participation in, the sessions of the Jesus Seminar from the Royce and Jane Reynolds Faculty Development Fund. During the summer of 1992, I received a Kathleen Price and Joseph M. Bryan Family Foundation Summer Fellowship which enabled me to begin the writing process in Sonoma, California, the home of the Westar Institute. Also, Mrs. Gay Shepherd, the reference/interlibrary loan librarian of the James Addison Jones Library at Greensboro College has been of great assistance in securing journal articles and monographs used in the writing of this report.

W. Barnes Tatum

The Scholars Version

The Scholars Version (SV) represents a new translation, not a revision, of the Bible. Only the gospels portion of the translation has appeared in print: *The Complete Gospels: Annotated Scholars Version* (1992). Since the translation has been undertaken independently of any ecclesiastical sponsorship, or control, the gospels volume includes many more than just the traditional four gospels.

Translations of the Bible into any language should, of course, be made from the original languages of those writings. Most of the gospels, including Matthew, Mark, Luke, and John, were first written in Greek. Most of those survived in Greek manuscripts from the earliest centuries. Others, such as the gospel of Thomas, have survived only in translation. Thomas has been preserved in its entirety only in Coptic, the language of ancient Egypt written in characters based on the Greek alphabet. Insofar as possible, the translators of the SV worked with original language manuscripts as the basis for their renderings into English.

The SV translators intentionally use the English language as spoken and written in North America. They do not follow the English phraseology of any other Bibles. They have attempted to remain faithful to the meaning of the original languages, but without repeating words and phrases that have lost their freshness.

This means that the Scholars Version is truly a new translation. As such, it belongs with other new translations such as the *New English Bible* (1970), the *New American Bible* (1970), and the *New International Version* (1978). Like these versions, the SV ignores the translation tradition represented by the *King James Version* (1611), the *Revised Standard Version* (1952), and the *New Revised Standard Version* (1989).

The gospel texts related to John the Baptist that are reproduced and cited in this book contain several words and expressions that reflect the distinctive phraseology of the SV. The most important turns of phrase are these:

Scholars Version	Traditional Translation
good news	gospel
Anointed	Christ
God's imperial rule, or God's domain	kingdom of God
Heaven's imperial rule, or Heaven's domain	kingdom of heaven
son of Adam	Son of man
Judeans	Jews
change of heart, or change of ways	repentance

Brief comments on these translation equivalents are in order.

The Greek word *euangelion* literally means "good news." The word was first used to refer to a message rather than a book. The choice of "good news" rather than "gospel" avoids this confusion (as in Mark 1:1,14).

The Greek word *christos* literally means "anointed." In turn the Greek *christos*, was itself a literal translation of the Hebrew *mashiah* which also meant "anointed." *Mashiah* comes into English as the similar sounding word "messiah." *Christos*, comes into English as "Christ" and often appears to be the last name of Jesus in the phrase "Jesus Christ" (again as in Mark 1:1). Originally, however, it was a title of honor meaning "the Anointed" (as Mark 8:29).

Throughout the gospels of Matthew, Mark, and Luke, the message of Jesus is summarized or epitomized by the Greek phrase *basileia tou theou*, "kingdom of God," although Matthew prefers the phrase *basileia tōn ouranōn*, "kingdom of heaven" (compare Mark 1:14–15 with Matt 4:17). "Kingdom" seems archaic and has spatial meaning whereas in Jesus' message the word often denotes more of an activity than a place. "Imperial rule" was used for those passages in which the phrase suggests an activity; but "domain" was adopted for those passages which require a spatial meaning.

Also, throughout the gospels of Matthew, Mark, and Luke, the Greek phrase *ho huios tou anthrōpou*, "the son of man" appears on Jesus' own lips seemingly as his own personal self-designation (as in Mark 8:31). The issues related to the different uses and the varied background to this phrase are very complicated. But *anthrōpos* in Greek means not a male, but a human being, as in the English word anthropology, the study of human beings, male and female. The Hebrew word *adam* also means a human being, neither man nor female (although it became the personal name of the first human Adam). In the SV, therefore, Jesus speaks of "the son of Adam."

The Greek expression word *Ioudaios* becomes the basis for the designation of those people who practice the religion known today as Judaism. Ultimately, the expression was derived from the Hebrew term which designated those who belonged to the Israelite tribe of Judah, and later those who inhabited the territory of Judea. The gospel of John often uses this expression to designate those who appear in dialogue with John and in opposition to Jesus (so John 1:19; 3:25). The SV uses the term "Judean" or "Judeans" to designate those who followed the precepts of Judaism during the period of the second temple, from ca 520 B.C.E. to 70 C.E. The word "Jew," therefore, is reserved for those who practice the teachings of the rabbis after the fall of Jerusalem in 70 C.E.

In the gospels of Matthew, Mark, and Luke, the message of John (Mark 1:4) and sometimes the message of Jesus (Matt 4:17) is characterized by a call for "repentance." The Greek verb *metanoeō*, and the related noun form, literally means "a change of mind." The Hebrew verb *shub*, presupposed by the Greek, has more to do with a reversal of direction. That repentance involves more than a change of mind is suggested in the SV by the phrases "change of heart" or "change of ways."

In quest of
JOHN *the*
BAPTIST

Scholarship is both cumulative and collaborative.
Scholars advance knowledge in their fields and sub-fields, and even across fields, by building upon the results of those who have gone before them: in physics, biology, sociology, psychology, history, linguistics, and so on. Scholars also interact with one another and even work together. Professional literature, learned societies, and research projects provide formal avenues for collaboration.

In the academic study of religion and in biblical studies, there are also cumulative and collaborative dimensions. In what follows, however, collaboration takes on a more intensive form. Here collaboration involves both face-to-face working sessions and a procedure for collective decision-making about specific items on the agenda. We will pursue this matter under three rubrics: collaborative biblical scholarship; the collaborative work of the Jesus Seminar; and the work of the Jesus Seminar in its deliberations about John the Baptist.

Collaborative biblical scholarship

Virtually all the English language versions of the Bible circulating today represent the fruit of collaborative scholarship, rather than the offspring of a solitary scholar's labor. The most recent major translation, *The New Revised Standard Version* (*NRSV*, 1989), required the collective efforts of the Standard Bible Committee, with Bruce M. Metzger as Chair, under the auspices of the National Council of Churches. The collaborative process has been documented in a lively volume written by three members of the committee: Bruce M. Metzger, Robert C. Dentan, and Walter Harrelson, *The Making of the New Revised Standard Version of the Bible* (Grand Rapids: Eerdmans, 1991).

At the time of the *NRSV*'s publication, the ecumenical committee was

1

comprised of thirty members. The work of revising the *RSV* (1952) proceeded over a fifteen-year period with occasional week-long meetings. The working sessions of the Old and New Testament Committees, and the subgroups, included both group discussion and decisions about specific readings. If a consensus could not be reached, votes were taken and a simple majority ruled.

In verbal and written comment about the *NRSV*, members of the committee have observed that many readings do not represent what one or more of their colleagues would have preferred. Such is the nature of collaborative scholarship!

This sketch of the organization and work of the committee which produced the *NRSV* could be duplicated with reference to those translation committees responsible for other English versions in the last half of the 20th century. *The New International Version* (*NIV*, 1978), sponsored by the New York Bible Society International, was the translation work of scholars representing an evangelical view of Scripture as infallible or inerrant. *The New American Bible* (NAB, 1970), a Catholic-sponsored translation, was initiated by the Bishops' Committee of Christian Doctrine, which delegated responsibility for the work to the Catholic Biblical Association. *The New English Bible* (NEB, 1970), initiated by five Protestant denominations in Great Britain, relied on a translation committee comprised of the leading Biblical scholars of the realm.

The model for collaborative translation work in this century was established nearly four centuries ago. In January, 1604, at the conference convened by him at Hampton Court, King James I agreed that another translation of the Bible into English should be undertaken in an attempt to reconcile competing religious parties. The result was the *King James Version* (1611), a distant ancestor of the *RSV* (1952) and the *NRSV* (1989). Records have survived which preserve the names of forty-six translators and the workings of the six so-called companies into which they were divided. Two of the companies met at Westminster, two at Oxford, and two at Cambridge. The procedural guidelines required the checking and rechecking of the work done within each company and each company's reviewing the work of the others.

English language Bibles, of course, are translations from the Hebrew Scriptures—for most of the Old Testament—and from Greek manuscripts for the New. But which Greek manuscripts for the New?

None of the so-called autographs of the New Testament, the original documents, have survived. In fact the oldest manuscripts in Greek of the entire NT date from the 4th and 5th centuries. Therefore, translators of the NT do not use any one manuscript; they employ a composite critical text. Scholars painstakingly study all the available manuscripts and then, on a reading-by-reading basis, decide what must have been in the original 1st century document. Unlike Humpty-Dumpty, the original Greek NT text is put back together again; but textual scholars perform this reconstructive procedure, not all the king's horses and all the king's men. Many translators themselves are not only linguists but textual critics.

Traditionally, printed critical texts of the Greek New Testament have been the work of an individual scholar, or two. The critical texts popular in this century have often carried the names of their originators: Tischendorf, von Soden, Souter, Nestle (later Nestle-Aland), and Westcott and Hort. Probably the most widely used critical text in this country in recent years has been the third edition of the *Greek New Testament* (1975) published by the United Bible Societies. Unlike many of its predecessors, this influential volume represents the product of collaborative scholarship.

The committee discussed the variant readings for specific texts in group meetings. The members voted individually on preferences for particular readings. There were majority and minority opinions about which readings to adopt for the reconstructed text and which readings to list as variants in the footnotes, the critical apparatus. On behalf of the entire committee, Bruce M. Metzger—himself a member—published a report of the work behind the third edition even before the edition appeared: *A Textual Commentary on the Greek New Testament* (London-New York: United Bible Societies, 1971).

In the United Bible Societies' third edition, the collective judgment of the committee about individual readings is indicated in the footnotes at the bottom of each page—in the critical apparatus itself. The symbols A, B, C, and D are used to indicate the levels of certainty about specific readings:

> A   virtually certain
> B   some degree of doubt
> C   a considerable degree of doubt
> D   a very high degree of doubt.

This graded scale can be illustrated by citing the readings for the very first reference to John the Baptist in the gospel of Mark. An English translation of the Greek text, not the text in Greek, will be used.

The Greek reading adopted for the original text of Mark 1:4 can be translated:

> John the Baptizer appeared in the wilderness
> and preaching a baptism of repentance
> for the forgiveness of sins.

Several variant readings for Mark 1:4 occur in other manuscripts. The variants in the apparatus can be translated:

> John the Baptizer appeared in the wilderness,
> preaching a baptism of repentance
> for the forgiveness of sins.

John appeared baptizing in the wilderness
and preaching a baptism of repentance
for the forgiveness of sins.

John appeared in the wilderness baptizing
and preaching a baptism of repentance
for the forgiveness of sins.

John appeared in the wilderness
and preaching a baptism of repentance
for the forgiveness of sins.

The grade given in the critical apparatus for the adopted reading: C.
Therefore, the committee has expressed considerable doubt about the reading adopted as the Greek text for Mark 1:4. Certainly one reason for the
doubt lies in the manuscript evidence itself. Of four of the oldest Greek NT
manuscripts, each contains a different reading for this text. The uncertainty
by the committee about the original Greek reading for Mark 1:4 is also
reflected in the uncertainty among the translators of this verse into English
about which reading should be translated for their English versions. The
translation of Mark 1:4 in the *NIV*, for example, rests upon a Greek text
different from that translated in the *NEB* and the *NAB*.

Therefore, collaborative scholarship has expressed itself formally both in
the arena of biblical translation and in the sphere of NT textual criticism.
The quest of the historical Jesus, pursued now for two centuries, has been
moved forward by the intensive research and the published monographs
of individual scholars. Again personal names come to the fore: Reimarus,
Strauss, Renan, Weiss, Schweitzer, Case, Käsemann, Bornkamm, Sanders,
Borg, Crossan, and so on. The roll lengthens annually.

Many members of the Jesus Seminar have made individual contributions
to the ongoing quest of the historical Jesus. Their names have appeared on
the title pages of books. They have published articles in academic journals
related to who Jesus was and what he did. They have also participated with
one another, and with other scholars, in the sessions and seminars of
learned societies. But it is the Jesus Seminar itself that has taken collaborative scholarship into the arena of Jesus research in special ways. To
the story of the Jesus Seminar we now turn.

The Jesus Seminar

The first meeting of the Jesus Seminar convened March 21–24, 1985, in
Berkeley, California. On that occasion, the founder, Robert W. Funk, described the plan of the Seminar in these words:

> We intend to examine every fragment of the traditions attached to the
> name of Jesus in order to determine what he really said—not his literal

words, perhaps, but the substance and style of his utterances. We are in quest of his *voice*, insofar as it can be distinguished from many other voices also preserved in the tradition. We are prepared to bring to bear everything we know and can learn about the form and content, about the formation and transmission, of aphorisms and parables, dialogues and debates, attributed or attributable to Jesus, in order to carry out our task.

As articulated by Funk later, in his own written story of the Seminar, this plan grew out of his experience as a biblical scholar. After more than thirty years of teaching at the undergraduate, graduate, and seminary levels, he had decided to write his own book about Jesus. In order to undertake this task, Funk sought two scholarly aids. First, he tried to locate a "raw list" of all the sayings by, and all of the stories about, Jesus reported in ancient literature—both within and without the New Testament. Secondly, he looked for a "critical list" of those words and deeds generally considered, after two hundred years of scholarly sifting, to have been actually said and done by Jesus. Funk intended to use the latter list as the basis for his own work on Jesus as a historical figure. He discovered partial, but no exhaustive, lists of either kind.

Consequently, Funk decided to solicit help from others. He wrote to thirty colleagues inviting them to participate in an ongoing Seminar focusing specifically on the question: which of the reported sayings of Jesus can be considered to have been actually spoken by him? Funk then convened that first meeting of the Jesus Seminar in Berkeley and outlined his plan in the words cited above.

Since that initial gathering, the Jesus Seminar has met twice each year— in the fall and in the spring. Currently the site of the fall meeting changes from year to year; but every spring the participants gather in California, in Sonoma or a nearby site, as harbingers of the return of the swallows to Capistrano. Sonoma, not Capistrano, is the home of the Westar Institute, the sponsoring organization.

Also since that first meeting, the number of participants has expanded from the thirty Charter Fellows to include more than two hundred participants, about evenly divided between Fellows (specialists with appropriate formal academic expertise) and Associates (interested non-specialists). Membership in both categories was, and remains, open to everyone who would seek inclusion.

But back to beginnings. In support of the foundational question of what Jesus really said, several supporting questions had to be answered up front. Where would the Jesus Seminar get its "raw list" of Jesus' words for evaluation? How would the meetings be organized? How would voting be conducted? How would the results be tabulated? How would the resulting "critical list" of so-called "authentic" sayings of Jesus be made public?

The Seminar set to work compiling a list of all the sayings of Jesus attested in literature through the third century. Seminar member J. Dominic Crossan designed and edited what became *Sayings Parallels: A Workbook for the Jesus Tradition* (Fortress, 1985). This volume contained more than a thousand versions of 503 items attributed to Jesus. The sayings were grouped into four categories: parables; aphorisms; dialogues; and stories. The Seminar now had its "raw list." This workbook with the sayings of Jesus in English translation was to be used, of course, in conjunction with the corresponding texts in the original languages.

With the Crossan volume as the official workbook, the Seminar organized itself around agendas of material to be reviewed at the semiannual meetings. One particularly lively meeting, for example, centered around the controversial "Son of man," or "son of Adam," passages. Prior to the meetings themselves, members of the Seminar, with expertise related to the sayings on the agenda, prepared and circulated papers about those items. In this way, the meetings—usually Thursday evening through noon Sunday—became working sessions devoted to discussion and debate. The papers circulated were position papers. The preparers were expected to make recommendations to the Seminar with regard to each individual saying under consideration: was it the *voice* of Jesus, or not?

Funk himself proposed that a vote be taken on every saying in order to establish the consensus or collective judgment of the group. Furthermore, harking back to the red letter Bibles of his youth (which printed the words of Jesus in red), he thought that a particular saying could be labeled either red or black: red meaning that Jesus said something like that; or black, that he did not. Critical judgments, however, are seldom black and white, or even red and black. So the Seminar decided upon four categories: red, pink, gray, and black. As one member later explained, with humorous phrasing but serious intent, the colors could be understood thus:

> Red   That's Jesus!
> Pink   Sure sounds like Jesus.
> Gray   Well, maybe.
> Black There's been some mistake.

For dramatic effect, and good press, voting on individual items was conducted not only with paper ballots but by the dropping of the appropriately colored bead into a small ballot box. A weighted scale and formula were adopted to calculate mathematically the collective vote of the Seminar on each item and to translate that vote into the appropriate color. (For particulars, see Appendix A, "Voting Guidelines and Calculation.")

One means of making the results of the Seminar's work on the sayings of Jesus available to the academic community, and the public at large, is the

Red Letter Series. Given the color scheme adopted by the Seminar, of course, these would *not* be, strictly speaking, just red letter editions, but editions with the words of Jesus printed in any one of the four colors: red, pink, gray, or black. These volumes would contain not just the gospel text but commentary explaining the reasons behind the colors. The intention to publish a series of so-called red letter volumes is in the process of being realized. *The Parables of Jesus: Red Letter Edition* (Polebridge, 1988) and *The Gospel of Mark: Red Letter Edition* (Polebridge, 1991) have already appeared. Works on the other individual gospels are well under way.

Another intended means of making the results of the Seminar's work known to the public was through the public media, both electronic and print. Journalists often attended working sessions. Members of the Seminar were available for interviews. Literally hundreds of news reports and feature articles have appeared in weekly news magazines, various religious publications, and daily newspapers. Headlines about the Seminar have appeared from Los Angeles to New York City, from Toronto to Atlanta— and in the Shreveport (LA) *Journal* and the Enid (OK) *News and Eagle*. This public face of the Seminar was consistent with one of its original commitments to make Jesus scholarship known beyond the confines of the academy and the campus.

The 1991 spring meeting of the Jesus Seminar, in Sonoma, marked a significant occasion. The Seminar completed the plan outlined at Berkeley six years earlier. All 503 items attributed to Jesus in more than a thousand versions, as displayed in *Sayings Parallels*, had been reviewed. The collective judgment of the Seminar had been rendered on each item.

A comprehensive report summarizing the results could now be prepared. *The Five Gospels. The Search for the Authentic Words of Jesus* (New York: Macmillan, 1993) is that report. Included between these covers are text and commentary not only related to the canonical gospels of Matthew, Mark, Luke, and John, but to the non-canonical gospel of Thomas as well. If *Sayings Parallels* constituted a "raw list" of Jesus' sayings, *The Five Gospels* represents a "critical list" (to use Funk's original distinction). Certainly this critical list does *not* represent the scholarly consensus about the teachings of Jesus. But the list does represent the collective judgment of a diverse group of scholars who worked collaboratively for more than half a decade asking and answering, on a saying-by-saying basis, whether or not this word expressed the *voice* of Jesus. No doubt every participant in the Seminar disagrees as an individual with this conclusion or that. But, again, such is the nature of collaborative scholarship!

Already before the Sonoma meeting in 1991, however, there was a move afoot within the Seminar to shift the focus from Jesus' words to his deeds, from the sayings attributed to him to the stories told about him. To that enlargement of the task of the Jesus Seminar we now turn.

The Jesus Seminar as John Seminar

Most of the sayings attributed to Jesus were preserved for later generations within the narrative framework of the four canonical gospels: Matthew, Mark, Luke, and John. These gospels represent narrative testimonies to Jesus as the Christ. All four tell the story of Jesus as a story leading to death—his death on a Roman cross in Jerusalem.

The observation has often been made that the four gospels agree most closely with one another in their presentations of the events just prior to Jesus' death: his arrival in Jerusalem at Passover time; the conspiracy against him by the local authorities; his betrayal by Judas, one of his disciples; a final meal with his disciples on the evening of his arrest; his subsequent arrest; his appearance that same evening before Jewish authorities; his appearance the next morning before Roman authorities; and his resulting execution.

There is, however, commonality not just toward the end of the gospel narratives. There is also commonality at the beginning. All four gospels begin their narratives of Jesus' public activity with one who had appeared publicly prior to Jesus—one with whom Jesus had in some way, or ways, interacted. That is, at the very outset of the Jesus story stands a man named John.

As the Jesus Seminar anticipated shifting its focus from Jesus' words to his deeds, the decision was made to begin a review of gospel stories where the gospel narratives themselves begin: with John the so-called Baptist, or Baptizer. The Jesus Seminar, at least for a season, would become the John Seminar. John became the principal subject for the meetings at Edmonton, Alberta, October 24–27, 1991, and at Santa Rosa, California, February 27-March 1, 1992.

The general format of the first working sessions of the deeds phase of the Seminar remained as that format had been developed during the previous words phase. Prior to the meetings, individual members were asked to develop and to circulate position papers related to items on the agenda. (For a bibliography, see Appendix B, "Seminar Papers on John the Baptist/Roster of Fellows.") The sessions themselves involved discussion and, finally, voting. Again there were four voting options: red; pink; gray; and black. The same weighted scale and formula were used to determine the color representative of the Seminar's judgment.

With the transition from sayings to stories, from Jesus to John, three issues became of paramount importance. The first issue had to do with the need for a "raw list" of texts pertaining to John. The second issue involved the methodological question of how to assess these texts historically, particularly for the deeds of John. The third issue had to do with a redefinition of the meaning of the colors.

First, Mahlon Smith, who had assumed the initial leadership for the deeds phase of the Seminar, assembled an inventory of texts which might be used as literary evidence for John as a historical figure. The inventory included passages from the canonical and the extra-canonical gospels. The inventory also included the important passage about John from the writings of Flavius Josephus, the 1st century Jewish historian.

Secondly, Robert Funk tackled the thorny issue of methodology and procedure. Out of the two-hundred-year quest of the historical Jesus, a number of principles or criteria had been articulated and refined for assessing the historical worth of Jesus' sayings. Members of the Jesus Seminar had often appealed to these well-established criteria even as they, knowingly or unknowingly, developed and appealed to other principles as well. Over the many years of the quest, however, less explicit attention had been given to methodology for assessing the historical worth of the stories about Jesus.

Based on his own study and writing in the theory and criticism of narrative texts, Funk proposed that the narrative texts be reduced to *narrative statements*. Therefore, the voting of the Seminar would *not* be on the narratives themselves but on the statements derived from the narratives. (For guidelines to be used in the development and assessment of narrative statements, see Appendix C, "Rules of Procedure.")

Take, as an example, the story of Jesus' baptism as narrated in three of the canonical gospels: Mark 1:9–11 par. (The use of the abbreviation par, for parallel, indicates that the story or saying in Mark has parallels in Matthew and/or Luke. Here the story of Jesus' baptism also oppears in Matthew 3:13–17 and Luke 3:21–22.) Among the three accounts of Jesus' baptism are some rather interesting, and not insignificant, differences in detail. In Matthew, John and Jesus engage in a brief conversation; and the words spoken by the heavenly voice do not agree exactly with the words reported in Mark and Luke. In Luke, mention is made of Jesus' praying; and, most strikingly, John is not even mentioned in the story itself. These similar but diverse narratives were reduced to this narrative statement:

John baptized Jesus.

This statement became the focal point of the Seminar's discussion although, of course, the discussion required references to the written texts as literary evidence for the attested event. The position paper on John's baptism of Jesus, by Walter Wink, referred to this event as "almost certain" and put forward a recommendation for a red vote. In this instance, but certainly not in all cases, the recommendation made to the Seminar was upheld by the collective vote of the Seminar's members. It could be said with certainty that John [hereafter often referred to as JB] had baptized Jesus. The narrative statement could be colored RED.

The third issue, therefore, had to with the meaning of the four colors. The traditional red letter Bibles had colored only Jesus' words, not his deeds. Now equivocating words characteristic of historical reasoning and discourse came to be associated with the colors:

Red   Certainty.
Pink   Probability.
Gray   Possibility.
Black   Improbability.

In the development of narrative statements, a distinction was made between two different kinds of statements: *action* statements and *status* statements. Action statements have to do with activities and events. The narrative statement about JB's having baptized Jesus represents an action statement. Status statements, however, have to do with participants and setting. In these statements the phrase "there was" means that so and so existed at such a time and place that makes possible the appearance of the person or persons in the events being narrated.

To expand on the earlier example, for JB to have baptized Jesus two historical figures identified by those names must have existed. Status statements about John and Jesus would have read thus:

There was a person named John the Baptist (Baptizer).

There was a person named Jesus.

For the Seminar to have been certain that John baptized Jesus, it should be assumed that the Seminar was just as certain that two historical figures bearing these names actually existed. In fact, the Seminar did vote upon the two status statements listed above and the collective judgment was colored RED.

Voting Record on John

The Jesus Seminar as John Seminar voted on more than 100 different narrative statements related to John the Baptist. The same weighted scale and formula adopted for the sayings phase of the Seminar were used to calculate the collective vote on each narrative statement and to translate the vote into the appropriate color. (For details, see Appendix A, "Voting Guidelines and Calculation.")

These statements are gathered together and listered here *in the colors* appropriate for their degrees of historical probability. They are arranged in what might be called a biographical order—under main headings pertaining to the life of JB. The S or A before each statement indicates whether the statement is a status statement or an action statement.

THE HISTORICAL SETTING

Locale
S: The wilderness is the region around the Jordan River.

Participants
S: There were Jerusalemites and Judeans.
S: There were Pharisees and Sadducees.
S: There were toll collectors and soldiers.
S: There was a tetrarch named Herod Antipas.
S: There was a woman named Herodias, who was married to Herod's brother.
S: There were Essenes.
S: There was a Jewish Sect at Qumran.
S: The Jews at Qumran were Essenes.

BIRTH, FAMILY, AND UPBRINGING

S: There was a person named John the Baptizer (Baptist).
S: **JB was the son of a priest named Zechariah.**
S: **JB's mother was a woman named Elizabeth.**
S: JB was a priest.
S: JB was circumcised.

MINISTRY

Locale
S: JB appeared in the wilderness and moved about in the region around the Jordan River.

Style
S: JB was an ascetic.
S: JB lived on locusts and raw honey.
S: JB dressed in camel hair.
S: JB wore a leather belt around his waist.

Characteristic Activities
A: JB baptized with water (characteristic activity).
A: JB preached (characteristic activity).
S: JB's characteristic activities took place in the wilderness.

Baptizing

A: **JB preached baptism.**

A: JB's baptism was a form of Jewish immersion rite.

A: **JB administered baptism himself.**

A: JB's baptism was done in flowing water.

A: **JB's baptism was understood to express repentance.**

A: JB's baptism was understood to mediate God's forgiveness.

A: JB's baptism was understood to be a protest against the temple establishment.

A: JB's baptism was understood to purify from uncleanness.

A: JB's baptism was understood as an initiation into a Jewish sectarian movement.

A: JB's baptism was understood to foreshadow an expected figure's baptism.

Preaching

A: **JB taught repentance.**

A: **JB taught repentance apart from baptism.**

A: Mark 1:4 and Matt 3:2 summarize the message of JB.

A: JB spoke the words in Mark 1:7, Luke 3:16b and Matt 3:11b (Q).

A: JB spoke the words in Mark 1:8, Luke 3:16a,c, and Matt 3:11a,c (Q).

A: JB spoke the words in Luke 3:17 and Matthew 3:12 (Q).

A: JB spoke the words in Luke 3:7-9 and Matt 3:7-10 (Q).

A: JB spoke the words in Luke 3:11 and Luke 3:13 and Luke 3:14.

A: **JB spoke the words reported in John 1:15, 19-24, 29-34, 35-42; 3:22-30.**

Response to his activities

A: **JB's exhortations and activities had a widespread appeal.**

A: In response, people repented.

A: In response, people were baptized.

A: JB had disciples.

A: Pharisees came to hear JB.

A: Sadducees came to hear JB.

A: Toll collectors came to hear JB.

A: Soldiers came to hear JB.

Relation to Contemporary Movements and Social Role

S: **JB was part of a broader baptizing phenomenon or movement.**

S: **JB was an Essene.**

S: **JB was a member (or former member) of the Qumran community.**

S: JB was a former Essene.
S: **JB was a lone Jewish sage and holy man (like Bannus).**
S: JB imitated Elijah.
S: JB acted as a prophet.
S: JB was an apocalyptic preacher.
A: **JB was perceived as a hellenistic moralist.**

JOHN THE BAPTIST AND JESUS

S: There was a person named Jesus.
S: **JB's mother Elizabeth was related to Jesus' mother Mary.**
S: **JB was related to Jesus.**
S: **JB's locale overlaps that of Jesus.**
S: **JB's time overlaps that of Jesus.**
S: Jesus began his public ministry at the time JB was imprisoned.
A: **JB baptized Jesus.**
A: **Jesus saw the heavens open and the spirit descend on him like a dove.**
A: **Jesus heard a voice from heaven at his baptism saying, "You are my favored son."**
A: Jesus had visionary experiences.
A: **Jesus had a visionary experience at the time of his baptism.**
A: **Jesus had a vision at his baptism.**
A: Jesus had a powerful religious experience at his baptism.
A: Jesus was a disciple of JB.
A: Jesus deliberately separated from JB's movement.
A: Some of JB's disciples became followers of Jesus.
A: JB wondered whether Jesus were his successor (Q 7:18–19).
A: **Jesus considered himself to be JB's successor.**
A: **The public considered Jesus to be JB's successor.**
A: Jesus' disciples considered Jesus to be JB's successor.
A: JB's supporters identified JB as Elijah.
A: **Jesus identified JB as Elijah.**
A: **Jesus' disciples identified JB as Elijah.**
A: Mark or Q identified JB as Elijah.
A: **Jesus identified JB as a great figure.**
A: Jesus contrasted his behavior with that of JB (Q 7:33–35; 16:16).

IMPRISONMENT AND DEATH

A: **Herod Antipas had JB imprisoned.**
A: **Herod Antipas had JB executed.**

A: JB denounced Herod Antipas.

A: JB criticized Herod Antipas' marriage to Herodias.

A: JB's activities posed a threat to Herod Antipas' ability to maintain peace and stability.

A: Herod Antipas had JB executed for political expediency.

S: Machaerus was the site of JB's execution.

A: Herodias requested the execution of JB.

A: Herodias used her daughter to get JB executed.

A: Herodias' daughter danced for Herod Antipas and his court.

A: Herodias' daughter asked for the head of JB on a platter.

JOHN THE BAPTIST MOVEMENT AFTER HIS DEATH

A: Disciples of JB continued to honor him after his death.

A: The movements of JB and Jesus were rivals during Jesus' lifetime.

A: The movements of JB and Jesus were rivals after Jesus' death.

A: JB's movement included hellenistic Jews (like Apollos).

APOCALYPTICISM, JESUS, AND JOHN THE BAPTIST

A: Apocalypticism was introduced into the Christian tradition after Jesus' death.

A: Apocalypticism was introduced into the Jesus tradition by some of his followers.

* * *

This report of the Jesus Seminar's collective judgment falls into three parts. PART ONE includes brief historical essays on the times and life of John. Although presented first, this section presupposes the next two parts. In other words, the volume begins, and does not end with conclusions. PART TWO surveys the literary evidence for the life, activity, and death of John. The texts themselves are reproduced, enabling the reader to see firsthand what was reported about John in ancient writings, both Christian and non-Christian, canonical and non-canonical. PART THREE repeats the narrative statements about John which were assessed for their relative historical value. Here, too, are the tabulated results of the voting of each statement and the historical reasoning reflected in those results.

The historical JOHN the BAPTIST

I

The writing of fiction and the writing of history require a goodly dose of the human imagination. It has been said that the only difference between the novelist and the historian is the claim by the historian that the events as narrated occurred off the written page among human beings within space and time. The historian weaves a story around those fixed points which have the highest degrees of historical certainty or historical probability.

The two chapters in PART ONE of our study represent historical essays. The first chapter describes in the broadest possible terms what can be considered common historical knowledge about Palestine under Roman rule during the 1st century C.E.. The second chapter has as its human subject the man named John, nicknamed "the Baptist," or "the Baptizer," who lived in Palestine under Roman rule during the opening decades of that century. This essay reflects the specific historical conclusions about John as determined by the collective judgment of the seminar. Imbedded in the essay are the narrative statements already listed in color format in the INTRODUCTION. The narrative also presupposes the literary evidence about John to be surveyed in PART TWO and the historical reasoning discussed in PART THREE.

Since historical narrative moves forward by recognizing varying degrees of historical probability, the essay about John will be punctuated by such qualifying words and phrases as "no doubt," "in all probability," "quite possibly," and "unlikely." The essay itself admittedly represents a skeleton. Nearly every sentence, with its verbal qualifier, represents a fixed point. Taken together these fixed points invite interpreters to weave historical narratives about John which might well differ from one another.

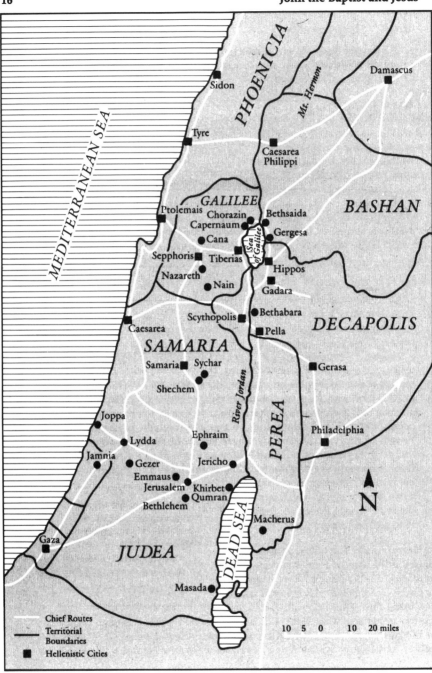

Palestine in the time of Jesus.

1   ROMAN PALESTINE

During the 1st century B.C.E., Roman legions marched into Palestine, the historic land of Israel, for the first time. From a Jewish point of view, the land promised of old by YHWH (Yahweh) to his chosen people first through Abraham and then through Moses had fallen once again under the rule of others. Jew was ruled by Gentile.

As was sometimes the way of imperial rule, the Romans established a patron-client relationship with a local notable and exercised control through him. In 40 B.C.E., the Senate in Rome proclaimed one Herod as "King of the Jews." Within three years he had established his rule over an expanse of territory that virtually equalled the kingdom established by David some nine centuries earlier.

It had been King David's son and successor Solomon who built in the royal city of Jerusalem the temple to Yahweh, Israel's covenant God. Although destroyed by the Babylonians around 586 B.C.E. and rebuilt later in the same century, beginning around 520 B.C.E., the Jerusalem temple had in many ways become the center of Judaism after the Babylonian exile. Here, in accordance with the law of Moses, a hereditary priesthood presided over the prescribed sacrifices to Yahweh, both daily sacrifices and sacrifices appropriate for the great pilgrimage festivals. At the center of the center stood the high priest. He always functioned as the chief liturgical figure within the temple cultus and, oftentimes, as the most powerful political broker among the Jews—at least in those areas of Palestine known as Judea and Samaria. By the time of Roman rule, however, the high priestly family in power was considered by many Jews not to be the one prescribed by the law of Moses. Individual high priests served at the pleasure of the Romans. Of note was the high priest named Caiaphas who managed to keep his office for nearly two decades (18–36 C.E.).

When Herod the so-called Great died in 4 B.C.E., the Romans divided his kingdom among his three sons. Archelaus received the title of ethnarch and ruled over Judea and Samaria (4 B.C.E.–6 C.E.). For a variety of reasons, Archelaus was eventually deposed and the Roman emperor placed his own Gentile governor directly over these territories. Of special note was the prefect Pontius Pilate who maintained the good favor of the emperor Tiberius for a decade (26–36 C.E.). Like his predecessors and successors, Pilate maintained his headquarters at Caesarea on the Mediterranean coast, sixty or so miles from Jerusalem. Another son of Herod, Herod Antipas, received the title tetrarch and ruled over Galilee and Perea (4 B.C.E.–39 C.E.). He built the city of Tiberias on the western shore of the Sea of Galilee and made it his principal residence in the north, but maintained Machaerus as a fortress-palace in Perea to the southeast. Still another son of Herod, Philip, also received the title tetrarch and ruled over territories northeast of the Sea of Galilee (4 B.C.E.–34 C.E.).

Palestine under the Romans was an agrarian society. If political jurisdiction were many-layered, how much more so the social stratification. Among the upper classes were the rulers, whether Roman or Roman-appointed, and those who directly served the rulers as retainers. Among the upper classes also were the priests, although even among the priests there was apparently a social division between representatives of the leading families and those whose ties were more to the countryside. The vast majority of the population, however, belonged to the peasant underclass. The economic demands made both by Jewish temple and Roman state, the latter through a bureaucratic system of taxation, fell heaviest on those who tilled the soil and lived in small villages. Little wonder then that Palestine, the land of religious promise, became a land of economic oppression and—eventually—political revolt. The Jewish-Roman War, climaxed by the fall of Jerusalem and the destruction of the temple in 70 C.E., would become a watershed in the history of Jew and Gentile alike.

2 THE MAN CALLED "BAPTIZER"

When Herod Antipas ruled over Galilee and Perea, when Pontius Pilate ruled over Judea and Samaria, and when Caiaphas served as high priest in Jerusalem, there came to public notice a man named John who attracted to himself the nickname "the Baptist," or "the Baptizer." As a Jew, he was in all probability circumcised as a sign that he belonged to Yahweh's covenant people. He may even have been of priestly lineage, although there is no evidence that he functioned as a priest in the temple in Jerusalem. It is unlikely, however, that the names by which his parents were later known—Zechariah and Elizabeth—have been accurately remembered.

This John appeared in the wilderness, the desert area astride the Jordan River and bordering the Dead Sea to the south. Separated by river and sea, the territories of Judea and Perea apparently served as the principal, if not exclusive, locale of his public activity. John was probably an ascetic whose diet included locusts and raw honey. He may even have dressed himself in a garment of camel hair with a leather belt around his waist. In this attire, he would have been clad in the traditional garb of a prophet (Zech 13:4). More specifically, he would have resembled the prophet Elijah, possibly in conscious imitation of Elijah (2 Kgs 1:8).

In John's day, the religious diversity of his people was evidenced through the existence of three principal sects each of which was committed to upholding the covenant law of Moses. The Sadducees, generally speaking, represented priestly interests. The Pharisees, primarily non-priests, committed themselves to applying the commandments to everyday life. The Essenes, whose members came from priestly and non-priestly backgrounds, tended to separate themselves from society at large.

It is certain that a Jewish sect had established a settlement in the Judean wilderness just off the northwest shore of the Dead Sea at a place called

Qumran. This sect, associated with what have become known as the Dead Sea Scrolls, was probably a community of Essenes. At one time John himself may have been an Essene even if not a member, or former member, of the community of Essenes at Qumran. At the time of his initial appearing and subsequent ministry, however, John was neither an Essene nor a lone sage and holy man like Bannus—mentioned by Josephus—who also withdrew into the wilderness to live an ascetic style of life.

Ministry of Baptizing and Preaching

John's characteristic activities took place in the wilderness. He baptized; and he preached.

John preached baptism. He administered baptism himself in some personal way, although the exact nature of his participation is not known. His baptism was probably a form of a Jewish immersion rite and was probably performed in flowing water, such as the water of the Jordan River. No doubt John's baptism was understood to be an expression of repentance by those who acccepted it. His baptism was also probably understood to mediate God's forgiveness, to purify from uncleanness, and to serve as an initiation into a sectarian movement. By implication, therefore, John's baptism—in all likelihood—was understood to be a protest against the temple establishment in Jerusalem, for his baptism provided an alternative to functions of the temple.

John also taught repentance, but not apart from baptism. His act of baptizing and his proclamation, therefore, were inextricably related to one another. John probably preached about one coming after himself in words similar to these:

> Someone more powerful than I will succeed me, whose sandal straps I am not fit to bend down and untie.
> (Mark 1:7; cf. Luke 3:16b, Matt 3:11b)

John may even have compared his own baptism with a baptism which would be effected by this coming powerful one. Such a comparison is expressed in these words:

> I have been baptizing with water, but he will baptize you with holy spirit.   (Mark 1:8; cf. Luke 3:16a,c, Matt 3:11a,c)

That this expected figure would bring a decisive judgment is expressed in these words probably spoken by John:

> His pitchfork is in his hand, to make a clean sweep of his threshing floor and to gather his wheat into the granary, but the chaff he'll burn in a fire that can't be put out.   (Luke 3:17; cf. Matt 3:12)

Other words of judgment declared by John were quite possibly amplified into an indictment of all those children of Abraham not bearing fruit worthy of repentance:

> You spawn of Satan! Who warned you to flee from the impending doom? Well then, start producing fruits suitable for a change of heart, and don't even start saying to yourselves, 'We have Abraham as our father.' Let me tell you, God can raise up children for Abraham right out of these rocks. Even now the axe is aimed at the root of the trees. So every tree not producing choice fruit gets cut down and tossed into the fire.   (Luke 3:7–9; cf. Matt 3:7–10)

John may also have issued ethical directives on interpersonal relations for those who responded to his call for repentance and baptism:

> Whoever has two shirts should share with someone who has none.
> (Luke 3:11)

> Charge nothing above the official rates.   (Luke 3:13)

> No more shakedowns! No more frameups either! And be satisfied with your pay!   (Luke 3:14)

John's message of judgment, repentance, right behavior, and an expected figure is reminiscent of the messages proclaimed by those great prophets in Israel's past whose words are preserved in the Hebrew Scriptures. But through John's words runs the theme of a transcendent judgment of fire characteristic of apocalyptic literature. Therefore, John can probably be described accurately as an apocalyptic preacher who acted like a prophet. However, it is unlikely that John the Jew, baptizing and preaching in the wilderness around the Jordan, would have been perceived in that place as a hellenistic moralist– as suggested by Josephus' account.

There can be no doubt that John had a widespread appeal among his contemporaries. Representatives of various religious and social groups would have come out into the wilderness to hear him. Among his hearers were probably Sadducees and Pharisees, toll collectors and soldiers. In response, people would have repented and received baptism. Among those who repented and received baptism were those who became his disciples. Even if John had not cast himself in the role of a returning Elijah, it is possible that his supporters so cast him.

John and Jesus

John had a contemporary named Jesus. Contrary to later claims, it is improbable that they were biologically related to each other through their mothers. But there can be little doubt that John baptized this Jesus, reportedly in the Jordan River.

On the occasion of his baptism, Jesus—who probably had visionary experiences—just as probably had a powerful religious experience, possibly even a visionary experience. But it is highly unlikely that he actually saw the heavens open and the spirit descend on him like a dove. It is just as unlikely that he heard a heavenly voice declaring him to be God's son. Later, his inner experience was objectified symbolically as a vision and an audition in the story as told in the church.

After his baptism by John, Jesus was probably in some sense a disciple of John. But later he must have deliberately separated from John's movement and inaugurated a ministry of his own, which for a while overlapped John's ministry in time and place. Some of John's disciples probably became followers of Jesus. There was possibly some relationship between the

---

Luke 1–2 and a Possible "Baptist" Source

Luke 1–2 contains information about JB found nowhere else in 1st century literature. Only here in the Lucan infancy stories does one read that JB came from a priestly family who lived in the hill country of Judea, that his parents were named Zechariah and Elizabeth, that he was related through his mother to Jesus, and that he apparently grew up in the wilderness.

These stories reflect two contrary tendencies. First, there can be no doubt that the stories have taken shape under the influence of similar stories of religious heroes in Hebrew Scripture and later Jewish lore. Secondly, there also can be no doubt that the stories contain incidental details—particularly about the temple and priesthood—that suggest their antiquity and, therefore, their potential historical worth for understanding the family background and origin of JB.

Therefore, a series of questions presents itself to the interpreter: Was Luke the one primarily responsible for shaping these stories in he light of earlier models? Or was the pattern already present in the traditions received? What *written sources* or *oral traditions* did Luke use in the composition of Luke 1–2? How did he proceed in the writing of these narratives?

Over the years, scholars have answered these questions by following one of three approaches:

Approach #1: Luke had access to a *developed written source about the birth of JB* which originated in Baptist circles, in a Palestinian Jewish environment, in the Hebrew or Aramaic language. Later the source was translated into Greek, and Luke modeled his narrative of the birth of Jesus on this account of the birth of JB. But the "Baptist" source already reflected the

imprisonment of John and the ministry of Jesus. If the imprisonment of John did not occasion the beginning of Jesus' ministry, it may have signaled the beginning of a new phase of his ministry. Whereas John's ministry was centered in the wilderness, Jesus would take his ministry to the villages of Galilee and eventually to Jerusalem itself. Jesus would also contrast his own behavior, or style of ministry, with that of John. John was an ascetic, neither eating nor drinking. Jesus was not an ascetic, for he both ate and drank.

John may have wondered whether Jesus were his successor in fulfillment of John's own proclamation of one who would come after him. Similarly, the public may have considered Jesus to be John's successor. Even Jesus may have considered himself to be John's successor. But it is more likely

---

patterns found in similar stories in Jewish lore. This general approach has recently been followed by Joseph A. Fitzmyer in his commentary on Luke in "The Anchor Bible" series. Earlier writers on the life of JB—Carl H. Kraeling and Charles H. H. Scobie–took this approach which also had been argued quite carefully by Paul Winter.

Approach #2: Luke had access to what were presumably *oral traditions about the births of both JB and Jesus* which had circlulated side by side within the church and which had come to reflect the pattern of similar stories in Jewish lore. Luke incorporated these already associated stories into his written gospel. This conclusion appears in Walter Wink's redaction study of JB's portrayal in the gospels.

Approach #3: Luke, Like Matthew, had access to *traditions about the birth and infancy of Jesus*. Luke, having shaped these Jesus traditions in accordance with OT stories, then modeled his narrative on the birth and infancy of JB on his own narrative account of the birth and infancy of Jesus. This view appears in Raymond Brown's detailed commentary on the biblical infancy traditions in Matthew 1–2 and Luke 1–2.

The Jesus Seminar took into account each of these approaches to the material about JB in Luke 1 in its consideration of JB's birth, family, and upbringing. Generally the Fellows were suspicious of the details about JB contained therein although they conceded by formal vote, a gray, that it was possible that JB was of priestly lineage. (Consult the bibliography for the works herein cited.)

that the recognition of Jesus as John's successor in fulfillment of John's proclamation first came from Jesus' own disciples, some of whom had been followers of John.

Jesus certainly considered John to be a great figure. His assessment of John is probably reflected in words like these:

> I tell you, among those born of women none is greater than John. . . .
> (Luke 7:28a; cf. Matt 11:11a)

> From Adam to John the Baptist, among those born of women, no one is so much greater that John the Baptist that his eyes should not be averted.   (Thom 46:1)

Jesus, or his disciples, also may have recognized John to be a prophet, even a prophet like Elijah. But it is more likely that the identification of John as Elijah first occurred within the early church as the church sorted out the relationship between John and Jesus. John became the Elijah-returned, or Elijah-like, the forerunner of Jesus the Messiah, the Christ, the Anointed.

The Death of John and Beyond

Throughout the ministries of John and Jesus, the tetrarch of Galilee and Perea was the man named Herod Antipas. There was also a woman named Herodias who had been married to Herod Antipas' brother. She married Herod Antipas forcing him to give up his longtime wife, the daughter of Aretas IV, the king of Nabatea. John the Baptist most assuredly denounced Herod Antipas. Specifically, he criticized Herod Antipas' marriage to Herodias. John's activities and his popularity posed a threat to Herod Antipas' ability to maintain peace and stability. Therefore, Herod Antipas had John imprisoned and executed for political expediency at Machaerus, his fortress-palace in Perea east of the Dead Sea.

It is possible that Herodias requested the execution of John. It is also possible that her daughter danced for Herod and his court and that she used her daughter—identified by the name Salome by Josephus—to manipulate Herod into putting John to death. It is improbable, however, that the daughter asked for and got John's severed head on a platter.

The disciples of John certainly continued to honor him after his death. In all probability the movement initiated by John came to include hellenistic Jews. Among them would have been Apollos, whose own activities intersected with the missionary work of Paul at Corinth and Ephesus some twenty or so years after the deaths of John and Jesus (Acts 18:24–19:1; 1 Cor 1:12, 3:4–6). Therefore, the movements initiated respectively by John and Jesus were probably rivals both during their lifetimes and after their deaths.

Literary sources for

II JOHN the BAPTIST

In biographical research, historians rely upon written documents by and about the person under investigation. Writings by that person, himself or herself, represent primary evidence. Writings about that person, by someone else, constitute secondary evidence. Historical assessment of primary and secondary evidence requires an understanding of the specific documents under scrutiny. What kind of document is it? Who wrote it? What were the interests and commitments of the author? Under what circumstances was it written? What sources, written or oral, were used by the author in producing the document?

JB left *no* writings by his own hand. Therefore, we are left only with secondary evidence about his words and deeds.

Also, the movement initiated by JB left *no* literary remains—although scholarly claims have been made that the New Testament contains portions of documents which originated in Baptist circles. These documents about JB are said to have been brought into early Christian circles by followers of JB who themselves became Christians. The first chapter of Luke, for example, has been said to preserve the remnants of a Baptist writing. (See cameo essay, "Luke 1–2 and a Possible 'Baptist' Source.") Revelation 4–11, for another example, has been said to contain the remains of a Baptist document. (See cameo essay, "The Book of Revelation as a 'Baptist' Apocalypse.") However, these proposals have not received wide acceptance, although the proposal for a Baptist source underlying Luke 1 continues to be taken seriously by many scholars. Therefore, we are left with secondary evidence about JB that originated in non-Baptist circles.

The writings gathered together and presented here in Part Two are those used by the members of the Jesus Seminar in their historical investigation into the activities of JB. The writings to be surveyed in consecutive chapters

25

include: the Gospel of Mark; so-called Q; the Gospel of Matthew; the Gospel of Luke and the Book of Acts; the Gospel of John; the Gospel of Thomas; other gospels (fragments of the Gospels of the Nazoreans, the Hebrews, and the Ebionites, plus the Infancy Gospel of James); and, finally, other writings (the Pseudo-Clementines, Josephus, and Mandaean literature). All these writings originated in Christian circles except the striking passage about JB from Josephus and the selections from the literature of the Mandaeans.

3   GOSPEL OF MARK

Mark, the shortest canonical gospel (only 16 chapters in modern Bibles), probably represents the earliest of the four canonical gospels to have been written. Without any knowledge of each other, the authors of Matthew and Luke then used Mark as their principal written source. As narratives, therefore, Matthew (28 chapters) and Luke (24 chapters) represent literary expansions of Mark. This claim of Marcan priority remains the dominant scholarly view, although some have argued for a return to the view that Matthew was written first and that Mark was a literary condensation of both Matthew and Luke.

Origin and Structure of Mark

Like the other canonical gospels, Mark is an anonymous document. The author is not identified by name. The heading often appearing over the book—"According to Mark"—comes from the 2nd century when the church had to distinguish among several narratives about Jesus. Also about that time there appears in Christian literature the tradition that this Mark was the Mark mentioned in other New Testament writings. In the Book of Acts, a John Mark serves as a companion of Paul on his travels to Cyprus (12:12, 25; 15:37–39). In 1 Peter, someone named Mark is identified as a close associate of Peter (5:13); and presumably Peter and Mark are together in Rome. The tradition also claims that Mark wrote down, after Peter's martyrdom, what he had learned about Jesus from Peter. Whatever might be said about the identity of the authors of Mark and the other gospels, we shall for convenience refer to them by their traditional names.

The Gospel of Mark also remains silent about the circumstances of its origin—its locale and date of composition. Clues within the book itself, however, suggest that it was written in a time of suffering for a suffering people. Some scholars have identified Rome itself as the place of origin and related its origin to the persecution of Nero (mid-60s C.E.). Others have preferred some area near Galilee, such as Syria, as the place of origin and connected its origin to the crisis precipitated by the Jewish-Roman War (66–70 C.E.). The author of the gospel does seem to allude to the Roman seige of Jerusalem and the impending destruction of temple in the great apocalyptic speech of Jesus on the events before the end (especially 13:14).

The literary structure, the narrative outline, and the plot movement of Mark all serve to highlight the suffering—or passion—of Jesus as the Christ. The gospel has no infancy account. The gospel, in its earliest version (concluding with 16:8), had no account of appearances by the resurrected Jesus. After Jesus' baptism and testing, he undertakes an initial ministry in Galilee (chs. 1–9), he journeys from Galilee to Jerusalem (ch. 10), and he experiences betrayal and death with only a hint of resurrection (chs. 11–16:8). The dramatic shift in the story occurs near Caesarea Philippi (8:27–33), when Jesus begins to prepare his disciples for his impending suffering and crucifixion through what have become known as the "passion predictions": ". . . the son of Adam was destined to suffer a great deal, and be rejected by the elders and the ranking priests and the scholars, and be killed, and after three days rise" (8:31; also 9:31; 10:32–34). His only words from the cross, words from Psalm 22:1, have the sound of desolation: "My God, My God, why did you abandon me?" (15:34). Diagrammatically, Mark appears thus:

> Introduction (1:1–13)
> I. Jesus in Galilee (1:14–9:50)
> II. Jesus on the road (10:1–52)
> III. Jesus in Jerusalem (11:1–16:8)

Within this framework, Mark has placed nine passages which refer to John the Baptist. The first three of these passages are combined into a continuous unit at the very outset of the gospel.

Texts in Mark about JB

1. Mark 1:2–6. Mark begins the gospel narrative with a conjoined pair of prophetic texts and the introduction of JB, in the wilderness baptizing and preaching, as their fulfillment:

2. . . Isaiah the prophet wrote:

> Here is my messenger,
> whom I send on ahead of you
> to prepare your way!
> 3A voice of someone shouting in the wilderness:
> "Make ready the way of the Lord,
> make his paths straight."

[4]So, John the Baptizer appeared in the wilderness calling for baptism and a change of heart that lead to forgiveness of sins. [5]And everyone from the Judean countryside and all the residents of Jerusalem streamed out to him and were baptized by him in the Jordan river, admitting their sins. [6]And John was dressed in camel hair [and wore a leather belt around his waist] and lived on locusts and raw honey.

2. Mark 1:7–8. Mark continues the narrative with a pronouncement by JB that Jesus himself will fulfill:

[7]And he began his proclamation by saying:
"Someone more powerful than I will succeed me, whose sandal straps I am not fit to bend down and untie. [8]I have been baptizing you with water, but he will baptize you with holy spirit."

3. Mark 1:9–11. Mark next introduces Jesus, who comes from Galilee and is baptized by JB:

[9]During that same period Jesus came from Nazareth in Galilee and was baptized in the Jordan by John. [10]And just as he got up out of the water, he saw the skies torn open and the spirit coming down toward him like a dove. [11]There was also a voice from the skies: "You are my favored son—I fully approve of you."

4. Mark 1:14. In the next brief reference to JB, Mark signals the important transition from Jesus' testing in the wilderness to the inauguration of his public ministry in Galilee:

[14]After John was locked up, Jesus came to Galilee proclaiming God's good news.

5. Mark 2:18–22. An inquiry by disciples of JB about fasting, and Jesus' response, has been placed by Mark near the outset of Jesus' ministry in Galilee:

[18]John's disciples and the Pharisees were in the habit of fasting, and they come and ask him, "Why do the disciples of John fast, and the disciples of the Pharisees, but your disciples don't?"
[19]And [Jesus] said to them: "The groom's friends can't fast while the groom is present, can they? So long as the groom is around, you can't expect them to fast. [20]But the days will come when the groom is taken away from them, and then they will fast, on that day."
[21]"Nobody sews a piece of unshrunk cloth on an old garment,

otherwise the new, unshrunk patch pulls away from the old and creates a worse tear.

²²"And nobody pours young wine into old wineskins, otherwise the wine will burst the skins, and destroy both the wine and the skins. Instead, young wine is for new wineskins."

6. Mark 6:14–29. Having noted the mounting speculation in Galilee about Jesus' identity, Mark narrates as a "flashback" the fascinating story of JB's tragic fate:

¹⁴King Herod heard about it—by now, ⟨Jesus'⟩ reputation had become well known—and people kept saying that John the Baptizer had been raised from the dead and that, as a consequence, miraculous powers were at work in him. ¹⁵Some spread the rumor that he was Elijah, while others reported that he was a prophet like one of the prophets.

¹⁶When Herod got wind of it, he started declaring, "John, the one I beheaded, has been raised!"

¹⁷Earlier Herod himself had sent someone to arrest John and put him in chains in a dungeon, on account of Herodias, his brother Philip's wife, because he had married her. ¹⁸You see, John had said to Herod, "It is not right for you to have your brother's wife!"

¹⁹So Herodias nursed a grudge against him and wanted to eliminate him, but she couldn't manage it, ²⁰because Herod was afraid of John. He knew that he was an upright and holy man, and so protected him, and, although he listened to him frequently, he was very confused, yet he listened to him eagerly.

²¹Now a festival day came, when Herod gave a banquet on his birthday for his courtiers, and his commanders, and the leading citizens of Galilee. ²²And the daughter of Herodias came in and captivated Herod and his dinner guests by dancing. The king said to the girl, "Ask me for whatever you wish and I'll grant it to you!" ²³Then he swore an oath to her: "I'll grant you whatever you ask for, up to half my domain!"

²⁴She went out and said to her mother, "What should I ask for?"

And she replied, "The head of John the Baptist!"

²⁵She promptly hastened back and made her request: "I want you to give me the head of John the Baptist on a platter, right now!"

²⁶The king grew regretful, but, on account of his oaths and the dinner guests, he didn't want to refuse her. ²⁷So right away the king sent for the executioner and commanded him to bring his head. And he went away and beheaded ⟨John⟩ in prison. ²⁸He brought his head on a platter and presented it to the girl, and the girl gave it to her

mother. [29]When his disciples heard about it, they came and got his body and put it in a tomb.

7. Mark 8:27–30. The name of JB appears on the lips of Jesus' disciples in that pivotal account of the exchange between them and Jesus that Mark has placed near Caesarea Philippi:

[27]Jesus and his disciples set out for the villages of Caesarea Philippi. On the road he started questioning his disciples, asking them, "What are people saying about me?"

[28]In response they said to him, "⟨Some say, 'You are⟩ John the Baptist,' and others 'Elijah,' but others 'One of the prophets.'"

[29]But he continued to press them, "What about you, who do you say I am?"

Peter responds to him, "You are the Anointed!" [30]And he warned them not to tell anyone about him.

8. Mark 9:9–13. The name of JB does not appear on Jesus' lips in his exchange with his disciples that Mark reports after Jesus' transfiguration; but Jesus implies that JB was Elijah-returned:

[9]And as they were walking down the mountain he instructed them not to describe what they had seen to anyone, until the son of Adam rise from the dead.

[10]And they kept it to themselves, puzzling over what this could mean, this "rising from the dead." [11]And they started questioning him: "The scholars claim, don't they, that Elijah must come first?"

[12]He would respond to them, "Of course Elijah comes first to restore everything. So, how does scripture claim that the son of Adam will suffer greatly and be the object of scorn? [13]On the other hand, I tell you that Elijah in fact has come, and they had their way with him, just as the scriptures indicate."

9. Mark 11:27–33. One of the conflict stories that Mark has set in Jerusalem involves hostile questioning of Jesus about his authority which leads him to counter with a question about the baptism of JB:

[27]Once again they come to Jerusalem. As he walks around in the temple area, the ranking priests and scholars and elders come up to him [28]and start questioning him: "By what right are you doing these things?" or, "Who gave you the authority to do these things?"

[29]But Jesus said to them: "I have one question for you. If you answer me, then I will tell you by what authority I do these things. [30]Tell me,

was the baptism of John heaven-sent or was it of human origin? Answer me that."

[31]And they conferred among themselves, saying, "If we say 'heaven-sent,' he'll say, 'Then why didn't you trust him?' [32]But if we say 'Of human origin. . . .'" They were afraid of the crowd. (You see, everybody considered John a genuine prophet.) [33]So they answered Jesus by saying, "We can't tell."

And Jesus says to them: "I'm not going to tell you by what authority I do these things either!"

Mark's Portrayal of JB

How has Mark presented JB? What details in his presentation may be of significance to the historian?

Simply put, *Mark presents JB as the prophetic, Elijah-returned forerunner to Jesus the Anointed, the Messiah, the Christ.* (See cameo essay, "Elijah and His Coming.") In fulfillment of God's scriptural promises, the rejection and death of JB prefigures the rejection and death of Jesus. This recognition,

---

Elijah and His Coming

There is no greater folk hero in Jewish tradition and lore than Elijah the prophet. How appropriate that his name in Hebrew means "Yahweh (is) my God"!

Even today a glass of wine is poured for Elijah during the Passover celebration and a chair is reserved for him at the circumcision ceremony. Both his cup and his chair recognize his role as the herald of the messiah and acknowledge his presence even by his absence. He is a protector of his people, with a special interest in the infant sons of his people.

We first encounter Elijah, of course, in Hebrew Scripture–the Old Testament. In those stories, which have as their setting the northern kingdom of Israel in the ninth century B.C.E., Elijah is assigned three roles (1 Kgs 17–2 Kgs 2). First, Elijah appears as the great defender of Yahweh. He stands in opposition to ill-fated King Ahab, treacherous Queen Jezebel, and the raving Baal prophets on Mt. Carmel. Secondly, Elijah also receives recognition as a miracle worker. He provides an endless supply of meal and oil for a non-Israelite widow of Zarephath and even revives her son when he dies. And then, thirdly, there is the matter of his departure from this earth. Like Enoch of old, he did not die. God came and took him into heaven by a whirlwind. Little wonder then that eventually there would be aroused the expectation of his return.

The later prophets, whose messages are preserved in the books bearing their names, often spoke about Yahweh's coming for judgment. Consequently, there emerged the notion of one who would prepare the way for Yahweh's coming— the expectation for an eschatological prophet. So, in Malachi 3:1, Yahweh de-

however, comes to the readers of the text rather than to the actors in the story, with the possible exception of JB and Jesus themselves. JB appears in fulfillment of a prophetic text associated with the prophet Elijah (1:2=Mal 3:1; cf. Mal 4:5) and attired like Elijah (cf. 1 Kgs 1:8). But within the narrative, it is Jesus about whom the popular speculation centers that he may be one of the prophets, perhaps Elijah, or even JB resurrected (6:14–15; 8:28). It is Jesus that *implicitly* accepts Peter's confession that he is not JB, nor Elijah, nor one of the prophets, but the Anointed (8:27–30). It is also Jesus, that *implicitly* identifies JB as Elijah (9:9–13). Just as there is in Mark a messianic secret about Jesus' true identity, so there is an Elijianic secret about JB's identity. The reader of the gospel, however, knows the secrets. JB is the prophetic, Elijah-returned forerunner; and Jesus is the Anointed, the Messiah, the Christ (already mentioned in 1:1).

A number of details in the Marcan presentation of JB raise intriguing possibilities for the historian.

The locale of JB's activity is the wilderness (1:4)—that desolate, desert area around the Jordan River (1:5, 9). His personal appearance and living style are that of an ascetic. He wears clothing of camel hair with a leather

---

clares that a messenger will be sent as a forerunner to prepare the way for judgment; and in Malachi 4:5, Yahweh identifies Elijah the prophet as that forerunner. But note that here the prophet prepares the way for the coming of Yahweh, not the coming of a messianic figure.

Whether or not there was already in JB's and Jesus' day the notion that Elijah would return specifically as a forerunner of the messiah has been much debated. But it is the expected eschatological role of Elijah that shines through the gospel texts as the writers, through their narrative presentations, interpret the relationship between JB and Jesus. Although in the synoptic stories it is the crowds who try to cast Jesus in the Elijah role (Mark 6:15 par; 8:28 par), it is just as clear that the narrators themselves give the Elijah role to JB as—in some sense—the forerunner of Jesus the messiah. For Mark and Matthew (Mark 9:13 par), JB is Elijah-returned, or Elijah *redivivus*; for Luke, Elijah-like.

Even apart from the JB/Jesus issue, however, Elijah appears in the gospels in each of the three roles assigned to him within Hebrew Scripture. First, Elijah is cast as a representative, if not a defender, of Yahweh. Such is his role when he appears alongside Moses to Jesus and Jesus' disciples on the mount of transfiguration (Mark 9:2–8 par). Secondly, Elijah is cast as a miracle worker. Such is his role, at least implicitly, when Jesus in his sermon at Nazareth refers to Elijah's having been sent to the widow of Zarephath during a famine (Luke 4:16–30). And, thirdly, Elijah is also portrayed as an eschatological deliverer. Such is his role when bystanders at Jesus' crucifixion mistake Jesus' cry to God, "Eloi, Eloi" or "Eli, Eli," as a call for Elijah (Mark 15:33–39 par).

belt around his waist; and he lives on a diet that includes locusts and raw honey (1:6).

The characteristic activities of JB are baptizing and preaching. Indeed, he preaches a baptism of repentance, or a change of heart, for the forgiveness of sins (1:4). His call for repentance seems so linked to baptism that he does not teach repentance apart from his water baptism. Apparently he personally, in some indeterminate way, administers baptism to those those who come forward, rather than having them baptize themselves (1:5, 9). His use of the Jordan River for his baptizing activity suggests that his baptizing was in running water, not standing water, and was an immersion, not a dipping nor simply a washing (1:5, 9). He also proclaims the coming of one mightier than he who will baptize with holy spirit (1:8).

Jesus, of course, was one of those baptized by JB. The experience of Jesus at his baptism has features of a vision and an audition, a seeing and a hearing (1:9–10). He sees the skies open and the spirit coming down like a dove. He hears a voice from the skies identifying him as God's favored son. Jesus does not return to Galilee until after JB suffers imprisonment (1:14). This suggests that JB precedes and Jesus succeeds in terms of public activity. Their public ministries do not overlap in time or place.

The response to JB from the general populace seems quite positive. Folk from the Judean countryside and Jerusalem come down to the Jordan River and submit to baptism (1:5). JB is said to receive universal recognition as a genuine prophet (11:32).

The response to JB by religious officials appears to be a begrudging acceptance. In Jerusalem, the priests and scholars and elders refuse to respond to Jesus' counter-question about the baptism of JB because they are fearful of the crowds (11:27–33).

The political response to JB by Herod Antipas, however, is negative. Herod Antipas, the Roman appointed ruler of Galilee and Perea, imprisons JB and has him beheaded (1:14, 6:14–29). Although the site of the execution is not identified, the text implies that JB is beheaded in Galilee (6:21). The immediate cause for JB's arrest and execution is his criticism of Herod Antipas' marriage to Herodias, his brother Philip's wife (6:17–18). Although Herod Antipas himself has some admiration and respect for JB, Herodias uses her fabled dancing daughter—not mentioned here by name—to manipulate her husband into acting against JB. The outcome is JB's head on a platter.

Apparently, JB not only baptized those who may have returned to their homeplaces and established tasks, but initiated a movement of followers during his lifetime which may have lasted beyond his death. Disciples of JB, along with disciples of the Pharisees, approach Jesus to ask him about fasting (2:18). Disciples of JB also care for his body and arrange for his burial (6:29).

4   SAYINGS GOSPEL Q

The gospel of Mark was used independently as the main written source for Matthew, on the one hand, and Luke, on the other. This accounts for the similarities among these three gospels. Mark, Matthew, and Luke, therefore, became known as the "synoptic" gospels because they together (syn-) view (optic) Jesus and his story. Matthew and Luke also share a sizable amount of material, primarily words of Jesus, not found in Mark. For example, both preserve versions of the Lord's prayer (Matt 6:9–13//Luke 11:2–4). From where did Matthew and Luke get this prayer and the other teachings by Jesus they share? The answer: they shared a common source no longer in existence. This source became known as Q, the first letter of the German word *Quelle* meaning "source."

Mark and Q, therefore, represent the two main sources referred to in the so-called "two-source hypothesis" which was developed to explain the obvious literary relationship among Mark, Matthew, and Luke. This hypothesis established itself as the dominant scholarly view beginning in the middle of the nineteenth century.

Character and Origin of Q

Is "Q" just a convenient symbol for the material common to Matthew and Luke, but not Mark? Is "Q" a name for a body of oral tradition obviously shared by Matthew and Luke? Is "Q" a name for a written document used by Mathew and Luke? If Q is a written document, should "Q" be called a gospel?

These questions have elicited differing answers as might be expected. In this report, however, "Q" is referred to as the Sayings Gospel Q. Since scholars accepting this viewpoint think that the order and wording of Q material are best preserved in Luke, references to Q customarily employ the chapter and verses of Luke. The Lord's prayer, for example, can be designated Q 11:2–4.

The traditions about what Jesus said and what he did, his words and deeds, circulated in oral form among his followers for decades after his life and death. Certainly the Jesus sayings and the occasional Jesus story reported both in Luke and Matthew, and thus designated Q, would have existed at some point in time only in oral form. The exact wording of Q passages in the Greek texts of Luke and Matthew, however, suggest that these writers were drawing upon a written Greek text when they composed their gospels. Words spoken by Jesus probably in Aramaic had already been translated into Greek.

It is appropriate to refer to Q not only as a source, but as a gospel—the Sayings Gospel Q. First, gospels customarily have been thought about as narrative accounts of Jesus' life, death, and resurrection. Before "gospel" was a book, however, "gospel" was a message—the message about what God was doing in and through Jesus. Those books now known as gospels probably became known as gospels because of the very opening verse of the narrative gospel Mark. But here the Greek noun *euangelion* can be translated not as "gospel" but as "good news" (its literal meaning in Greek), since the word designates not book but message: "The good news of Jesus the Anointed begins . . ." (Mark 1:1). Forms of the Greek verb for preaching the good news (*euangelizomai*) are found on Jesus' own lips in Q 7:22 and Q 16:16, supporting the notion that this reconstructed document consisting primarily of Jesus sayings can appropriately be called a gospel, the Sayings Gospel Q. Secondly, and more briefly, the so-called Gospel of Thomas unearthed in Egypt in 1945 also consists primarily of sayings attributed to Jesus. Sayings Gospel Q now has a literary companion which has been preserved in documentary form—the sayings Gospel of Thomas. More will be said about Thomas later. There are therefore sayings gospels as well as narrative gospels.

Sayings Gospel Q is an extensive collection of Jesus' teachings containing many of his most memorable words. These include not only the Lord's prayer (Q 11:2–4), but the beatitudes (Q 6:20b–23), the golden rule (Q 6:31), the sayings on not being anxious about food and clothing (Q 12:22–31), the twin parables of the mustard seed and leaven (Q 13:18–21), and the saying about God and mammon (Q 16:13). Many of the teachings in Q have been gathered together into discourses bound together by a common theme. Among these discourses are those which focus on missionary outreach (Q 10:1–16), exorcisms (Q 11:14–26), Pharisees (Q 11:39–52), and the coming of the Son of man, that is the son of Adam, for final judgment (Q 17:23–24 , 25, 26–30, 34–35, 37).

Even this brief, and incomplete, survey of Jesus' sayings in Q supports the observation of scholars that Q has preserved two different kinds of teaching. In some passages, Jesus speaks like a sage—or wise man—challenging his hearers to new views of reality and disciplined lifestyles. The emphasis is upon instruction. In other passages, Jesus speaks more like a prophet announcing an apocalyptic message of threat and judgment. The emphasis is more polemical. Therefore, some scholars even contend that Q developed in two or more stages. The earliest collection of Jesus' teachings contained words of wisdom. This collection was later enlarged to accommodate Jesus' prophetic and apocalyptic words.

Although primarily a sayings collection, Q does contain at least two brief narratives: the story of Jesus' testing in the wilderness (Q 4:1–13) and the miracle story about Jesus' healing of the centurion's slave (Q 7:1–10). There are, however, neither passion nor resurrection narratives. Q itself, therefore, reflects no interest in the saving significance of Jesus' death and resurrection, a surprise to those familiar with the Christian proclamation in Paul's letters and in the narrative gospels.

What could have been the origin of Sayings Gospel Q? Q was known to the authors of Matthew and Luke, but not Mark. Since Mark was written no later than the Jewish-Roman War (66–70 C.E.), Sayings Gospel Q can claim a date of origin no later than the 60s, possibly even the 50s given what retrospectively seems to be its relatively undeveloped form. Although Q contains a reference to Jerusalem in the south (Q 13:34), most of the few place names are towns in Galilee and neighboring territory: Capernaum (Q 7:1; 10:15), Chorazin and Bethsaida (Q 10:13), Tyre and Sidon (Q 10:13, 14). Consequently, scholars undestanding Q to be a written document point to Galilee or Syria as possible locales of origin. Those people who lived out Jesus' teachings in Q must have subsisted economically on the margin of life, engaged in an itinerant ministry, and had a profound sense of being persecuted and rejected (Q 6:20–49; 10:2–12; 12:22–31, 12:33–34; 16:13).

Within Sayings Gospel Q are six passages that refer to JB. Scholars who believe that Q developed in two stages often claim that these JB passages were added at the second stage when the original collection of wisdom teachings attributed to Jesus was expanded to include prophetic and apocalyptic teachings from both Jesus and JB. Therefore, the teachings in Q attributed to JB may have been brought into the Q community by followers of JB who had become members of the Jesus movement.

The narrative gospel Mark opens with JB. So does the Sayings Gospel Q, with two passages at the outset summarizing JB's message. A discourse comprised of three passages and still another passage come later. Instead of showing a reconstructed single text of Q, the following reproduces both the Matthean and the Lucan texts with the Lucan text first, since scholars think that Luke preserves the more original sequence.

Texts in Q about JB

1. Luke 3:7–9//Matt 3:7–10. Q reports a JB saying which threatens imminent judgment and calls for repentance:

> ⁷So ⟨John⟩ would say to the crowds that came out to be baptized by him, "You spawn of Satan! Who warned you to flee from the impending doom? ⁸Well then, start producing fruits suitable for a change of heart, and don't even start saying to yourselves, 'We have Abraham as our father.' Let me tell you, God can raise up children for Abraham right out of these rocks. ⁹Even now the axe is aimed at the root of the trees. So every tree not producing choice fruit gets cut down and tossed into the fire."

* * *

> ⁷When he saw that many of the Pharisees and Sadducees were coming for baptism, ⟨John⟩ said to them, "You spawn of Satan! Who warned you to flee from the impending doom? ⁸Well then, start producing fruit suitable for a change of heart, ⁹and don't even think of saying to yourselves, 'We have Abraham as our father.' Let me tell you, God can raise up children for Abraham right out of these rocks. ¹⁰Even now the axe is aimed at the root of the trees. So every tree not producing choice fruit gets cut down and tossed into the fire.

2. Luke 3:16–17//Matt 3:11–12. Q immediately carries forward the judgment theme with a JB saying about one coming more powerful than he:

> ¹⁶John's answer was the same to everyone: "I baptize you with water; but someone more powerful than I is coming, whose sandal straps I am not fit to untie. He'll baptize you with [holy] spirit and fire. ¹⁷His pitchfork is in his hand, to make a clean sweep of his threshing floor and to gather his wheat into the granary, but the chaff he'll burn in a fire that can't be put out."

* * *

> ¹¹"I baptize you with water to signal a change of heart, but someone more powerful than I will succeed me. I am not fit to carry his sandals. He'll baptize you with holy spirit and fire. ¹²His pitchfork is in his hand, and he'll make a clean sweep of his threshing floor, and gather his wheat into the granary, but the chaff he'll burn in a fire that can't be put out."

3. Luke 7:18–20, 22–23//Matt 11:2–6. In the first of a cluster of three passages about JB, Q reports a pronouncement story in which JB's disciples ask Jesus whether or not he is the coming one:

¹⁸The disciples of John brought reports of all these things to him. ¹⁹John summoned two of his disciples and sent them to the Lord to ask: "Are you the one who is to come, or are we to wait for someone else?" ²⁰And when the men came to ⟨Jesus⟩, they said, "John the Baptist sent us to you to ask: 'Are you the expected one, or are we to wait for someone else?'" ²²And so he answered them, "Go report to John what you have seen and heard:

> the blind see again,
> the lame walk,
> lepers are cleansed,
> the deaf hear,
> the dead are raised,
> and the poor have the good news preached to them.

²³Congratulations to those who don't take offense at me."

* * *

²While John was in prison he heard about what the Anointed had been doing and he sent his disciples ³to ask, "Are you the one who is to come or are we to wait for another?"

⁴And so Jesus answered them, "Go report to John what you have heard and seen:

> ⁵The blind see again and the lame walk;
> lepers are cleansed and the deaf hear;
> the dead are raised,
> and the poor have the good news preached to them.

⁶Congratulations to those who don't take offense at me."

4. Luke 7:24–28//Matt 11:7–11. In the second passage in the cluster about JB, Q preserves sayings in which Jesus gives his eulogy about JB:

²⁴After John's messengers had left, ⟨Jesus⟩ began to talk about John to the crowds: "What did you go out to the wilderness to gawk at? A reed shaking in the wind? ²⁵What did you really go out to see? A man dressed in fancy clothes? But wait! Those who dress fashionably and live in luxury are found in palaces. ²⁶Come on, what did you go out to see? A prophet? Yes, that's what you went out to see, yet someone more than a prophet. ²⁷This is the one about whom it was written:

> Here is my messenger,
> whom I send on ahead of you
> to prepare your way before you.

²⁸I tell you, among those born of women none is greater than John; yet, the least in God's domain is greater than he."

* * *

⁷After ⟨John's disciples⟩ had departed, Jesus began to talk about John to the crowds: "What did you go out to the wilderness to gawk at? A reed shaking in the wind? ⁸What did you really go out to see? A man dressed in fancy ⟨clothes⟩? But wait! Those who wear fancy ⟨clothes⟩ are found in regal quarters. ⁹Come on, what did you go out to see? A prophet? Yes, that's what you went out to see, yet someone more than a prophet.

¹⁰"This is the one about whom it was written:

> Here is my messenger,
> whom I send on ahead of you
> to prepare your way before you.

¹¹"I swear to you, among those born of women no one has arisen who is greater than John the Baptist; yet the least in Heaven's domain is greater than he."

5. Luke 7:31–35//Matt 11:16–19. In the third passage in the cluster about JB, Q has Jesus render judgment on this generation through a parable and other sayings which explain the negative responses to JB and Jesus:

³¹"What do members of this generation remind me of? What are they like? ³²They are like children sitting in the marketplace and calling out to one another:

> We played the flute for you,
> but you wouldn't dance;
> we sang a dirge,
> but you wouldn't weep.

³³"Just remember, John the Baptist appeared on the scene, eating no bread and drinking no wine, and you say, 'He is demented.' ³⁴The son of Adam appeared on the scene both eating and drinking, and you say, 'There is a glutton and a drunk, a crony of toll collectors and sinners!' ³⁵Indeed, wisdom is vindicated by all her children."

* * *

¹⁶"What does this generation remind me of? It is like children sitting in marketplaces who call out to others:

> ¹⁷We played the flute for you,
> but you wouldn't dance;
> we sang a dirge
> but you wouldn't mourn.

¹⁸Just remember, John appeared on the scene neither eating nor drinking, and they say, 'He is demented.' ¹⁹The son of Adam came both

eating and drinking, and they say, 'There's a glutton and a drunk, a crony of toll collectors and sinners!' Indeed, wisdom is vindicated by her deeds."

6. Luke 16:16//Matt 12–13. Q also includes a saying of Jesus which assesses JB's place in salvation history:

16"Right up to John's time you have the Law and the Prophets; since then God's imperial rule has been proclaimed as good news and everyone is breaking into it violently."

* * *

12"From the time of John the Baptist until now Heaven's imperial rule has been breaking in violently, and violent men are attempting to gain it by force. 13You see, the Prophets and even the Law predicted everything that was to happen prior to John's time."

Q's Portrayal of JB

How does JB appear in Q? How does the presentation of JB in Q, a sayings gospel, compare to the presentation of JB in Mark, a narrative gospel? What details may be of interest to the historian?

Although independent of Mark, *Q also presents JB as the prophetic Elijah-returned forerunner to Jesus*—although Q generally avoids using for Jesus the designation of the Anointed, the Messiah, the Christ.

There is in Q a coherent characterization of JB. In the two passages with which Q begins, JB looks forward with a prophet-like message of impending judgment, which includes the anticipation of a more powerful one who will baptize not with water but with holy spirit and fire (Q 3:1–7, Q 3:16–17). Varied material about Jesus follows these two passages, including the narratives of his testing in the wilderness and his healing of the centurion's slave.

The next block of three passages that refers to JB opens with JB's question about Jesus' identity, contains Jesus' eulogy about JB, and concludes with Jesus' comment on their common rejection albeit for different reasons (Q 7:18–23, Q 7:24–28, Q 7:31–35). In its sequencing of material, Q makes it clear to the reader that Jesus is the more powerful one about whom JB spoke and the coming one about whom JB inquired. It is Jesus himself in Q that, on one level, leaves no doubt about JB's identity. Jesus calls JB "a prophet," but even "more than a prophet," since JB is said to fulfill the prophecy of Mal 3:1 where God declares: "Here is my messenger, whom I send on ahead of you to prepare your way before you" (Q 7:26–27). This scriptural citation applied to JB by Jesus (also cited in Mark 1:2) is an Elijah text (cf. Mal 4:5). Although the name of the prophet Elijah does not appear, Jesus has *implicitly* identified JB as Elijah-returned. However, Jesus only builds JB up in order to let him down; for he immediately adds, "I tell you, among those born of women none is greater than John; yet the least in God's domain is greater than he" (Q 7:28).

The implications of Jesus' assessment of JB are taken up in the final passage, which refers to JB's position in salvation history (Q 16:16). At least the Lucan form of the Q saying can be read to suggest that JB may be the greatest of those born prior to Jesus, but who is still not associated with God's imperial rule as proclaimed by Jesus.

The basic contours of the way Mark and Q present JB are similar. There is a coherence in Q's own presentation of JB. But there are distinctive features about Q's portrayal which are related to its character as a sayings gospel and which could have implications for the historian.

First, a couple of omissions. Q does not contain any reference to, or story about, Jesus' baptism by JB, so far as one can tell. Some scholars have argued, however, that Q probably had some kind of report of Jesus' baptism by JB, since, in the synoptic gospels, baptism and testing are linked and Q does have an account of Jesus' testing in the wilderness (Q 4:1–13). Also, Q does not contain any reference to JB's execution, although JB's imprisonment seems presupposed and possibly mentioned (Q 7:18–20, 22–23). JB's rejection also elicits comment by Jesus (Q 7:31–35).

Secondly, the locale of JB's ministry. Only in a saying on Jesus' lips is JB explicitly associated with the wilderness; but that same complex of sayings does suggest that JB carries on away from towns and population centers (Q 7:24–28). The Jordan River may not be mentioned at all as a site for JB's baptizing (but note Q 4:1).

Thirdly, the characterization of JB's activity and style of life. Q focuses so sharply on JB's preaching activity that his baptizing activity is mentioned only in passing. JB the prophet is foremost a preacher. He calls for repentance in anticipation of impending doom (Q 3:7–9). He acknowledges his own baptism with water but announces the coming of one who will baptize with holy spirit and fire (Q 3:16–17). That JB lived as an ascetic is suggested by Jesus' words contrasting JB's refusal to eat and drink with his own propensity for eating and drinking (Q 7:31–35).

5 GOSPEL OF MATTHEW

The author of Matthew has undertaken a creative rewriting of the gospel of Mark. Matthew has access not only to Mark but to Sayings Gospel Q. Matthew also utilizes a variety of traditions peculiar to this gospel. The letter M will be used to designate substantial material peculiar to Matthew, whether inherited tradition or imaginative formulation by the writer.

Structure and Origin of Matthew

Matthew has prefaced to his Marcan material M traditions related to the birth and infancy of Jesus (chs. 1–2). He has also supplemented his Marcan material with M traditions related to the resurrection appearances of Jesus (ch. 28). As in Mark so in Matthew, Jesus' public ministry reflects a geographical pattern of activity in Galilee (chs. 3–19), travel from Galilee to Jerusalem (chs. 19–20), and activity in Jerusalem climaxed by his crucifixion (chs. 21–27).

It has long been recognized, however, that the most distinctive literary features of Matthew are the five collections of Jesus' teachings superimposed by the author on the geographical outline of Jesus' ministry. Much of this teaching material has be adapted from the Sayings Gospel Q. The first collection (located in Galilee, chs. 5–7), the well-known Sermon on the Mount, contains the higher righteousness or religion required by Jesus of those who would be his disciples (5:20). The second collection (also placed in Galilee, ch. 10) contains what Jesus expects his disciples to do and experience as they go forth under his authority (10:1). The third collection (in Galilee, ch. 13), a collection of Jesus' parables, contains the secrets of the kingom of heaven or Heaven's imperial rule (13:11). The fourth collection (also in Galilee, ch. 18) contains Jesus' guidelines for discipline within the church or congregation (18:17). The fifth and last collection (set in Jerusalem, chs. 24–25) contains Jesus' teachings on what must occur before the close or end of the age (24:3). The Gospel of Matthew, therefore, emphasizes Jesus' teachings. The literary structure of the body of the gospel can be diagrammed thus:

    I. On Righteousness or Religion
       (in Galilee, chs. 5–7)
    II. On Discipleship
      (in Galilee, ch. 10)
    III. On the Secrets of Heaven's Rule
       (in Galilee, ch. 13)
    IV. On the Church or Congregation
      (in Galilee, ch. 18)
    V. On the End or Close of the Age
     (in Jerusalem, chs. 24–25)

The church tradition that this gospel was the work of Matthew the toll collector, one of the twelve disciples, begins to appear in Christian literature in the middle of the 2nd century C.E. The stated tradition includes the notation that the gospel was first written in the Hebrew language. But the original language of the gospel of Matthew was most certainly Greek as was the original language of Mark, its foundational documentary source. Most scholars find the tradition of authorship by Matthew implausible.

Many of the theological and literary characteristics of the book suggest that it was written by someone well versed in traditional Jewish scholarly tradition.

The book opens with emphasis upon Jesus' descent from David and Abraham (1:1). The five-fold division of the body of the gospel recalls the first five books of Scripture, the five books of the Law—the books of Moses. In the so-called Sermon on the Mount (chs. 5–7), Jesus gives his own interpretations over against the commandments of the law of Moses: "We once were told. . . . But I tell you. . . ." Here Jesus also describes the right way to observe customary expressions of piety—almsgiving, prayer, and fasting. The author also prefers to avoid the divine name by changing Jesus' characteristic phrase "kingdom of God" to the expression "kingdom of heaven," that is, "God's imperial rule" to "Heaven's imperial rule" (compare Matt 13 with Mark 4). Throughout the gospel the author formally introduces prophetic scriptural texts which have found their fulfillment in the events of Jesus'life and ministry (1:23; 2:6, 15, 18, 23; 4:15–16; 8:7; 12:18–21; 13:35; 21:5; 27:9–10).

Whoever composed this gospel writes not as a toll collector named Matthew but as an unnamed scholar trained for Heaven's imperial rule. A saying of Jesus about just such a scholar is reported only in this gospel: ". . . every scholar who is schooled in Heaven's Imperial rule is like some toastmaster who produces from his cellar something mature and something old" (13:52). This saying accurately describes what has been wrought by the author of Matthew.

When was the gospel written? Where? Why? Written after Mark (late 60s C.E.), and no doubt after the Jewish-Roman War (66–70 C.E.), Matthew was possibly written in the 80s C.E. Modern scholars often look to Syria, even Antioch, as a possible place of origin. The gospel, therefore, was written during the period when emerging Christianity and rabbinic Judaism were in the process of defining themselves, often over against one another.

In a world without the Jerusalem temple, ancient Jewish scholars representative of the Pharisaic party gathered at the Judean village of Jamnia. Their awesome task was to create new forms of faith. Scripture, what Christians know as Old Testament, would finally be considered closed once and for all for Judaism. Within a century or so, the interpretations of the commandments would be codified in a writing known as the Mishnah. Rabbi and synagogue had replaced priest and temple.

Clues within Matthew indicate that the gospel was written for a Jewish-Christian community, possibly even defining itself consciously in relation to the developments occurring at Jamnia. Separated from the synagogues (4:23; 6:2; 10:17; 12:9), the members of the Matthean church or congregation (16:16; 18:17) bitterly attack those scholars and Pharisees as hypocrites or imposters (23:1ff).

The Mishnah became the guide for rabbinic Judaism. The Dead Sea Scroll known as the Manual of Discipline had been the guide for the sect at Qumran. The gospel of Matthew was written as a similar guidebook for the Matthean community. Like the Pharisees at Jamnia and what were probably Essenes at Qumran, the members of the Matthean community understood themselves to be the true Israel. Unlike their kinsfolk, however, they confessed Jesus to be the fullfilment of God's promises to Israel. Their guidelines for living, therefore, are the words of Jesus himself conveniently arranged in five great collections.

The gospel of Matthew has sixteen passages related to JB. All but two are derived from either Mark or Q.

Texts in Matthew about JB

1. Matt 3:1–6 (source: Mark 1:2–6 and M). Matthew begins his narrative of Jesus' ministry with the account of JB's preaching and baptizing in the wilderness; but, significantly, his added summary of JB's message coincides exactly with his later summaries of the messages of Jesus and Jesus' disciples (3:1; 4:17; 10:7):

[1]In due course John the Baptist appears in the wilderness of Judea, [2]calling out: "Change your ways because Heaven's imperial rule is closing in."
[3]No doubt this is the person described by Isaiah the prophet:

A voice of someone shouting in the wilderness:
"Make the way of the Lord ready;
make his paths straight."

⁴Now this same John wore clothes made of camel hair and had a leather belt around his waist; his diet consisted of locusts and raw honey. ⁵Then Jerusalem, and all Judea, and all the region around the Jordan streamed out to him, ⁶and they were baptized in the Jordan [river] by him, admitting their sins.

2. Matt 3:7–10 (source: Q 3:7–9). Matthew has inserted into the block of Marcan material about JB a saying of judgment addressed by him to representatives of leading religious sects:

⁷When he saw that many of the Pharisees and Sadducees were coming for baptism, ⟨John⟩ said to them, "You spawn of Satan! Who warned you to flee from the impending doom? ⁸Well then, start producing fruit suitable for a change of heart, ⁹and don't even think of saying to yourselves, 'We have Abraham as our father.' Let me tell you, God can raise up children for Abraham right out of these rocks. ¹⁰Even now the axe is aimed at the root of the trees. So every tree not producing choice fruit gets cut down and tossed into the fire.

3. Matt 3:11–12 (source: Mark 1:7–8 and Q 3:16–17). Matthew has amplified the Marcan saying by JB about a coming one by adding words from Q that carry forward the theme of judgment:

¹¹"I baptize you with water to signal a change of heart, but someone more powerful than I will succeed me. I am not fit to carry his sandals. He'll baptize you with holy spirit and fire. ¹²His pitchfork is in his hand, and he'll make a clean sweep of his threshing floor, and gather his wheat into the granary, but the chaff he'll burn in a fire that can't be put out."

4. Matt 3:13–17 (source: Mark 1:9–11 and M). Matthew has inserted into the Marcan story of Jesus' baptism by JB a significant verbal exchange between Jesus and JB (3:14–15):

¹³Then Jesus comes from Galilee to John at the Jordan to be baptized by him. ¹⁴And John tried to stop him with these words: "I'm the one who needs to be baptized by you, yet you come to me?"
¹⁵In response, Jesus said to him, "Let it go for now. After all, in this way we are doing what is fitting and right." Then John deferred to him.
¹⁶After Jesus had been baptized, he got right up out of the water,

and—amazingly—the skies opened up, he saw God's spirit coming down on him like a dove, perching on him, [17]and—listen!—there was a voice from the skies, which said, "This is my favored son—I fully approve of him!"

5. Matt 4:12 (source: Mark 1:14). As in Mark so in Matthew, Jesus begins his own public activity only after the imprisonment of JB:

[12]When Jesus heard that John had been locked up, he headed for Galilee.

6. Matt 9:14–17 (source: Mark 2:18–22). Appropriately, Matthew has placed the Marcan story about JB's disciples and fasting between Jesus' own advice of fasting in his discourse on religion (chs. 5–7) and his collection of Jesus' teaching on discipleship (ch. 10):

[14]Then the disciples of John come up to him, and ask: "Why do we fast, and the Pharisees fast, but your disciples don't?"

[15]And Jesus said to them, "The groom's friends can't mourn as long as the groom is present, can they? But the days will come when the groom is taken away from them, and then they will fast. [16]Nobody puts a piece of unshrunk cloth on an old garment, since the patch pulls away from the garment and creates a worse tear. [17]Nor do they pour young wine into old wineskins, otherwise the wineskins burst, the wine gushes out, and the wineskins are destroyed. Instead, they put young wine in new wineskins and both are preserved."

7. Matt 11:2–6 (source: Q 7:18–23). Immediately after the collection of Jesus' teaching on discipleship (ch. 10), Matthew begins a series of interesting Q passages which provide commentary on how JB and Jesus viewed each other:

[2]While John was in prison he heard about what the Anointed had been doing and he sent his disciples [3]to ask, "Are you the one who is to come or are we to wait for another?"

[4]And so Jesus answered them, "Go report to John what you have heard and seen:

[5]The blind see again and the lame walk;
lepers are cleansed and the deaf hear;
the dead are raised,
and the poor have the good news preached to them.

[6]Congratulations to those who don't take offense at me."

8. Matt 11:7–11 (source: Q 7:24–28). Having reported Jesus' response to the inquiry from JB about him, Matthew now provides Jesus' assessment of JB:

⁷After ⟨John's disciples⟩ had departed, Jesus began to talk about John to the crowds: "What did you go out to the wilderness to gawk at? A reed shaking in the wind? ⁸What did you really go out to see? A man dressed in fancy ⟨clothes⟩? But wait! Those who wear fancy ⟨clothes⟩ are found in regal quarters. ⁹Come on, what did you go out to see? A prophet? Yes, that's what you went out to see, yet someone more than a prophet.
    ¹⁰"This is the one about whom it was written:

Here is my messenger,
whom I send on ahead of you
to prepare your way before you.

¹¹"I swear to you, among those born of women no one has arisen who is greater than John the Baptist; yet the least in Heaven's domain is greater than he."

9. Matt 11:12–13 (source: Q 16:16). Matthew continues with a somewhat enigmatic saying of Jesus about JB that explains JB's place in salvation history:

¹²"From the time of John the Baptist until now Heaven's imperial rule has been breaking in violently, and violent men are attempting to gain it by force. ¹³You see, the Prophets and even the Law predicted everything that was to happen prior to John's time.

10. Matt 11:14–15 (source: M). Into the block of material about Jesus and JB from Q, Matthew has added this startling pronouncement of Jesus about JB's identity:

¹⁴And if you are willing to admit it, John is the Elijah who was expected. ¹⁵Anyone here with two ears had better listen!"

11. Matt 11:16–19 (source: Q 7:34–35). Matthew concludes his sequence of passages on the relationship between JB and Jesus with a brief parable and added sayings from Q that explain the negative responses to JB and Jesus:

¹⁶"What does this generation remind me of? It is like children sitting in marketplaces who call out to others:

¹⁷We played the flute for you,
but you wouldn't dance;

we sang a dirge
but you wouldn't mourn.

[18]Just remember, John appeared on the scene neither eating nor drinking, and they say, 'He is demented.' [19]The son of Adam came both eating and drinking, and they say, 'There's a glutton and a drunk, a crony of toll collectors and sinners!' Indeed, wisdom is vindicated by her deeds."

12. Matt 14:1–12 (source: Mark 6:14–29). The story of JB's fate represents the first of three Marcan passages involving JB that Matthew has placed between Jesus' speeches on the secrets of Heaven's rule (ch. 13) and on the congregation (ch. 18):

[1]On that occasion Herod the tetrarch heard the rumor about Jesus [2]and said to his servants, "This is John the Baptizer. He has been raised from the dead, that's why miraculous powers are at work in him."

[3]Herod, remember, had arrested John, put him in chains, and thrown him in prison, on account of Herodias, his brother Philip's wife. [4]John, for his part, had said to him, "It is not right for you to have her."

[5]And while ⟨Herod⟩ wanted to kill him, he was afraid of the crowd because they regarded ⟨John⟩ as a prophet. [6]On Herod's birthday, the daughter of Herodias danced for them and captivated Herod, [7]so he swore an oath and promised to give her whatever she asked.

[8]Prompted by her mother, she said, "Give me the head of John the Baptist right here on a platter."

[9]The king was sad, but on account of his oath and his dinner guests, he ordered that it was to be done. [10]And he sent and had John beheaded in prison. [11]⟨John's⟩ head was brought on a platter and presented to the girl, and she gave it to her mother. [12]Then his disciples came and got his body and buried him. Then they went and told Jesus.

13. Matt 16:13–20 (source: Mark 8:27–30 and M). Matthew reports the Marcan account of the events near Caesarea Philippi, but inserts words of Jesus' acceptance of Peter's confession about his identity (16:17–19):

[13]When Jesus came to the region of Caesarea Philippi, he started questioning his disciples, asking, "What are people saying about the son of Adam?"

[14]They said, "Some ⟨say, 'He is⟩ John the Baptist,' but others 'Elijah,' and others 'Jeremiah or one of the prophets.'"

[15]He says to them, "What about you, who do you say I am?"

¹⁶And Simon Peter responded, "You are the Anointed, the son of the living God!"

¹⁷And in response Jesus said to him, "You are to be congratulated, Simon son of Jonah, because flesh and blood did not reveal this to you but my Father who is in heaven. ¹⁸Let me tell you, you are Peter, 'the Rock,' and on this very rock I will build my congregation, and the gates of Hades will not be able to overpower it. ¹⁹I shall give you the keys of Heaven's domain, and whatever you bind on earth will be considered bound in heaven, and whatever you release on earth will be considered released in heaven."

²⁰Then he ordered the disciples to tell no one that he was the Anointed.

14. Matt 17:9–13   (source: Mark 9:9–13). Matthew has taken over the Marcan conversation between Jesus and his disciples after the tranfiguration, but with the added comment that the disciples fully understand Jesus' words about JB's identity (17:13):

⁹And as they came down from the mountain, Jesus ordered them: "Don't tell anyone about this vision until the son of Adam has been raised from the dead."

¹⁰And the disciples questioned him: "Why, in the light of this, do the scholars claim that Elijah must come first?"

¹¹In response he said, "Elijah does indeed come and will restore everything. ¹²But I tell you that Elijah has already come, and they did not recognize him but had their way with him. So the son of Adam is also going to suffer at their hands."

¹³Then the disciples understood that he had been talking to them about John the Baptist.

15. Matt 21:23–27   (source: Mark 11:27–33). After Jesus' discourse on the congregation (ch. 18) and before his fifth and final speech on the end of the age (chs. 24–25), Matthew repeats with little alteration Mark's account of the verbal exchange Jesus had with the temple authorities involving the authority of JB:

²³And when he came to the temple area, the ranking priests and elders of the people approached him while he was teaching, and asked, "By what right are you doing these things?" and "Who gave you this authority?"

²⁴In response Jesus said to them, "I also have one question for you. If you answer me, I'll tell you by what authority I do these things. ²⁵The baptism of John, what was its origin? Was it heaven-sent or was it of human origin?"

And they conferred among themselves, saying, "If we say 'heaven-sent,' he'll say to us, 'Why didn't you trust him?' ²⁶And if we say 'Of human origin . . . !' We are afraid of the crowd." (Remember, everybody considered John a prophet.) ²⁷So they answered Jesus by saying, "We can't tell."

He replied to them in kind: "I'm not going to tell you by what authority I do these things either!"

16. Matt 21:28–32 (source: M). Matthew's final reference to JB occurs in Jesus' application of his parable of Two Sons, which immediately follows the verbal exchange between Jesus and the temple authorities:

²⁸Now what do you think? A man had two children. He went to the first, and said, "Son, go and work in the vineyard today."

²⁹He responded, "I'm your man, sir," but he didn't move.

³⁰Then he went to the second and said the same thing.

He responded, "I don't want to," but later on he thought better of it and went ⟨to work⟩.

³¹Which of the two did what the father wanted?

They said, "The second."

Jesus said to them, "I swear to you, the toll collectors and prostitutes will get into God's domain, but you will not. ³²After all, John came to you advocating justice, but you didn't believe him; yet the toll collectors and prostitutes believed him. Even after you observed ⟨this⟩, you didn't think better of it later and believe him."

Matthew's Portrayal of JB

How has Matthew presented JB? How does Matthew's treatment of JB differ from that of his sources, especially Mark? What details in the presentation may be of interest to the historian?

Matthew portrays JB as the prophetic, Elijah-returned forerunner to Jesus the Anointed, the Messiah, the Christ. Matthew's basic understanding of JB follows along the lines already established in his Marcan and Q sources. But Matthew goes beyond them. In Mark and Q, Jesus only implicitly identified JB as Elijah the prophet to his own disciples. In Matthew, Jesus *explicitly* identifies JB as Elijah even to the crowds (11:14–15); and later, Jesus' disciples are said to understand his identification (17:13). According to Matthew, therefore, Jesus' messiahship (16:13–20) and JB's Elijahship (11:14–15; 17:13) are not secretive.

The details of JB's ministry incorporated in Matthew also correspond rather closely to the details offered in Mark.

The locale of JB's ministry is the wilderness, although Matthew has added an explanatory phrase—wilderness "of Judea" (3:1). In the wilderness, the Jordan River is the stated site of JB's baptizing activity (3:6, 13). JB maintains the personal appearance and living style of an ascetic by wearing attire of camel hair with a leather belt and by eating locusts and raw honey (3:4). That JB is an ascetic is further underscored in Matthew by the addition of Q sayings. One saying of Jesus compares the simple dress of JB with the fancy attire of the upper classes (11:8). Another saying of Jesus contrasts JB's refusal to eat and drink with his own practice of eating and drinking (11:18–19).

The characteristic activities of JB in Matthew remain baptizing and preaching. But there are developments in Matthew beyond Mark because of Matthew's use of Q and Matthew's own special traditions and comments. First, there are developments in Matthew's reporting both of JB's message and of the activity of the coming one promised by JB. Secondly, there are also developments in Matthew's treatment of JB's baptism of Jesus.

First, Mark summarizes, in indirect speech, the content of JB's message as a baptism of repentance; and he reports, in direct speech, a saying by JB that a coming one will baptize with holy spirit. Matthew, however, has formulated a summary of JB's message that corresponds word for word with the later summaries of Jesus' message and the message of Jesus' disciples: "Change your ways because Heaven's imperial rule is closing in" (3:1; 4:17; 10:7; also 11:12–13). Furthermore, Matthew has added Q material that makes both JB and his promised coming one into apocalyptic figures proclaiming and bringing judgment. JB speaks about "impending doom," and "the axe aimed at the root of the tree" (3:7–10). The coming one will baptize with "holy spirit and fire" and "burn with fire" (3:11–12).

Secondly, Mark matter of factly states that JB baptized Jesus. Taken at face value, the reader might infer that Jesus went to be baptized as an act of repentance in order to receive God's forgiveness. Matthew protects Jesus from any notion of sinfulness by inserting M material into the Marcan story. Now JB himself acknowledges his subordination to Jesus and baptizes Jesus only because Jesus expressly commanded him to do so (3:14–15). Matthew has appropriately changed the opening word of the heavenly voice from the Marcan personal "You . . ." to the demonstrative "This, . . ." thereby suggesting that not only Jesus but also JB heard the divine pronouncement (3:17).

In Matthew, the responses to JB by various sectors of Palestinian society are described similarly to the presentations in Mark.

The general populace responds positively to JB. Matthew mentions not only Jerusalem and all Judea but "all of the region around the Jordan" as coming forth to be baptized (3:5). Matthew repeats the Marcan notation that everyone considers JB to be a prophet (21:26), but continues by singling out toll collectors and prostitutes as groups who believed JB (21:32).

The religious leaders respond to JB with a certain resignation. Matthew repeats the Marcan story how in Jerusalem they refuse to answer Jesus' question about the authority of JB (21:23–27). Matthew, however, specifically mentions only priests and elders, not scholars.

The political leadership responds to JB with hostility. Matthew retells, but condenses in characteristic fashion, the Marcan account of JB's arrest and execution by Herod Antipas (14:1–12). Matthew also alters the Marcan portrayal of Herod Antipas as one who respects JB as a holy and just man. In Matthew, only fear of the crowds who view JB as a prophet restrains Herod's hand until the trickery of Herodias through her dancing daughter forces him to act.

Mark contains evidence that JB had established a movement of disciples during his lifetime: JB's disciples ask Jesus about fasting and also take care of their master's body for burial. Matthew retains these two references to JB's disciples (9:14; 14:12) and adds the Q account of those inquiring disciples sent to Jesus by JB during the latter's imprisonment (11:2).

6 GOSPEL OF LUKE– BOOK OF ACTS

The Gospel of Luke and the Book of Acts constitute a massive two-volume work on Christian origins. The Gospel of Luke narrates the story of Jesus' ministry. The Book of Acts narrates the story of the earliest church. Like the author of Matthew, this writer uses the Gospel of Mark and the Sayings Gospel Q as written sources for telling the story of Jesus. There is also a considerable amount of material peculiar to the gospel which can be identified by the symbol L, whether created or inherited by the author. The writer must have had access to a variety of traditions, even written sources, for telling the story of the church. But a designation of sources underlying the material in Acts will not be made since no scholarly consensus exists. Most of what is said about JB in Acts could have been created by the gospel writer based on the information about JB derived from Mark and Q.

Origin and Structure of Luke-Acts

In the style of Graeco-Roman history writing, the author of Luke-Acts begins his two-volume narrative with a formal preface giving some information about the origin of the work (Luke 1:1–4); and he opens the second volume with a reference back to the first volume (Acts 1:1–2). Both volumes are addressed to "Theophilus," a Greek name meaning "friend of God" or "God-lover." The name could be either the personal name of an individual or a symbolic name referring to any person in the Greek or Gentile world interested in the events narrated. The stated purpose of this ambitious undertaking is to instill confidence in Theophilus of the truth or reliability of what he has been taught about Christianity.

Whoever wrote Luke-Acts was not a participant in the events recorded, at least in the gospel. In the preface, the writer sharply distinguishes between himself and earlier "eyewitnesses" and "ministers of the word." Indeed, the writer acknowledges the existence of other narratives which, from the perspective of modern scholarship, would be an allusion to the gospel of Mark and the Sayings Gospel Q, among others.

Early church tradition attributed the authorship of Luke-Acts to Luke the Gentile physician and companion of Paul. Such a Luke is mentioned in letters attributed to Paul (Phlm 24; Col 4:14; 2 Tim 4:11). Luke does not appear by name anywhere in the Book of Acts. But some scholars have found support for Lucan authorship in those strange "we"-passages in the Book of Acts (16:10–17; 20:5–15; 21:1–18; 27:1–28:16). In the midst of the narration of Paul's travels around the Mediterranean, the writer suddenly shifts from the third person "they" to the first person "we," suggesting that the writer is accompanying Paul.

Other scholars argue that the "we"-passages simply indicate that the writer was using a diary of Paul's travels as a source, although the diary itself may have been the jottings of Luke. Still other scholars think that the claim of Lucan authorship for this two-volume work is as suspect as the claims for Marcan authorship of Mark and Matthean authorship of Matthew.

Suggestions of the place of writing of Luke-Acts have also varied widely. There has been a general recognition of an origin somewhere outside Palestine. Specific sites mentioned range from Antioch in Syria to Rome. Luke-Acts was a work roughly contemporary with the Gospel of Matthew, since the authors of Matthew and Luke-Acts depended upon Mark but wrote independently of each other. The dates for the writing of these two volumes, therefore, would have been sometime during the mid 80s to the early 90s.

What about the overall literary structure of Luke-Acts? The theological plan?

Since the Lucan gospel narrative relies upon the Marcan story, Jesus' public ministry in Luke reflects a geographical pattern of activity in Galilee (chs. 3–9), travel from Galilee to Jerusalem (chs. 9–19), and activity in Jerusalem (chs. 19–23). But already there appears a significant development beyond Mark. In Mark the journey of Jesus from Galilee to Jerusalem takes only one chapter; but in Luke, Jesus winds his way up to Jerusalem for some ten chapters. Furthermore, notations within the narrative suggest that for Luke the travels of Jesus take him through the territory of Samaria (9:51–56; 10:30–37; 17:11–19). Luke has prefaced his Marcan material with L traditions related to the birth and infancy of Jesus (chs. 1–2) and supplemented his Marcan material with L traditions about the resurrection appearances of Jesus (ch. 24).

Luke, however, does not stop with the story of Jesus. Alone among the gospel writers he continues with a narration of the story of the earliest church. Jesus himself had traveled from Galilee by way of Samaria to Jerusalem. Now the church travels from Jerusalem by way of Samaria to

Rome, from the center of the Jewish world to the center of the Gentile world. In the first half of the book of Acts, the church under the leadership of Peter moves from Jerusalem through Samaria to Antioch in Syria (chs. 1–12). In the second half, the church moves out of Antioch by way of Cyprus, Asia Minor, and Greece to Rome through the missionary travels of Paul (chs. 13–28).

Even the geographical scheme of Luke-Acts, therefore, recognizes the universality of Jesus' ministry and the mission of the church. Jesus and the church are for all folk—Samaritan and Jew, Jew and Gentile. This universal emphasis is all the more understandable if the two volumes were written by a Gentile, such as Luke, to Theophilus, also a Gentile.

Among scholars there is general recognition that the geographical movement throughout Luke-Acts occurs within an overarching framework of salvation history. Luke sees the way of God as working itself out within history in terms of three periods: (1) the period of Israel; (2) the period of Jesus; and (3) the period of the church.

Literarily, therefore, Luke 1–2 mark the transition from the period of Israel to the period of Jesus; and Acts 1–2 mark the period of transition from the period of Jesus to the period of the church. Throughout Luke-Acts, Luke uses the theme of God's spirit, the holy spirit, to link these periods. During the transition period from Israel to Jesus (Luke 1–2), the holy spirit inspires selected individuals including JB (1:15, 41, 67; 2:25, 26, 27). During the period of Jesus (Luke 3–24), that spirit which created him (1:35) descends (3:22) and rests upon him throughout his life (especially 4:14–30 and 23:46). During the transition from Jesus to the the church (Acts 1–2), the church awaits and receives the spirit (1:4–5; 2:4, 17, 18). Throughout the period of the church (Acts 3–28), the spirit empowers and guides the church in its missionary outreach (for example, 10:44–48; 13:1–4).

Diagrammatically the literary-geographical-theological structure of Luke-Acts appears thus:

     Preface (Luke 1:1–4)
    I. Transition—Period of Israel to Period of Jesus (Luke 1–2)
   II. Period of Jesus (Luke 3–24)
     A. Galilee (3–9)
     B. Journey through Samaria (9–19)
     C. Jerusalem (19–24)
     Preface (Acts 1:1–2)
    I. Transition—Period of Jesus to Period of Church (Acts 1–2)
   II. Period of Church (Acts 3–28)
     A. From Jerusalem through Samaria to Antioch (1–12)
     B. From Antioch through Greece to Rome (13–28)

Scattered throughout Luke-Acts are twenty-eight passages that make reference to JB. Twenty-one of the passages appear in the Gospel of Luke, seven in the book of Acts. The passages vary greatly in length.

Texts in Luke-Acts about JB

1. Luke 1:5–25 (source: L). In this the first of five passages about JB in the infancy narratives, Luke describes the angel Gabriel's annunciation of his birth to Zechariah and his conception in the womb of Elizabeth:

⁵In the days of Herod, king of Judea, there happened to be this priest named Zechariah, who belonged to the priestly clan of Abijah. His wife, a descendant of Aaron, was named Elizabeth. ⁶They were both scrupulous in the sight of God, obediently following all the commandments and ordinances of the Lord. ⁷But they had no children, because Elizabeth was infertile, and both were well along in years. ⁸While he was serving as priest before God, when his priestly clan was on temple duty, ⁹it so happened that he was chosen by lot, according to the custom of the priesthood, to enter the sanctuary of the Lord and burn incense.

¹⁰At the hour of incense, while a huge crowd was praying outside, ¹¹there appeared to him a messenger of the Lord standing to the right of the altar of incense. ¹²When he saw him, Zechariah was shaken and overcome by fear. ¹³But the heavenly messenger said to him, "Don't be afraid, Zechariah, for your prayer has been heard, and your wife Elizabeth will bear you a son, and you are to name him John. ¹⁴And you will be joyful and elated, and many will rejoice at his birth, ¹⁵because he will be great in the sight of the Lord; he will drink no wine or beer, and he will be filled with holy spirit from the very day of his birth. ¹⁶And he will cause many of the children of Israel to turn to the Lord their God. ¹⁷He will precede him in the spirit and power of Elijah: he will turn the hearts of the parents back towards their children, and the disobedient back towards the ways of righteousness, and will make people ready for their lord."

¹⁸But Zechariah said to the heavenly messenger, "How can I be sure of this? For I am an old man and my wife is well along in years."

¹⁹And the messenger answered him, "I am Gabriel, the one who stands in the presence of God. I was sent to speak to you, and to bring you this good news. ²⁰Listen to me: you will be struck silent and speechless until the day these things happen, because you did not trust my words, which will come true at the appropriate time."

²¹Meanwhile, the people were waiting for Zechariah, wondering why he was taking so long in the sanctuary. ²²And when he did come

out and was unable to speak to them, they realized that he had seen a vision inside. And he kept making signs to them, since he could not speak. [23]And it so happened, when his time of official service was completed, that he went back home.

[24]Afterwards, his wife Elizabeth conceived, and went into seclusion for five months, telling herself: [25]"This is how the Lord has seen fit to deal with me in his good time in taking away the public disgrace ⟨of my infertility⟩."

2. Luke 1:36 (source: L). In the midst of the angel Gabriel's annunciation of Jesus' birth to Mary appears a brief reference to her relative Elizabeth's conception of JB:

[36]Further, your relative Elizabeth has also conceived a son in her old age. She who was said to be infertile is already six months along

3. Luke 1:39–45 (source: L). Having paralleled the annunciations and conceptions of JB and Jesus, Luke reports this meeting between their mothers, and thus between them:

[39]At that time Mary set out in haste for a city in the hill country of Judah, [40]where she entered Zechariah's house and greeted Elizabeth. [41]And it so happened, when Elizabeth heard Mary's greeting, the baby jumped in her womb. Elizabeth was filled with holy spirit [42]and proclaimed at the top of her voice, "Blessed are you among women, and blessed is the fruit of your womb! [43]Who am I that the mother of my lord should visit me? [44]You see, when the sound of your greeting reached my ears, the baby jumped for joy in my womb. [45]Congratulations to her who trusted that what the Lord promised her would come true."

4. Luke 1:57–79 (source: L). Luke reports JB's birth, circumcision, and naming followed by Zechariah's prophecy about his son:

[57]The time came for Elizabeth to give birth and she had a son. [58]Her neighbors and relatives heard that the Lord had shown her great mercy, and they rejoiced with her. [59]And so on the eighth day they came to circumcise the child; and they were going to name him Zechariah after his father.

[60]His mother spoke up and said, "No; he is to be called John."

[61]But they said to her, "No one in your family has this name." [62]So they made signs to his father, asking what he would like him to be called.

[63]He asked for a writing tablet and to everyone's astonishment he

wrote, "His name is John." [64]And immediately his mouth was opened and his tongue loosed, and he began to speak, blessing God.

[65]All their neighbors became fearful, and all these things were talked about throughout the entire hill country of Judea. [66]And all who heard about these things took them to heart and wondered: "Now what is this child going to be?" You see, the hand of the Lord was with him.

[67]Then his father Zechariah was filled with holy spirit and prophesied: [68]"Blessed be the Lord, the God of Israel, for he has visited and ransomed his people. [69]He has raised up for us a horn of salvation in the house of David his servant. [70]This is what he promised in the words of his holy prophets of old: [71]deliverance from our enemies, and from the hands of all who hate us; [72]mercy to our ancestors, and the remembrance of his holy covenant. [73]This is the oath he swore to Abraham our ancestor: [74]to grant that we be rescued from the hands of our enemies, to serve him without fear, [75]in holiness and righteousness before him all our days. [76]And you, child, will be called a prophet of the Most High; for you will go before the Lord to prepare his way, [77]to give his people knowledge of salvation through the forgiveness of their sins. [78]In the heartfelt mercy of our God, the dawn from on high will visit us, [79]to shine on those sitting in darkness, in the shadow of death, to guide our feet to the way of peace."

5. Luke 1:80 (source L). Luke concludes his presentation of JB's infancy with this summary statement of his later years:

[80]And the child grew up and became strong in spirit. He was in the wilderness until the day of his public appearance to Israel.

6. Luke 3:1–6 (source: Mark 1:2–6). Luke begins his narrative of Jesus' ministry with a block of six passages about JB with the first passage an adaptation of the Marcan account of JB's activity in the wilderness:

[1]In the fifteenth year of the rule of Emperor Tiberius, when Pontius Pilate was governor of Judea, Herod tetrarch of Galilee, his brother Philip tetrarch of the district of Iturea and Trachonitis, and Lysanias tetrarch of Abilene, [2]during the high-priesthood of Annas and Caiaphas, the word of God came to John, son of Zechariah, in the wilderness. [3]And he went into the whole region around the Jordan, calling for baptism and a change of heart that lead to forgiveness of sins. [4]As is written in the book of the sayings of Isaiah the prophet,

The voice of someone shouting in the wilderness:
"Make ready the way of the Lord,

make his paths straight.
⁵Every valley will be filled,
and every mountain and hill leveled.
What is crooked will be made straight,
and the rough ways smooth.
⁶Then the whole human race will see the salvation of God."

7. Luke 3:7–10 (source: Q 3:7–9). Luke reports a Q saying of judgment addressed by JB to the crowds, not to Sadducees and Pharisees as in Matthew:

⁷So ⟨John⟩ would say to the crowds that came out to be baptized by him, "You spawn of Satan! Who warned you to flee from the impending doom? ⁸Well then, start producing fruits suitable for a change of heart, and don't even start saying to yourselves, 'We have Abraham as our father.' Let me tell you, God can raise up children for Abraham right out of these rocks. ⁹Even now the axe is aimed at the root of the trees. So every tree not producing choice fruit gets cut down and tossed into the fire."
¹⁰The crowds would ask him, "So what should we do?"

8. Luke 3:10–14 (source: L). Luke adds L material which includes injunctions by JB not only to the crowds but to toll collectors and soldiers:

¹⁰The crowds would ask him, "So what should we do?"
¹¹And he would answer them, "Whoever has two shirts should share with someone who has none; whoever has food should do the same."
¹²Toll collectors also came to be baptized, and they would ask him, "Teacher, what should we do?" ¹³He told them, "Charge nothing above the official rates." ¹⁴Soldiers also asked him, "And what about us?" And he said to them, "No more shakedowns! No more frame-ups either! And be satisfied with your pay."

9. Luke 3:15–18 (source: Mark 1:7–8 and Q 3:16–17). Luke has amplified the Marcan saying about a coming one by adding words from Q that carry forward the theme of judgment:

¹⁵The people were filled with expectation and everyone was trying to figure out whether John might be the Anointed.
¹⁶John's answer was the same to everyone: "I baptize you with water; but someone more powerful than I is coming, whose sandal straps I am not fit to untie. He'll baptize you with [holy] spirit and fire. ¹⁷His pitchfork is in his hand, to make a clean sweep of his threshing floor

and to gather his wheat into the granary, but the chaff he'll burn in a fire that can't be put out."

¹⁸And so, with many other exhortations he preached to the people.

10. Luke 3:19–20 (source: Mark 1:14, 6:17–18). Rearranging the sequence found in Mark, Luke notes JB's arrest before the baptism of Jesus:

¹⁹But Herod the tetrarch, who had been denounced by John over the matter of Herodias, his brother's wife, ²⁰topped off all his other crimes by shutting John up in prison.

11. Luke 3:21–22 (source: Mark 1:9–11). Having just noted the arrest of JB, Luke does not even mention JB in his retelling of the Marcan account of Jesus' baptism:

²¹And it so happened when all the people were baptized, and after Jesus had been baptized and while he was praying, the sky opened up, ²²and the holy spirit came down on him in bodily form like a dove, and a voice came from the sky, "You are my son; today I have become your father."

12. Luke 5:33–39 (source: Mark 2:18–22). Midway through his presentation of Jesus' ministry in Galilee, Luke retells the Marcan story about JB's disciples and fasting:

³³They said to him, "The disciples of John are always fasting and offering prayers, and so are those of the Pharisees, but yours just eat and drink."

³⁴And Jesus said to them, "You can't make the groom's friends fast as long as the groom is present, can you? ³⁵But the days will come when the groom is taken away from them, and then they will fast, in those days."

³⁶He then gave them a proverb: "Nobody tears a piece from a new garment and puts it on an old one, since the new one will tear and the piece from the new will not match the old. ³⁷And nobody pours young wine into old wineskins, otherwise the young wine will burst the wineskins, it will gush out, and the wineskins will be destroyed. ³⁸Instead, young wine must be put into new wineskins. ³⁹Besides, nobody wants young wine after drinking aged wine. As they say, 'Aged wine is just fine!'"

13. Luke 7:18–23 (source: Q 7:18–23). Luke has also incorporated into the broader setting of Jesus' work in Galilee a series of four passages which offer comment on how JB and Jesus relate to each other:

¹⁸The disciples of John brought reports of all these things to him. ¹⁹John summoned two of his disciples and sent them to the Lord to ask: "Are you the one who is to come, or are we to wait for someone else?" ²⁰And when the men came to ⟨Jesus⟩, they said, "John the Baptist sent us to you to ask: 'Are you the expected one, or are we to wait for someone else?'"

²¹Jesus had just cured many of their diseases and plagues and evil spirits, and restored sight to many who were blind. ²²And so he answered them, "Go report to John what you have seen and heard:

> the blind see again,
> the lame walk,
> lepers are cleansed,
> the deaf hear,
> the dead are raised,
> and the poor have the good news preached to them.

²³Congratulations to those who don't take offense at me."

14. Luke 7:24–28   (source: Q 7:24–28). Having reported Jesus' response to the inquiry from JB about him, Luke now gives Jesus' assessment of JB:

²⁴After John's messengers had left, ⟨Jesus⟩ began to talk about John to the crowds: "What did you go out to the wilderness to gawk at? A reed shaking in the wind? ²⁵What did you really go out to see? A man dressed in fancy clothes? But wait! Those who dress fashionably and live in luxury are found in palaces. ²⁶Come on, what did you go out to see? A prophet? Yes, that's what you went out to see, yet someone more than a prophet. ²⁷This is the one about whom it was written:

> Here is my messenger,
> whom I send on ahead of you
> to prepare your way before you.

²⁸I tell you, among those born of women none is greater than John; yet, the least in God's domain is greater than he."

15. Luke 7:29–30   (source: L). Luke himself, thus the designation L for the source, makes a parenthetical statement about the divided response to God:

²⁹All the people, even the toll collectors, who were listening and had been baptized by John, vindicated God's plan; ³⁰but the Pharisees and

the legal experts, who had not been baptized by him, subverted God's plan for themselves.

16. Luke 7:31–35 (source: Q 7:31–35). Luke concludes the series of four passages on the relationship between JB and Jesus with a brief parable and other sayings from Q which explain the negative response to JB and Jesus:

³¹"What do members of this generation remind me of? What are they like? ³²They are like children sitting in the marketplace and calling out to one another:

> We played the flute for you,
> but you wouldn't dance;
> we sang a dirge,
> but you wouldn't weep.

³³"Just remember, John the Baptist appeared on the scene, eating no bread and drinking no wine, and you say, 'He is demented.' ³⁴The son of Adam appeared on the scene both eating and drinking, and you say, 'There is a glutton and a drunk, a crony of toll collectors and sinners!' ³⁵Indeed, wisdom is vindicated by all her children."

17. Luke 9:7–9 (source: Mark 6:14–29). Before shifting the scene of Jesus' ministry away from Galilee, Luke makes reference to the beheading of JB but without retelling the dramatic Marcan story:

⁷Now Herod the tetrarch heard of all that was happening. He was perplexed because some were saying that John had been raised from the dead, ⁸some that Elijah had appeared, and others that one of the ancient prophets had come back to life. ⁹Herod said, "John I beheaded; but this one about whom I hear such things—who is he?" And he was curious to see him.

18. Luke 9:18–21 (source: Mark 8:27–30). In his version of the conversation between Jesus and his disciples that involves the mention of JB, Luke omits the Marcan place name Caesarea Philippi, leaving the impression that the verbal exchange occurred in Galilee:

¹⁸And on one occasion when Jesus was praying alone the disciples were with him; and he questioned them asking: "What are the crowds saying about me?"
¹⁹They said in response, "⟨Some say, 'You are⟩ John the Baptist,' while others ⟨say,⟩ 'Elijah,' and still others ⟨claim,⟩ 'One of the ancient prophets has come back to life.'"
²⁰Then he said to them, "What about you, who do you say I am?"

And Peter responded, "God's Anointed!"
²¹Then he warned them, and forbade them to tell this to anyone.

19. Luke 11:1-4 (source: L and Q 11:2-4). Luke has used Jesus' journey through Samaria as the setting for the so-called Lord's Prayer from Q and provides the prayer with an introduction that mentions the disciples of JB:

¹On one occasion he happened to be praying someplace. When he had finished, one of his disciples said to him, "Lord, teach us how to pray, just as John taught his disciples."
²He said to them, "When you pray, you should say:

Father, your name be revered.
Impose your imperial rule.
³Provide us with the bread we need day by day.
⁴Forgive our sins, since we too forgive everyone in debt to us.
And please don't subject us to test after test."

20. Luke 16:16 (source: Q 16:16). Jesus' journey through Samaria also serves as the setting of the Q saying about JB's place in salvation history which Luke has Jesus address to the Pharisees:

¹⁶"Right up to John's time you have the Law and the Prophets; since then God's imperial rule has been proclaimed as good news and everyone is breaking into it violently."

21. Luke 20:1-8 (source: Mark 11:27-33). Luke's final reference to JB in the gospel occurs in the Marcan story about the exchange between Jesus and the temple authorities in Jerusalem:

¹One day as he was teaching the people in the temple area and speaking of the good news, the ranking priests and the scholars approached him along with the elders, ²and put this question to him: "Tell us, by what right are you doing these things? Who gave you this authority?"
³In response Jesus said to them, "I also have a question for you: tell me, ⁴was John's baptism heaven-sent or was it of human origin?"
⁵And they started conferring among themselves, reasoning as follows: "If we say, 'Heaven sent,' he'll say, 'Why didn't you trust him?' ⁶But if we say, 'Of human origin,' the people will all stone us." Remember, ⟨the people⟩ were convinced John was a prophet. ⁷So they answered that they couldn't tell where it came from.
⁸And Jesus said to them, "Neither am I going to tell you by what authority I do these things!"

22. Acts 1:4-5. Luke reports a saying of Jesus uttered to his disciples or apostles during the forty-day period he appeared to them between his resurrection and his ascension:

> ⁴And while staying with them he enjoined them not to depart from Jerusalem, but to wait for the promise of the Father, which, he said, "you heard from me, ⁵for John baptized with water, but before many days you shall be baptized with the holy spirit."

23. Acts 1:21-22. Luke has Peter address believers after the ascension within which address these words state the criterion for the selection of a successor to the dead Judas:

> ²¹One of our companions must become a witness with us to his resurrection, and that person must have been with us all during the time the Lord Jesus came and went among us, ²²from his baptism at the hands of John until the day he ascended from us.

24. Acts 10:34-38. Luke has Peter speak to Cornelius the Gentile at Caesarea, on the occasion of the latter's conversion, with a speech to all present that begins with these words:

> ³⁴Peter spoke up and said, "I perceive for a fact that God does not have favorites, ³⁵but anyone, no matter the race, who fears God and does what is right will find divine approval. ³⁶You are aware of the message of peace God sent to the children of Israel through the agency of Jesus Christ (the one who is lord of all) ³⁷and of what transpired throughout the whole of Judea, beginning in Galilee following the John's call for baptism, ³⁸namely, how God anointed Jesus with holy spirit and power and how he went about performing good deeds and healing everyone tyrannized by the devil, since God was with him.

25. Acts 11:15-17. After the conversion of Cornelius, and the resultant outpouring of the holy spirit, Luke has Peter in Jerusalem defend his mission to Gentiles with a speech that concludes with these words:

> ¹⁵When I began to talk, the holy spirit came over them just as it did over us at the beginning. ¹⁶And I remembered what the Lord had said: "John baptized with water, but you will be baptized with holy spirit." ¹⁷If, therefore, God gave to them the same gift that was given to us at the time we began to trust in the Lord Jesus Christ, who was I to stand in God's way?

26. Acts 13:23-25. In the missionary speech of Paul in the synagogue at

John the Baptist in Film

In the twentieth century, Jesus took John with him to Hollywood. Frescoes and mosaics, stone sculptures and wood carvings, were superseded by celluloid. Perhaps more than any other medium, the passion play prepared the way for the presentation of Jesus and John on film.

The standard for the Jesus epic was set in the silent film period by Cecil B. De Mille's black and white "The King of Kings" (1927). But therein John has no role. John first assumed roles befitting his traditional place in the Christian story in those great Jesus epics that appeared shortly after mid-century: Samuel Bronston's "King of Kings" (1961), directed by Nicholas Ray; George Steven's "The Greatest Story Ever Told" (1965), with Stevens himself as producer and director; and Franco Zeffirelli's "Jesus of Nazareth" (1977), a film made not for the theatre but for home viewing via television. Each of these films, in its own way, used all four gospels as the basis for its script and, with varying degrees of effectiveness, wove the gospels together into one story.

In these films John appears in the guise of Robert Ryan, Charlton Heston, and Michael York respectively. Each characterization of John has its own distinctiveness, its memorable moments, whether dramatic or simply silly. In the "King of Kings," Jesus' mother Mary is present for her son's baptism by John and, in a conversation with John, assures him that her son is who he is. In "The Greatest Story," John is effectively introduced by his own words. The viewer sees a scene of sacrifice in the temple but hears as a voiceover John's call for repentance; and this scene dissolves into a scene of John's baptizing in the Jordan River. But when Jesus suddenly presents himself to John, John interrogates Jesus about his name and birthplace in a manner appropriate for an induction. Jesus responds: "Jesus" and "Bethlehem." In "Jesus of Nazareth," generally recognized to be the best of these films cinematically and theologically, Zefferelli introduces John with a careful harmonization of the fourth gospel and the synoptics. When a delegation from the Sanhedrin in Jerusalem visits John at the Jordan and asks him who he is, he responds "I am the voice of one crying in the wilderness." John's baptism is shown with a dove circling overhead and the sound of the heavenly voice. Then, in the presence his disciples, John declares Jesus to be the "lamb of God."

All three of these epics, therefore, include the baptism of Jesus by John. All three also include John's arrest and subsequent execution involving the threesome of Herod Antipas, Herodias, and Herodias' daughter, Salome. "King of Kings" conveys the execution of John to the viewer through the sound of John's cry; and the execution is communicated by the dull thud of the executioner's axe in "The Greatest Story." Zeffirelli, in "Jesus of Nazareth," has the camera cut away from the face of John in prison to the digging of his grave outside for his burial.

A glance at the credits would suggest that Pier Paolo Pasolini's "The Gospel According to St. Matthew" (1964 release in Italy, 1966 in the United States) and "Jesus" (1979), produced by director John Heyman's so-called Genesis Project, have little in common. Pasolini was an Italian Marxist; the Genesis Project had a Christian evangelistic purpose. The Heyman film continues to be shown throughout the world in more than a hundred languages by many mission organizations and denominations. However, each film represents an alternative to the epic tradition because it claims to follow the Jesus story as narrated by a single gospel. "The Gospel According to St. Matthew" follows the Jesus story as presented in the Gospel of Matthew; and "Jesus" follows the story as presented in the Gospel of Luke. In each film, therefore, John the Baptist appears in accordance with the presentation of John in the gospel on which it is based. For example, as we have noted, it is in "Jesus" that John does not touch Jesus at the latter's baptism. Jesus kneels and baptizes himself. Furthermore, in neither film is John played by a recognizable Hollywood actor.

The Jewison/Lloyd Webber/Rice "Jesus Christ Superstar" and the Greene/ Tebelak/Schwartz "Godspell" (both 1973) represent alternative approaches to the Jesus story. "Godspell," set in New York City, is also a John story. The film opens with the John figure, played by David Haskell, crossing the Brooklyn Bridge singing "Prepare Ye the Way of the Lord." John later baptizes the clown-faced Jesus in the the Bethesda Fountain in Central Park. "Superstar," in the tradition of a passion play, focuses on the last days of Jesus' life. John the Baptist has already passed from the scene, and does not appear.

The word "provocative" can certainly be used to describe Martin Scorsese's film "The Last Temptation of Christ" (1989), which was based on the Nikos Kazantzakis novel of the same name. The word "provocative" can also be used to describe the presentation of John the Baptist played by Andre Gregory. The viewers encounter a manic figure who has an formative impact on Jesus. After Jesus' baptism, at night, John and Jesus engage one another in a striking discussion over God's way. John identifies the God of Israel as the God of the desert. He speaks of the rottenness of the tree. He speaks of the axe as symbolic of his mission. By contrast, Jesus speaks of the heart—of love. But John has his way with Jesus. Jesus abandons his message of love and takes up the axe of judgment. Only toward the end of his ministry does Jesus set aside the axe and commit himself to his own God-ordained self-sacrifice in fulfillment of Isaiah 53.

John's screen appearances have not been confined to the titles mentioned here; and John has not seen his last cinematic embodiment. Filmmaker Paul Verhoeven has distinguished himself by a series of films of his own that can also be described by "provocative": "Robocop" (1987), "Total Recall," (1990), and "Basic Instinct" (1992). In recent years, he has immersed himself in the scholarly literature about Jesus. He has become an active participant in the Jesus Seminar in order to prepare for his own prospective Jesus film. He has expressed a special interest in the John/Jesus relationship and asked the members of the Seminar for reasoned speculation about the impact John must have had on Jesus. Individual members have expressed a high level of certainty about the trauma Jesus must have experienced on the execution of John the Baptist. Verhoeven's own resolution of the question will become public when his film takes its place alongside the others in the ongoing tradition of Jesus films.

Pisidian Antioch, Luke has Paul introduce Jesus to his hearers with these words:

> [23]As promised, out of ⟨David's⟩ descendants God has produced a savior for Israel, namely Jesus. [24]However, before ⟨Jesus⟩ appeared on the scene, John called for baptism signifying repentance among all the people of Israel. [25]When John was about to complete his work, he would announce: "What do you think I am? I am not the one. No, you are looking for someone who will succeed me, whose sandal straps I am not fit to untie."

27. Acts 18:24–28. The next to last reference to JB in Acts appears in a narrative by which Luke introduces Apollos:

> [24]Now this Jew named Apollos, a native of Alexandria, showed up in Ephesus. He was well educated and a competent interpreter of scripture. [25]He had been taught the way of the Lord and was on fire with the spirit; he used to speak and teach about Jesus correctly, except that he knew only the baptism of John. [26]He began to speak freely in the synagogue. But when Priscilla and Aquila heard him, they took him aside and explained the way of God more precisely to him. [27]And when he decided to go over to Achaia, his friends encouraged him and wrote to the disciples there to welcome him. When he arrived, he was of considerable assistance to those who had become believers through grace. [28]You see, he delivered a powerful and effective refutation of the Jews publicly, demonstrating on the basis of the scriptures that the Anointed was Jesus.

28. Acts 19:1–7. The last reference to JB in Acts appears in a story involving Paul, by which Luke again associates the gift of the holy spirit with the church:

> [1]It so happened, during the time Apollos was at Corinth, that Paul traveled through the interior and came to Ephesus. There he found some disciples. [2]He asked them, "When you came to have faith, did you receive holy spirit?" They ⟨responded⟩ to him: "Of course not. We didn't even know there was such a thing as holy spirit." [3]He continued, "What, then, was the point of your baptism?" They replied, "The point of John's baptism." [4]Paul said, "The baptism John practiced was a baptism of repentance; he told the people to trust in the one who was to come after him, namely, Jesus." [5]When they heard this, they were baptized in the name of the Lord Jesus. [6]When Paul laid his hands on them, the holy spirit came upon them. They would speak in tongues and prophesy. [7]There were about a dozen of them altogether.

Luke's Portrayal of JB

How has Luke presented JB? How does the presentation of JB in Luke-Acts differ from the presentations in his principal sources, Mark and Q, and in the Gospel of Matthew? What features and details in his presentation may be of interest to the historian?

Luke certainly offers the most comprehensive portrayal of JB of any ancient writer. Because Luke uses traditions both about JB's infancy and about issues related to JB in the church's mission to Gentiles, he goes beyond Mark, Q, and Matthew in a number of ways. *Luke does carry forward the presentation of JB as the prophetic, Elijah-like forerunner to Jesus the Anointed, the Messiah, the Christ.* For Luke, however, JB is *Elijah-like, not Elijah-returned.* Furthermore, Luke is less preoccupied with the Elijah-like status of JB throughout his work because JB, as well as Jesus, has been accommodated to his three-epoch view of salvation history.

In the infancy narratives, which mark the transition from the period of Israel to the period of Jesus (Luke 1–2), Luke does present *JB as the prophetic, Elijah-like forerunner to Jesus the Christ.* God begins a new initiative within Israel through the sending of the angel Gabriel to announce respectively the comings of JB and Jesus, JB of priestly lineage and Jesus of royal descent. The stories reporting their annunciations, births, circumcisions, namings, and upbringings are paralleled to one another even as the stories are intertwined. Indeed, their mothers, and thus they themselves, are relatives (1:36). Biologically, JB is a forerunner to Jesus, being six months older (1:36). But even in their mothers' wombs JB recognizes his subordination to Jesus by jumping for joy when the pregnant Mary approaches Elizabeth (1:44). Theologically, JB also appears as a forerunner to Jesus. But here, too, JB is clearly subordinated to Jesus. JB will be filled with the "holy spirit" from the moment he leaves the womb (1:15) and be called "a prophet of the Most High" (1:75). But Jesus will be conceived within the womb by the "holy spirit" (1:35) and, therefore, will be appropriately called "son of the Most High" (1:32) and "son of God" (1:35).

Within the infancy narratives, it is the angel Gabriel who associates JB with the prophet Elijah. Gabriel declares to Zechariah that JB will not only be filled with the holy spirit from the womb of his mother, but he will go forth in "the spirit and power of Elijah" (1:17).

In the narratives which describe the period of Jesus (Luke 3–24), Luke continues to cast *JB as a prophetic forerunner to Jesus as the Christ.* Luke opens the body of his gospel just as the prophetic books in scripture begin. There the writers often date God's call of the prophets in relation to the reigns of the kings of Israel and Judah. Luke similarly provides a date for when JB first received the "word of God." It was "in the fifteenth year of the rule of Tiberius Caesar . . ."(3:1–2). First comes the ministry of JB, only subsequently the ministry of Jesus—when he is "about thirty years old"

(3:23). Later during the ministry of Jesus, Luke reports the Q saying in which Jesus affirms JB to be not only "a prophet," but "more than a prophet" (7:24–28).

Also in the body of the gospel, Luke separates JB from Jesus with several bold strokes of the pen, thereby suggesting that the time of JB as prophetic forerunner has been superseded by the time of Jesus as the Christ. With one pen stroke Luke transposes the Marcan story of Jesus' baptism by JB and JB's arrest by Herod Antipas. Luke reports the imprisonment of JB by Herod Antipas (3:19–20) *before* he retells the story of Jesus' baptism (3:21–22). In the story of Jesus' baptism, therefore, he omits any reference to JB and does not even say that Jesus is baptized by JB. This explains the striking presentation of Jesus' baptism in the widely circulated film called *Jesus* (1979). In this film, based exclusively on the text of Luke, Jesus baptizes himself. (See the cameo essay, "John the Baptist in Film.") With another stroke, Luke also omits the engaging Marcan account of how Herodias and her dancing daughter conspired to have Herod execute JB. Luke simply reports that Herod Antipas had beheaded JB and thereby deemphasizes any correlation between the passion of JB and the passion of Jesus (9:7–9). With still another stroke, Luke gives another version of the Q saying about JB's place in salvation history which separates JB from Jesus (16:16). Jesus' word associates JB with the Law and the Prophets in contrast to the proclamation of God's imperial rule, which, of course, begins with Jesus.

Perhaps it is understandable, therefore, that in the body of the gospel Luke suppresses the association between JB and the prophet Elijah. He omits the Marcan description of JB's appearance in Elijah-like attire of animal skins and a leather belt. He also omits the Marcan conversation between Jesus and the disciples after the transfiguration during which Jesus implicitly identifies JB as Elijah.

In the opening chapters of Acts, which mark the transition from the epoch of Jesus to the epoch of the church (chs. 1–2), and in the body of Acts, which portrays the epoch of the church (chs. 3–28), *JB continues to be linked to Jesus as forerunner.* In their speeches, both Peter and Paul introduce the ministry of Jesus with references to JB as one having gone before him (1:21–22; 10:34-38; 13:23-25). Now, however, the emphasis falls not so much upon JB's prophetic role itself but upon his having had a ministry of water baptism, whereas the church has a ministry of baptism by the holy spirit. During the forty days between resurrection and ascension, the risen Jesus anticipates the outpouring of the holy spirit at Pentecost when he promises his followers: ". . . John baptized with water, but before many days you shall be baptized with holy spirit" (1:4-5). And Peter much later recalls Jesus' words when he defends his conversion of the Cornelius the Gentile: ". . . John baptized with water, but you shall be baptized with holy spirit . . ." (11:15–17). The stories about Apollos (18:24–25) and the twelve disciples at Ephesus (19:1–7) serve to indicate how JB's baptism with water has been superseded by the church's baptism of holy spirit. From the vantage point of the church now established in the Gentile world, neither the prophetic role nor the Elijah-like status of JB is of any importance. What are the details about JB reported in Luke-Acts that reinforce, supplement, or contradict the presentations of JB in Mark, Q, or Matthew?

Luke is comfortable with the designation of the wilderness and the region around the Jordan River as the locale of JB's activity (1:2, 3). Although he has removed from JB the attire and diet of Elijah, Luke does preserve references to JB that suggest an ascetic lifestyle, particularly JB's scruples about eating and drinking (5:35; 7:33; also 1:15).

For Luke, JB's characteristic activities remain baptizing and preaching. Like Mark, he summarizes JB's message as a baptism of repentance for the forgiveness of sins (3:3) and repeats JB's saying about one coming after him (3:16). Like Matthew, he has added Q material that makes both JB and the promised coming one into apocalyptic figures proclaiming and bringing judgment (3:7–10, 16–17). Unlike Matthew, however, Luke does not place on JB's lips nor associate JB with the theme of God's imperial rule, which characterizes the message of Jesus (16:16). Luke does report ethical teaching by JB found in no other writings (3:10–14).

In Luke, the responses to JB by the various segments of Palestinian society are described similarly to the presentations in the narrative gospels of Mark and Matthew, but with occasional differences.

The populace at large responds to JB positively. Among those receiving his baptism and teaching are not only the crowds (3:7, 10) but toll collectors (3:12; 7:29) and soldiers (3:14), the latter mentioned only in Luke. Also, only Luke includes the brief notation that there was among the people speculation as to whether or not JB was the messiah (3:15).

The religious leadership responds to JB with less favor. Pharisees and legal experts, who had evidently refused baptism, work in opposition to God's plan (7:30), while the priests, scholars, and elders in Jerusalem remain publicly non-committal on the issue of JB's authority (20:1–8).

The political leadership responds to JB with deadly force. For Luke, Herod Antipas assumes responsibility for the beheading of JB in his own words, with neither Herodias nor her daughter around to assume or share the responsibility (9:7–9). Earlier Luke had referred to the cause of JB's imprisonment as simply "the matter of Herodias, his brother's wife" and had summarily ranked JB's imprisonment among the tetrarch's "other crimes" (3:19–20).

In two specific areas, however, Luke goes significantly beyond Mark, Q, and Matthew in providing information about JB.

The first area has to do with the movement apparently initiated by JB during his lifetime that continued alongside the Jesus movement during Jesus' lifetime. Luke carries forward from Mark and Q references to disciples of JB (5:33; 7:18f). Luke also adds a reference to disciples of JB in his introduction to the so-called Lord's prayer (11:1); and he inserts a reference to prayer by JB's disciples in his introduction to the Marcan story about fasting (5:33). But the successive stories in Acts about Apollos the Jew from Alexandria (18:24–28) and the twelve disciples at Ephesus (19:1–7), all of whom knew only the baptism of JB, may provide evidence for the JB movement's having continued well after the lifetimes of JB and Jesus, and having established a presence outside of Palestine.

The second area has to do with the background and early years of JB. Here the infancy material about JB in Luke may make a contribution historically (1:5–24, 36, 39–45, 57–79, 80). Among the claims made on behalf of JB are these: JB was from a family of rural priests who lived in the hill country of Judea. His aged parents were named Zechariah and Elizabeth. His mother was a kinswoman to Mary, the mother of Jesus. He experienced the traditional rites of circumcision and naming. His upbringing was apparently in the wilderness.

7   GOSPEL OF JOHN

Even a cursory reading of the Gospel of John discloses its sharp differences in contrast to the synoptic gospels of Mark, Matthew, and Luke. Although ancient as well as modern scholars have claimed that the author of John was familiar with the synoptic gospels, most scholars in recent decades have concluded otherwise. John provides a literarily independent account of the Jesus story. How is John so different?

Difference of John

John differs from the synoptic gospels both in its outline of the Jesus story and in its portrayal of Jesus and his teaching.

In the synoptics, Jesus goes from Galilee to Jerusalem only once during his ministry. On that occasion he creates a commotion in the temple. He celebrates a meal with his disciples on Passover evening, using bread and wine as symbols of his impending death. He suffers crucifixion on Passover day. Since the synoptics mention only one Passover, the ministry of Jesus could have lasted one year, or less. In John, however, Jesus cleanses the temple at the outset of his ministry (2:13–25). On a later occasion in Jerusalem, he celebrates a meal with his disciples during which he anticipates his death by washing their feet (13:1–20). He dies not on Passover day but on the day of preparation for the Passover (19:14). He reportedly goes to Jerusalem four times (2:13; 5:1; 7:10; 12:12). Since John mentions at least three Passovers, the ministry of Jesus possibly lasted three years (2:13; 6:4; 12:1).

In the synoptics, Jesus proclaims the kingdom of God—God's imperial rule. He uses parables and aphorisms as his characteristic forms of discourse. Generally he refuses to talk about his identity to friend and foe alike. In John, however, Jesus talks about himself incessantly, in long discourses, to anyone who will listen. Woven throughout these discourses are the themes of "love" and "eternal life" (e.g. 3:16; 13:1, 34–35; 15:12–13). But the central theme therein is Jesus himself. The discourses are punctuated with declarations by Jesus that begin with the words "I am, . . ." such as "I am the bread of life" (6:35, 38; also 8:12; 9:5; 10:7; 10:11, 14; 11:25; 14:6; 15:1). Jesus in John, therefore, talks like God talks in the Hebrew Scriptures (Ex 3:14; Isa 44:6).

Structure and Origin of John

That the identity of Jesus himself provides the focus of the Gospel of John appears in the literary structure of the gospel. The magnificent prologue opens with talk about that Word in the beginning with God which became flesh (1:1–18).

The gospel then presents Jesus' activity in the world at large as a series of "signs" (1:19–12:50). For John, "signs" (translated "miracles" in SV) is a technical term for those deeds of Jesus which disclose his identity as the one from God. The story of the feeding of the five thousand, for example, provides the point of departure for Jesus' discourse about himself as "the bread of life" (6:1–15, 22–71).

The gospel next presents Jesus' activity in preparation for his death and his return as Son to the Father (13:1–20:29). His so-called farewell discourses with his disciples on the night of his betrayal (13:1–17:26) are followed by his arrest, trial, crucifixion, and resurrection (18:1–20:29).

The gospel concludes with a statement of its purpose (20:30–31). The subsequent post-resurrection narrative is generally recognized to be a later addition to the gospel (21:1–25). Simply diagrammed, the gospel of John looks like this:

> Prologue (1:1–18)
> I. In the World (1:19–12:50)
> II. In Preparation for Return (13:1–20:29)
> Purpose (20:30–31)
> Appendix (21:1–25)

The peculiar emphasis in the gospel on Jesus' deeds as "signs" has led some scholars to suggest that underlying the present gospel may be what has been called the Signs Gospel. According to this view, the author of the present gospel has expanded this narrative gospel by the addition of Jesus' discourses. Whether or not they accept the hypothesis of a Signs Gospel, however, a number of scholars do believe that John may preserve historically accurate narrative details about Jesus' ministry—such as his several visits to Jerusalem. Also, whether or not they accept the hypothesis of a Signs Gospel, many scholars, including members of the Jesus Seminar, have come to a shared opinon about Jesus' discourses in John. Because of the differences between Jesus' words in John and the synoptics, Jesus' discourses in John represent the creative work of John and his community. In their creativity, of course, John and his community may have understood themselves to be guided by the "advocate," John's special name for the "holy spirit," also called "the spirit of truth" (14:16, 26; 15:26; 16:13). But Jesus' discourses contain little reminiscence of the *voice* of Jesus the historical figure of Galilee, although they may be considered profound and true from a theological point of view.

What can be said about John and his community? In the second century, the authorship of this gospel came to be attributed to John, the son of Zebedee, one Jesus' twelve disciples. That mysterious figure in the gospel known popularly as the "beloved disciple" (13:23; 18:15; 19:26, 35; 20:2; also 21:7, 20, 24) was identified as John. But as in the other gospels so in John, the author is not identified by personal name and must remain unknown.

Into this century John was often considered to be the most Greek, or hellenistic, of the canonical gospels. Particularly since the discovery of the Dead Sea Scrolls beginning in 1947, however, such paired themes as "light" and "darkness," "truth" and "falsehood," are understood to be thoroughly Jewish. Like the community for which Matthew was written, so the community of John seems to be engaged in a kind of spiritual warfare: Jew against Jew. It would appear that this community consisted of Christian Jews whose members had experienced expulsion from the synagogue (9:22; 12:42; 16:2). This would date the gospel some time in the 80s or 90s—after the fall of Jerusalem and after the beginning of the Jewish reforms at Jamnia. The term "Jews" ("Judeans," in SV) therefore, has become for this gospel a blanket name for those who reject Jesus as the Anointed, the Son of God (especially 8:12–59). Sharply focusing on the identity of Jesus, the author of John writes for his readers ". . . so you will come to believe that Jesus is the Anointed, God's son—and by believing this have life in his name" (20:30–31). Traditionally, Ephesus in Asia Minor was said to be the site of this gospel's origin since Ephesus was associated with the disciple named John. As with the identity of the author, however, the place of origin must remain unknown.

No less than the synoptic gospels, John underscores the relationship between Jesus and JB although here, too, significant differences will appear between the synoptics and the fourth gospel. John has ten passages which refer to JB. The first two passages appear in the prologue. The next four passages serve to introduce Jesus' work in the world; and the remaining four passages appear later in that first half of the gospel.

(In what follows the name John will be used for the author of the gospel, and JB will continue to designate John the Baptizer, although the gospel writer never uses the nickname "the Baptizer" for the John who baptizes. Also, those passages about JB that may be derived from the reconstructed Signs Gospel in the Scholars Version are designated SG with a question mark.)

Texts in John about JB

1. John 1:6–8 (source: SG? only vs. 6). John already introduces JB as a witness to the light coming into the world without having yet mentioned Jesus by personal name:

> [6]There appeared a man sent from God named John. [7]He came to testify—to testify to the light—so everyone would believe through him. [8]He was not the light; he came only to attest to the light.

2. John 1:15. John reintroduces JB as a witness—this time to the superiority of the one having come, but still without having mentioned Jesus by name:

> [15]John testifies on his behalf and has called out, "This is the one I was talking about when I said, 'He who is to come after me is actually my superior, because he was there before me.'"

3. John 1:19–24 (source: SG? vss. 19–23). John opens his narrative with representatives from Jerusalem asking JB about his identity:

> [19]This is what John had to say when the Judeans sent priests and Levites from Jerusalem to ask him, "Who are you?"
> [20]He made it clear—he wouldn't deny it—"I'm not the Anointed."
> [21]And they asked him, "Then what are you? Are you Elijah?"
> And he replies, "I am not."
> "Are you the Prophet?"
> He answered, "No."
> [22]So they said to him, "Tell us who you are so we can report to those who sent us. What have you got to say for yourself?"
> [23]He replied, "I am the voice of someone shouting in the wilderness, 'Make the way of the Lord straight'—that's how Isaiah the prophet put it."
> ([24]It was the Pharisees who had sent them.)

4. John 1:25–28 (source: SG? vss. 26b-27). Only now does John make reference to JB's baptizing activity as the questioning of JB continues:

> [25]"So," they persisted, "why are you baptizing if you're not the Anointed, not Elijah, and not the Prophet?"
> [26]John answered them, "I baptize, yes, but only with water. Right there with you is someone you don't yet recognize; [27]he is the one who is to be my successor. I don't even deserve to untie his sandal straps."
> [28]All this took place in Bethany on the far side of the Jordan, where John was baptizing.

5. John 1:29–34 (source: SG? vss. 29a, 31bc, 32b, 33d, 34c). John reports how JB witnesses to Jesus' identity including a contrast between his own water baptism and the spirit baptism of Jesus:

²⁹The next day John sees Jesus approaching and says, "Look, the lamb of God, who does away with the sin of the world. ³⁰This is the one I was talking about when I said, 'Someone is coming after me who is actually my superior, because he was there before me.' ³¹I didn't know who he was, although I came baptizing with water so he would be revealed to Israel."

³²And John continued to testify: "I have seen the spirit coming down like a dove out of the sky, and it hovered over him. ³³I wouldn't have recognized him, but the very one who sent me to baptize with water told me, 'When you see the spirit come down and hover over someone, that's the one who baptizes with holy spirit.' ³⁴I have seen this and I have certified: This is God's son."

6. John 1:35–42 (source: SG? vss. 35, 37–42). John concludes his series of passages about JB by reporting how two of JB's disciples, in response to his witness to Jesus, leave him and follow Jesus:

³⁵The next day John was standing there again with two of his disciples. ³⁶When he noticed Jesus walking by, he says, "Look, the lamb of God."

³⁷His two disciples heard him ⟨say this⟩, and they followed Jesus. ³⁸Jesus turned around, saw them following, and says to them, "What are you looking for?"

They said to him, "Rabbi" (which means Teacher), "where are you staying?"

³⁹He says to them, "Come and see."

They went and saw where he was staying and spent the day with him. It was about four in the afternoon.

⁴⁰Andrew, Simon Peter's brother, was one of the two who followed Jesus after hearing John ⟨speak about him⟩. ⁴¹First he goes and finds his brother Simon and tells him, "We have found the Messiah" (which is translated, Anointed), ⁴²and he took him to Jesus.

When Jesus laid eyes on him, he said "You're Simon, John's son; you're going to be called Kephas" (which means Peter ⟨or Rock⟩).

7. John 3:22–30. After Jesus' first sign of changing water into wine and his first trip to Jerusalem, John tells how parallel baptizing ministries by JB and Jesus prompt JB's final verbal witness to Jesus:

²²After this Jesus and his disciples went to Judea, and he extended

his stay with them there and began to baptize. ²³John was baptizing too, in Aenon near Salim, since there was plenty of water around; and people kept coming to be baptized. (²⁴Remember, John hadn't yet been thrown in prison.)

²⁵A dispute over purification broke out between John's disciples and one of the Judeans. ²⁶They came to John and reported: "Rabbi, that fellow who was with you across the Jordan—you spoke about him earlier—guess what! He's now baptizing and everyone is flocking to him."

²⁷John answered, "You can't lay claim to anything unless it's a gift from heaven. ²⁸You yourselves can confirm this: I told you I was not the Anointed but had been sent on ahead of him. ²⁹The bride belongs to the groom, and the best man stands with him and is happy enough just to be close at hand. So I am content. ³⁰He can only grow in importance; my role can only diminish."

8. John 4:1–4. John includes another narrative note on the parallel baptizing ministries by JB and Jesus:

> ¹Jesus was aware of the rumor that had reached the Pharisees: Jesus is recruiting and baptizing more disciples than John. (²Actually, Jesus himself didn't baptize anyone; his disciples did the baptizing.) ³So he left Judea again for Galilee. ⁴His route took him through Samaria.

9. John 5:30–38. On the occasion of Jesus' second trip to Jerusalem, John has Jesus defend himself with an argument that includes a reference to JB as a witness to him:

> ³⁰"I can do nothing on my own authority. I base my decision on what I hear; and my decision is the right one, because I don't consider what I want but what the one who sent me wants. ³¹If I give evidence on my own behalf, my testimony is not reliable. ³²Someone else testifies on my behalf, and I am certain the evidence he gives about me is reliable. ³³You've sent ⟨messengers⟩ to John, and he has provided reliable testimony. ³⁴I'm not interested in evidence from a human source; rather, I make these statements so you will be rescued. ³⁵⟨John⟩ was a bright shining light, and you were willing to bask in that light of his for a while. ³⁶But I have given evidence that is even weightier than John's: the tasks the Father gave me to carry out. These very tasks I am performing are evidence that the Father has sent me. ³⁷The one who sent me has himself also given evidence on my behalf. You've never heard his voice, you've never seen his image, ³⁸and his message doesn't find a home in you, since you don't believe the one he has sent."

10. John 10:40–42. After Jesus' third visit to Jerusalem, John makes his final reference to JB:

> [40]He went away once more, to the place across the Jordan where John had first baptized, and there he stayed. [41]Many people came to him; they kept repeating, "John didn't perform any miracle, but everything John said about this man was true." [42]And many believed in him there.

John's Portrayal of JB

As a document literarily independent of the Sayings Gospel Q and the synoptic gospels, how has John presented JB? What details in his presentation may be of interest to the historian?

Each of these other gospels interprets JB in relation to Jesus by associating JB with the eschatological expectation of Elijah's return as prophetic forerunner. Both Mark and Q implicitly identify JB as the prophetic, Elijah-returned forerunner. Matthew makes the identification quite explicit. Luke also associates JB with Elijah but not as Elijah-returned, rather as the Elijah-like eschatological prophet empowered by the spirit. All of these gospels present JB as the fulfillment of the Elijah text, Malachi 3:1.

In John, the question of JB's identity serves as a foil for the question of Jesus' identity so central to the gospel. In the first narrative scene involving JB, the priests and Levites immediately ask him: "Who are you?" JB responds by denying that he is the Anointed or Elijah or the prophet (1:19–24). John does not apply Malachi 3:1, the Elijah text, to JB . But John has JB identify himself with his own "I am" saying: "I am the voice of someone shouting in the wilderness, 'Make the way of the Lord straight'." JB is the "voice" of Isa 40:3! Therefore, how has John presented JB? With singular focus, *John presents JB as a witness testifying to Jesus' identity as the One from God.* Here JB appears quite differently than in Q. JB in Q asks whether or not Jesus is the coming one; and Jesus subsequently praises JB, but declares the least in God's domain to be greater than he. JB in John has become the first Christian. Only on the basis of the portrayal of JB in John could the later church have made JB into a Christian saint, as the church did. (See the cameo essay, "John the Baptist as Saint.")

JB's witness to Jesus is manifold. JB testifies to Jesus as the coming light (1:6–8). JB testifies to Jesus as the word become flesh, the one about whom he said, "He who is to come after me is actually my superior, because he was there before me" (1:15). JB also testifies to Jesus, in words reminiscent of a saying found in Mark and Q, as ". . . the one who is to be my successor. I don't even deserve to untie his sandal straps" (1:27).

John does not report Jesus' baptism by JB; but in John, JB testifies about Jesus in words that seem to allude to Jesus' baptism as reported in the synoptics: "I have seen the spirit coming down like a dove out of the sky, and it hovered over him." Note that JB, not Jesus, sees the spirit descending like a dove; and JB, not God, says of Jesus, "This is God's son" (1:29–34). Twice in a saying peculiar to John, JB declares about Jesus: "Look, the lamb of God, who does take away the sin of the world" (1:29, 36). In his final discourse about Jesus, JB relates himself to Jesus as the best man to the groom; and he ends with this declaration: "He can only grow in importance; my role can only diminish" (3:30). These very words, in Latin, appear on the crucifixion panel of Matthias Grünewald's Isenheim Altarpiece as JB stands beneath the cross, with the symbolic lamb, pointing his crooked finger at the dying form of Jesus. (See the cameo essay, "John the Baptist in Art.")

John's sharp emphasis upon JB as witness leads to a deemphasis on other dimensions of his ministry, including his characteristic activities of preaching and baptizing. Since Jesus as the One from God constitutes the subject matter of JB's preaching, JB does not proclaim a baptism of repentance. JB certainly engages in water baptism (1:25–26, 31, 33; 3:23, 25; 4:1; 10:40). Nowhere, however, is the meaning of this water baptism explained, except that JB's water baptism has been mandated by God and in some sense has prepared for Jesus' revelation to Israel and his baptizing with holy spirit (1:29–34).

John's stress upon JB's role as witness may also account for the deemphasis upon his lifestyle and fate. John does not highlight the ascetic lifestyle of John nor contrast his lifestyle with that of Jesus. Remember, JB in John is neither Elijah nor the prophet and so does not appear in the attire of a prophet. Although John makes a passing reference to JB's imprisonment, he relates no particulars related to his death—no accusation again Herod Antipas, no Herodias, no dance, no head (3:24).

What other features of the treatment of JB might have historical significance?

Of some importance could be the specific social and religious categories of people depicted interacting with JB. These include priests, Levites, and Pharisees (1:19, 24; also 4:1).

Of greater importance could be the place names connected with JB's baptizing ministry. The wilderness and the Jordan River continue to be mentioned. John, however, always refers to JB's activity in relation to the Jordan River as "across" or "on the far side of" the Jordan, that is the east bank in the territory of Perea, although Perea receives no mention (1:23, 28; 3:26; 10:40). Also only John makes specific references to "Bethany on the far side of the Jordan" (1:28) and "Aenon near Salim" (3:23) as sites of JB's baptizing activity.

Of still greater importance could be the way the ministries of JB and Jesus relate to one another. First, the ministries of JB and Jesus overlap both in terms of time and locale. According to the synoptics, JB is imprisoned before Jesus' begins his own ministry in the northern territory of Galilee.

But according to John, there is a period during which Jesus conducts a ministry in the southern territory of Judea simultaneously with the ministry of JB (especially 3:22–26). Secondly, the activity of Jesus and his disciples is said to have included water baptism (3:22–26; 4:1–3). Perhaps the added denial that Jesus himself actually baptized comes from a later hand, not the gospel writer (4:2). Thirdly, some of those who became disciples of Jesus had been disciples of JB. As one of these, Andrew, Simon Peter's brother, is identified by name (1:35–42).

John the Baptist as Saint

Midway between Baton Rouge and New Orleans lies St. John the Baptist Parish, as counties are called in Louisiana. This parish has received national publicity in recent years for its struggles against industrial pollution. In Charleston, South Carolina, stands the gothic Roman Catholic Cathedral of St. John the Baptist. The San Juan whose name designates the capital of Puerto Rica is the same Juan whose name identifies the local cathedral—San Juan Bautista, St. John the Baptist. No less than his successor, JB has left a lasting cultural mark. But now the honorific title associated with JB is not prophet but saint. JB the Jew has become a Christian.

The veneration of JB as a saint began in the earliest centuries of the church's life. Eventually St. JB was remembered with two feast days. As with many saints, he came to be honored on the day of his death. In our calendar this falls on August 29, the alleged day of his beheading. But perhaps even earlier, he was also honored on the day of his birth. In our calendar this falls on June 24, appropriately six months before the birthday of Jesus on December 25 since JB—according to Luke—was six months older than his kinsman Jesus.

Among others, the great Latin church father Augustine (died 430 c.e.) comments at some length on the celebration of JB's nativity. He affirms the appropriateness of the celebration since JB was sanctified at his birth. The angel Gabriel affirmed this—again in Luke—when he said to Zechariah about his promised son: ". . . he will be filled with holy spirit from the very day of his birth," or "from the womb of his mother" (Luke 1:15). Based on JB's sanctification in the womb, claims were even made for JB's sinlessness. Augustine also gave a rather ingenious interpretation of JB's words set forth in the Gospel of John when JB says of Jesus: "He can only grow in importance; my role can only decrease," or as sometimes translated, "He must increase, but I must decrease" (John 3:30). Augustine observes that JB got it right: the days do increase in length after the birthday of Jesus while the days decrease in length after his own birthday.

John the Baptist in Art

John the Baptist stands at the beginning of the narrative story of Jesus as recounted in the Christian gospels. Visual representations of JB, usually in association with Jesus, also make their appearance near the beginning of Christian art—as early as the 2nd and 3rd centuries. JB's baptism of Jesus often provides the subject matter. So it is with the wall paintings in in the catacombs of Rome, and with the later mosaics in the baptistries of churches in Ravenna, also in Italy.

Constantine made Christianity a religion of state in 313 c.e. and moved toward the establishment of what would emerge as Christian "orthodoxy" by convening the Council of Nicea in 325 c.e. Constantine himself built the Lateran Basilica in Rome and dedicated it to the one now known as St. John the Baptist. Thereafter, the emerging Christian artistic tradition surged forward carrying JB with it.

By the Middle Ages, JB and scenes from his life had become the focus for visual artists in various media. Statues of JB adorn many of the great gothic cathedrals. Among them are the cathedrals of Amiens, Reims, and Chartres in France. At Chartres JB stands in the company of Isaiah, Jeremiah, Simeon, Peter, and Elijah over the center door of the north transept portal.

By the Middle Ages, not only in sculpture but in paintings, a recognizable iconographic tradition about JB had emerged. Common motifs and attributes—or symbols–begin to appear, many based on biblical and apocryphal texts. JB often appears as an ascetic dressed in animal skins with a leather girdle around his waist. In this attire, JB represents not simply a prophet but, no doubt, the prototypical Christian anchorite or hermit who goes into the wilderness to seek Christ. JB often has a thin reed staff in his hand, sometimes in the shape of a cross. In depictions of his baptizing activity, JB often has a small baptismal bowl in his hand for the holy water. Another dish, actually a platter with his head thereon, also becomes one of his attributes. However, JB's chief attribute is the lamb. This we noted in our discussion of the Gospel of John–in our comment on the depiction of JB on the crucifixion panel of Matthias Grünewald's Isenheim altarpiece (1515 c.e.). The lamb of God—or *agnus dei*—became the attribute for JB because it is JB in scripture who bears witness to Jesus with the declaration: "Look, the lamb of God. . . ." (John 1:29, 36).

By the Middle Ages, JB had also become venerated not only for his association with Jesus but for his own sake. Entire cycles of frescoes (much like cartoon strips, but on a grander scale) were devoted to portraying the principal events of his life. Some twenty or more scenes from JB's life were available to the artist. These included: the annunciation to Zechariah in the temple; the visitation of Mary to Elizabeth; his birth, circumcision, and naming; the flight of his mother

Elizabeth with him as an infant into the mountains to escape Herod the Great; his own withdrawal into the wilderness; the axe laid to the root of the tree; his baptism of Jesus; his bearing witness to Jesus as the Christ; his arrest and imprisonment; his appearance before Herod Antipas and Herodias; the feast of Herod and the dance of Salome; his beheading; and his burial.

Two of the best known JB cycles are in the cathedral church of St. Blasius in Braunschweig, Germany, and in the church of Santa Croce in Florence, Italy. The presence of this cycle in Florence is understandable. JB was the patron saint of that city. The cycle of the life of JB in the church of Santa Croce was by Giotto (died 1337); and it matches Giotto's magnificent cycle of the life of Jesus in the chapel at Padua.

Artistic representations of JB were not confined to western Europe and those areas nurtured by the faith and practice of the Catholic Church. In the regions of the eastern Mediterranean where Greek Orthodox customs prevailed, Christian art came to express itself primarily through the icon, or sacred image.

Within this Christian artistic tradition, there emerged a distinctive way of portraying JB. He is depicted as the forerunner with two large wings on his back, like an angel. The textual basis for this detail is the passage in Malachi 3:1. Mark and the other synoptics cite this verse as having been fulfilled by JB. Therein God speaks through the prophet Malachi: "Here is my messenger (Greek, *angelos*) whom I send on ahead of you to prepare your way!" (Mark 1:2; Matt 11:10=Luke 7:27). JB is the "messenger" or, in Greek, the "angel." This portrayal of JB appears in a fresco in Serbia, and in manuscript illuminations, as early as the 13th century; but it is not until the 16th century that icons of JB as the angelic forerunner with wings become more common.

One of the best known icons of this type evidently originated on Crete in the 16th or 17th century and now resides in the Byzantine Museum in Athens. On the icon, the winged figure of JB stands with a full-length frontal view but slightly turned to his right. His left hand extends upward as if in supplication or prayer. His right hands holds a cross and open scroll. He wears a camel hair garment and a cloak. In the upper left-hand corner of the icon appears a small half-length image of Christ, in the heavens, toward whom JB has lifted his gaze. In the lower left corner of the icon lies a severed head—symbolic of JB's coming martyrdom. In the background are rocks, bushes, and an axe.

Representations of JB continued to proliferate in eastern and western art from the Middle Ages, through the Renaissance, and beyond. Somewhere among the works of those whose names are prominent in art history appear images of JB. Rafael and Donatello. El Greco and Rembrandt. Even Joshua Reynolds who depicts JB as a playful child, and Gustave Doré who included several wood engavings of JB in his popular illustrated Bible which appeared in its first French edition in 1865.

8 GOSPEL OF THOMAS

Like Q, the Gospel of Thomas is a sayings gospel. In its printed form, the gospel consists of 114 sayings of Jesus most of which are introduced with the formula, "Jesus said." Many of these sayings correspond to similar sayings of Jesus in Q and the synoptic gospels. Of fifteen parables in Thomas, for example, twelve also appear in Q and the synoptics.

Literary Relationships and Character

This commonality raises the question of the literary relationship between Thomas and the other gospels. Some scholars consider Thomas to be, in some sense, literarily dependent upon the synoptics. Therefore, Thomas would be a collection of teachings abstracted from these gospels and other traditions. Others, however, think that Thomas represents an independent source that developed over time without reference to our known written gospels. Based on the assumption of Thomas as an independent source, for example, the Jesus Seminar collectively considered the parable of the mustard seed in Thomas (20:2) to be closer to the *voice* of Jesus than the versions of the same parable in Q and the synoptics (Mark 4:31–32; Matt 13:31b-32; Luke 13:19): red, for the parable in Thomas; pink, in the other gospels.

Although Thomas may represent an independent source and contain genuine words of Jesus, it is also clear to scholars that in its present form Thomas contains two different kinds of teachings. In some passages, such as those containing the traditional parables, Jesus speaks like a sage, or wise man, challenging his hearers to new views of reality and radical lifestyles.

But in other passages, Jesus speaks like a gnostic revealer, sharing with his readers a hidden knowledge about one's origin and one's identity from beyond this world. Gnosticism is a name for the complicated movement during the hellenistic period which assumed a dualistic worldview sharply contrasting this lower world of matter with the spirit world beyond. Salvation was to be attained by *gnosis*, literally "knowledge" in Greek.

Q and Thomas are sayings gospels containing teachings attributed to Jesus. But they differ in their orientations. Q represents a mixture of wisdom and apocalyptic traditions, Thomas a blend of wisdom and gnostic traditions.

Discovery and Origin

Only one complete manuscript of Thomas exists today. This manuscript resurfaced among those writings of that ancient Christian library discovered in 1945 near the Egyptian village of Nag Hammadi, where they had been buried since the 4th century. The fifty-two documents bound in thirteen codices, or volumes, are written on papyrus in Coptic, the common language of Egypt in the hellenistic period. Many of these tractates represent translations into Coptic from other languages. Thomas itself had been translated from Greek. It is now recognized that papyrus fragments disovered at Oxyrhynchus in Egypt at the end of last century represent the remains of manuscripts of Thomas written in Greek. These fragments have received the designations POxy 1, POxy 654, and POxy 655. The handwriting suggests a date for the Greek text to be as early as 200 C.E.

What can be said about the origin of the gospel itself? Its author? Locale? Date?

The Gospel of Thomas opens with these words: "These are the secret sayings that the living Jesus spoke and Didymos Judas Thomas recorded." The gospel has been associated with Thomas, one of Jesus' twelve disciples. Although this ascription cannot be considered historically reliable, the form of the name itself has suggestive implications. The apostle Thomas came to be associated with the church in Syria. The three-fold form of his name appears only in the Acts of Thomas, a work probably from eastern Syria. Therefore, scholars often look also to Syria as the place of origin for the Gospel of Thomas. A saying by Jesus about the authority of James the Just (12:1–2), Jesus' brother, who was a leader of the church in Jerusalem, has prompted the suggestion that a core of the teachings in Thomas may even have been assembled in Jerusalem. The Greek fragments of Thomas make a date later than the end of the 2nd century an impossibility. The literary independence of Thomas from Q and the synoptic gospels moves its possible date of composition back to the 60s of the 1st century. An earlier core collection could date from the 50s.

Within Thomas, there is only one passage which explicitly refers to JB. Another passage may contain an allusion to JB. Three other sayings of Jesus that make no references to JB are similar to sayings that are applied to JB in the other gospels.

Texts in Thomas about JB

1. Thom 46:1–2. Thomas reports a saying of Jesus, similar to a Q saying (Q 7:28), which praises JB:

> ¹Jesus said, "From Adam to John the Baptist, among those born of women, no one is so much greater than John the Baptist that his eyes should not be averted. ²But I have said that whoever among you becomes a child will recognize the ⟨Father's⟩ imperial rule and will become greater than John."

2. Thom 47:2–5. Thomas reports a saying of Jesus that in the synoptics has been used in conjuction with his reply to the question about fasting by JB's disciples but not his (Mark 2:18–22 par.):

> ²And a slave cannot serve two masters, otherwise that slave will honor the one and offend the other.
> ³"Nobody drinks aged wine and immediately wants to drink young wine. ⁴Young wine is not poured into old wineskins, or they might break, and aged wine is not poured into a new wineskin, or it might spoil. ⁵An old patch is not sewn onto a new garment, since it would create a tear."

3. Thom 52:1–2. In response to praise of Jesus by his disciples, Thomas reports a saying of Jesus not found elsewhere that may allude to JB:

> ¹His disciples said to him, "Twenty-four prophets have spoken in Israel, and they all spoke of you."
> ²He said to them, "You have disregarded the living one who is in your presence, and have spoken of the dead."

4. Thom 78:1–3. Thomas reports a saying of Jesus that seemingly refers to Jesus himself but which in Q refers to JB (Q 7:24–28):

> ¹Jesus said, "Why have you come out to the countryside? To see a reed shaken by the wind? ²And to see a person dressed in soft clothes, [like your] rulers and your powerful ones? ³They are dressed in soft clothes, and they cannot understand truth."

5. Thom 104:1-2. Thomas reports another saying of Jesus that has been used in the synoptics also to reply to the question about fasting by JB's disciples but not his (Mark 2:18-22 par):

> ¹They said to Jesus, "Come, let us pray today, and let us fast."
> ²Jesus said, "What sin have I committed, or how have I been undone?"

Portrayal of JB in Thomas

It can hardly be said that the Gospel of Thomas presents a portrayal of JB. Thomas shows virtually no interest in JB himself. In this disinterest, Thomas stands alone among the gospels considered above.

The one explicit reference to JB, however, may offer independent evidence for Jesus' having praised JB while at the same time having elevated over JB those who respond affirmatively to his own proclamation of God's imperial rule (46:1-2). The possible allusion to JB in Jesus' response to his disciples could offer support for the portrayal of JB in the other gospels in two ways (Q 52:1-2). If originally a response to the question as asked, and if an allusion to JB, this saying involves Jesus' recognition of JB as a prophet. This supports the claims made by Jesus for JB as a prophet in the synoptics. If an allusion to JB, this saying also assumes that JB was still alive when Jesus declared it and possibly still engaged in a ministry simultaneous with the ministry of Jesus. This supports the presentation in the Gospel of John that the ministries of Jesus and JB overlapped in time and place. The other sayings of Jesus cited above, without any reference to JB, may be used in a consideration of the authenticity of Jesus' teaching. They offer minimal support for an understanding of JB.

9 OTHER GOSPELS

Thus far we have surveyed six gospels for their references to JB: Mark, Sayings Gospel Q, Matthew, Luke (and Acts), John, and Thomas. Each of these gospels either represents an independent written source for understanding JB or possibly contains independent traditions about JB. Mark, Sayings Gospel Q, John, and Thomas are documents written independently without copying one another. Matthew and Luke used Mark and Q as written sources. However, they include passages about JB which are designated M and L, with Luke's special traditions appearing not only in the infancy portion of the gospel but also in the Book of Acts.

We continue this survey of early Christian literature by citing references to JB found in other gospels, which were probably written no later than the middle of the 2nd century. These gospels include: the Gospel of the Nazoreans; the Gospel of the Hebrews; the Gospel of the Ebionites; and the Infancy Gospel of James. The first three of these gospels are known only through references to them in other ancient Christian writings. The Infancy Gospel of James has been preserved in more than a hundred manuscripts in Greek (25 chapters long in modern translations). However, these four gospels appear to be—in some sense—literarily dependent upon earlier gospels, especially the four canonical gospels of Matthew, Mark, Luke, and John. Passages in them related to JB are reproduced here not to provide additional sources for understanding JB as a historical figure, but to illustrate how JB was viewed in Christian literature of the 2nd century.

GOSPEL OF THE NAZOREANS

Quotations from the Gospel of the Nazoreans first appear in Christian writings beginning in the latter half of the 2nd century.

Based on a variety of evidence, scholars have concluded that this work originated as an expanded version of the Gospel of Matthew when that gospel was translated from Greek into Aramaic or Syriac. Like the Gospel of Matthew itself, the Gospel of the Nazoreans was written for Jewish Christians, probably in Syria. Most of the fragments from this gospel have been preserved in the writings of Jerome (died 420). In his treatise against Pelagius the theological adversary of Augustine, Jerome preserves a verbal exchange between Jesus and his family, an exchange that evidently occurred prior to his baptism by JB. As in Matthew's account of Jesus' baptism, so here Jesus is protected from any implication that his accepting baptism by JB involved sin on his part:

> Behold, the mother of the Lord and his brothers said to him, "John the Baptist baptized for the remission of sins; let us go and be baptized by him." But he said to them, "Wherein have I sinned that I should go and be baptized by him? Unless what I have said is (itself) ignorance."
>
> Jerome, *Against Pelagius*, 3.2

GOSPEL OF THE HEBREWS

Quotations from the Gospel of the Hebrews also begin to appear in writings of church leaders beginning in the latter half of the 2nd century, many of whom who lived in Alexandria, Egypt. Evidently composed in Greek, this gospel was probably—as its name suggests—written by and for Jewish-Christians. It is also Jerome who preserves in his Commentary on Isaiah, in the comment on Isa 11:2, a passage from the Gospel of the Hebrews that describes Jesus' baptismal experience but without specific reference to JB himself:

> And it came to pass when the Lord came up out of the water, the whole fount of the Holy Spirit descended upon him and rested on him and said to him, "My Son, in all the prophets was I waiting for you that you should come and I might rest in you. For you are my rest; you are my first-begotten Son who reigns forever."
>
> Jerome, *Commentary on Isaiah* 4

GOSPEL OF THE EBIONITES

This gospel receives its current name from its apparent use by the Ebionites, a sect of Greek-speaking Jewish-Christians. This sect flourished in the 2nd and 3rd centuries, probably east of the Jordan River. The gospel itself must have been created by harmonizing, or combining, into one document the story of Jesus as presented in the synoptic gospels of Matthew, Mark, and Luke. All the fragments preserved from this gospel are found in the writings of the Christian writer Epiphanius (died 403), Based on three fragments preserved in his *Heresies* 30:13, the Gospel of the Ebionites evidently began with three passages each of which contains a reference to JB.

The opening passage makes reference to JB's ministry of baptizing:

> It happened in the days of Herod, king of Judaea, that John came baptizing a baptism of repentance in the river Jordan. It was said of him that he was of the tribe of Aaron the priest, a son of Zechariah and Elizabeth. And all went out to him.   Epiphanius, *Heresies*, 30.13.6

The next passage reports JB's ascetic style of ministry but omits mention of his eating locusts since the Ebionites were vegetarians:

> It happened that John was baptizing; and Pharisees and all Jerusalem went out to him and were baptized. And John had a garment of camel's hair and a leather belt about his waist. And his food was wild honey, which had the taste of manna, like a cake ⟨made⟩ with oil.
> Epiphanius, *Heresies*, 30.13.4–5

The third passage describes an expanded account of Jesus' baptism by JB:

> When the people were baptized, Jesus also came and was baptized by John. And as he went up out of the water, the heavens opened and he saw the Holy Spirit in the form of a dove descending and entering into him. And there was a voice from heaven saying, "You are my beloved Son, in you I am well pleased. Today I have begotten you." And immediately a great light illuminated the place.
> When John saw this, he said to him, "Who are you, Lord?"
> And again a voice (came) from heaven to him, "This is my beloved Son, in whom I am well pleased."
> John fell down before him and said, "I beg you, Lord, you baptize me."
> But he prevented him, saying, "Let it be, for thus it is fitting that everything should be fulfilled."   Epiphanius, *Heresies*, 30.13.7–8

INFANCY GOSPEL OF JAMES

The Infancy Gospel of James claims to have been written by James the half-brother of Jesus (ch. 25). Traditionally called the Protevangelium of James, this work begins by recounting events that occurred before those narrated in the infancy accounts in Matthew and

Luke. The story centers around Mary the virgin chosen by God to bear God's son. The story opens by telling about Joachim and Anna, the parents of Mary, and the miraculous events related to Mary's own birth and childhood (chs. 1–8). The story continues with an account of Mary's coming of age in the temple and the decision to betroth her to Joseph (chs. 9–16). The story concludes by retelling the events surrounding Mary's giving birth to Jesus and Jesus' escape from the murderous clutches of Herod (chs. 17–24). It is in the third portion of the gospel that the story-teller borrows most heavily from the canonical stories of Jesus' birth.

Although not identified as the parents of JB, both Zechariah and Elizabeth are introduced to the reader midway through the gospel: Zechariah as high priest officiating in the temple (8:1–9) and Elizabeth as a pregnant relative of the sixteen-year old, pregnant Mary (12:3–9). Two consecutive passages near the end of the gospel contain references to JB. But little emphasis in Infancy James falls upon JB himself. Nothing is reported of his conception or birth, his circumcision or naming. Nothing is announced about his role in God's plan as prophet or baptizer.

1. InJas 22:5–9. Immediately following a notation of how Mary had fled with her child from the murderous clutches of Herod, this passage makes similar comment about Elizabeth and her child:

> ⁵When Elizabeth heard that they were looking for John, however, she took him and went up into the hill country. ⁶She kept searching for a place to hide him, but there was none to be had. ⁷Then she groaned and said, "Mountain of God, please take in a mother with her child." You see, Elizabeth was unable to keep on climbing. ⁸Suddenly the mountain split open and let them in. That mountain was a transparent light to her, ⁹since a heavenly messenger of the Lord was with them for protection.

2. InJas 23:1–9. The next passage reports the murder, in the temple, of Zechariah the father of JB, after which the entire gospel narrative concludes with the discovery of Zechariah's body and the election of Simeon as his high priestly successor:

> ¹Herod, though, kept looking for John ²and sent his agents to Zechariah ⟨serving⟩ at the altar with this message: "Where have you hidden your son?"
> ³But he answered them, "I am a minister of God and am attending to his temple. How should I know where my son is?"
> ⁴And so the agents went away and reported all this to Herod, who became angry and said, "Is his son going to rule over Israel?"

⁵And he sent his agents back with this message: "Tell me the truth. Where is your son? Don't you know that I have your life in my power?"

⁶And the agents went and reported this message to him.

⁷⟨Zechariah⟩ answered and said, "I am a martyr for God. Take my life. ⁸The Lord, though, will receive my spirit because you are shedding innocent blood at the entrance to the temple of the Lord."

⁹And so at daybreak Zechariah was murdered, but the people of Israel did not know that he had been murdered.

With these passages from the Infancy Gospel of James, we have concluded our survey of the gospel evidence for the life and activity of JB.

10 Other writings

The figure of JB is mentioned in sources other than the gospels. These sources include the Pseudo-Clementines, the works of Josephus, and the traditions of the Mandaeans.

PSEUDO-CLEMENTINES

The group of writings known as the Pseudo-Clementines claim to be the work of Clement, who, according to tradition, succeeded Peter as bishop of Rome. Among these writings are the so-called *Recognitions* and *Homilies*, which were written no later than the 4th century. Both writings originated in Greek; but the former has been preserved in Latin and Syriac, not Greek.

The *Recognitions* and the *Homilies* recount Clement's story: his birth in Rome; his intellectual quest as a non-Christian; his attraction to Christianity; and his subsequent association with Peter.

The similarities between these two works have generated much discussion about their literary relationship. Perhaps the most satisfactory hypothesis about the relationship claims that these two works independently used a common source. Accordingly, this older basic writing (sometimes designated by the letter B) was written in Greek, perhaps in Syria, around 220 C.E. The unknown author of this basic source (B) was dependent upon still older sources which, according to some interpreters, originated in Jewish-Christian circles. Therefore, the *Recognitions* and the *Homilies* may preserve traditions that extend back to the 1st century.

A few passages in these works mention JB. It is possible that the Pseudo-Clementines provide evidence that JB continued to be honored by his disciples after his death. Indeed, the texts in their present form even claim that the disciples of JB looked to him as the Anointed, the Messiah, the Christ.

1. Rec. 1.53.5–54.1–3, 8. Peter speaks to Clement about the origin of Jewish sects:

53 [5]For the people were divided into many beliefs that began in the days of John the Baptist.

54 [1]For as the Messiah was ready to be revealed for the abolition of sacrifices and in order to reveal and show forth baptism, the slanderer who was opposed recognized from predestination the point in time and created sects and divisions, so that if the former sin should receive renunciation and correction, a second vice would be able to obstruct redemption.

[2]The first of these then are the ones called Sadducees, who arose in the days of John when they separated from the people as righteous ones and renounced the resurrection of the dead. They put forward their unbelieving doctrine speciously when they said, namely, "It is not right to worship and fear God in prospect of a reward for goodness." [3]In this doctrine, as I have said, Dositheus began and, after Dositheus, Simon who also started to create differences of opinions in the likeness of the former.

[8]Now the pure disciples of John separated themselves greatly from the people and spoke to their teacher as if he were concealed (or: said that their master was, as it were, concealed).

2. Rec. 1.60.1–4, 63:1. Peter reports to Clement a discussion between the disciples of JB and the disciples of Jesus about the relative status of their masters:

60 [1]One of the disciples of John approached and boasted regarding John, "He is the Christ, and not Jesus, just as Jesus himself spoke concerning him, namely that he is greater than any prophet who had ever been. [2]If he is thus greater than Moses, it is clear that he is also greater than Jesus for Jesus arose just as did Moses. Therefore, it is right that John, who is greater than these, is the Christ."

[3]Simon the Canaanite testified against this one, "John was greater than the prophets who were begotten of women but not greater than the Son of Man. [4]Hence, Jesus, in addition, is the Christ, while he was only a prophet. The matters of Jesus are as far removed when compared with the matters of John as is the one who is sent out and proceeds ahead from the one who sends him to run out before him and as is the one who performs the service of the law from the one who institutes the law." Now he spoke these things, witnessed to related matters, and then was silent.

63 [1]Thus we the ignorant fishermen testified against the priests concerning God who alone is in the heavens; against the Sadducees con-

cerning the resurrection of the dead; in truth against the Samaritans concerning Jerusalem, though we did not enter into their city but rather spoke publicly outside; against the scribes and the Pharisees concerning the kingdom of heavens; against the disciples of John in order that they not be tripped up by him. Against all we said that Jesus is the eternal Christ.

Like the gospels, the Pseudo-Clementines represent Christian literature. Now we turn our attention to references to JB in non-Christian sources.

JOSEPHUS

From a Jewish point of view, the inhabitants of the world were and are divided into two groups: Jews and non-Jews, or Jews and Gentiles. Jesus was a Jew, not a Gentile. Those earliest followers of Jesus who first confessed him to be the Anointed, the Messiah, the Christ, were all Jews. Paul, who came to share that confession and became an apostle to Gentiles, views the world from a Jewish point of view and repeatedly refers to himself as a Jew.

Quite possibly, among those twenty-seven writings now known as New Testament only Luke and Acts were written by a non-Jew, a Gentile. Perhaps it is understandable that two of only three uses of the word "Christian" (from the Greek word now rendered Christ and meaning Anointed) in the New Testament appear in Acts. The author of Acts also notes that the followers of Jesus were first called Christians in Antioch (11:26; also Acts 26:48; 1 Pet 4:16). Therefore, several of the Christian writings already surveyed for their references to JB were in fact written by Jews, but Jews confessing Jesus to be the Anointed, the Messiah, the Christ.

There is, however, a reference to JB in the writings of a 1st century Jew who was not Christian. His name was Joseph ben Mattathias, better known by his adopted Graeco-Roman name—Flavius Josephus.

Life and Writings of Josephus

Joseph ben Mattathias (around 38–100 C.E.) was born of a priestly aristocratic family in Jerusalem within a decade of the deaths of Jesus and JB. Joseph took seriously his upbringing within Judaism. According to his own testimony he carefully investigated each of the three sects—the Pharisees, the Sadducees, and the Essenes—before associating himself with the Pharisaic way of life. Along the way, he spent three years in the wilderness as a disciple of Bannus, a holy man and ascetic. This Bannus reportedly undertook daily and nightly ablutions of cold water to purify himself. His clothing and diet came from the natural vegetation of his surroundings.

At the outset of the Jewish-Roman War in 66 C.E., Joseph was appointed as the military leader of the Jewish forces in Galilee. During the conflict, however, he surrendered to the Romans and allied himself with them. Joseph found favor with the Roman military commander Vespasian, who was acclaimed emperor during the war and returned to Rome (69–79 C.E.). Joseph then served Vespasian's son Titus, who had succeeded his father as military commander in Palestine. With Joseph as an advisor and eyewitness, Titus successfully executed the seige of Jerusalem, climaxed by the fall of the city and the destruction of the temple in 70 C.E. Later Titus himself became emperor (79–81 C.E.).

After the war, Joseph left his homeland never to return. He took up residence in Rome. Thanks to the ongoing patronage of the Flavian rulers, Joseph ben Mattathias, their client, became Flavius Josephus, man of letters.

Josephus produced two major historical works. His first work *The Jewish War*, divided into seven books, was written in the early 70s. This work appeared in an Aramaic edition, now lost, as well as the version or edition written in Greek. Josephus surveys the history of the recent unpleasantness, from the unrest which resulted in the rise of the Herods as vassal rulers under the Romans, through the Roman capture of Masada, three years after the fall of Jerusalem. His second work the *Jewish Antiquities*, a monumental undertaking divided into twenty books, appeared some twenty years later during the reign of the Flavian emperor Domitian (81–96 C.E.). Here Josephus surveys the history of the Jews from creation through the time of the patriarchs down into his own lifetime. Thus, in the latter book, he retells much of the story recorded in his earlier history of the war.

Josephus was a historian. His narratives recalled past events. Much has been written, however, about Josephus' use of the conventions of ancient historiography. Graeco-Roman historians imaginatively created speeches appropriate for the occasions on which they were spoken rather than scrupulously retelling what had been said. Much has also been written about Josephus' perspective or perspectives in narrating the past.

Josephus wrote as an apologist—a defender and an advocate. He was an apologist on behalf of Rome. Certainly one of the objectives of *The Jewish War* was to warn other provincials about the futility of rebelling against the might of Rome. He was also an apologist on behalf of his own people. In a day when antiquity meant superiority, one of the objectives of the *Jewish Antiquities* was to extol the great age and the grand achievements of the Jews. Josephus was also an apologist on behalf of himself. Little modesty here! He even appended to the *Jewish Antiquities* a brief autobiography— his *Vita*, or *Life*—from which were taken our earlier statements about his upbringing within Judaism. Throughout his writings, Josephus commends Jewish beliefs and practices to his Graeco-Roman readers in categories familiar to them. He speaks of the traditional Jewish sects as schools of philosophy, for example, and compares the Pharisees to the Stoics. It is in the *Jewish Antiquities*, book 18, that Josephus refers to JB—and to Jesus.

Texts Related to JB

1. Ant 18:63–64. Within the broader context of book 18, Josephus has been narrating a series of events in the political history of Palestine, and neighboring territories, to demonstrate the ongoing unrest among the people. These events span the first four decades of the 1st century. Among several incidents involving Pontius Pilate, the Roman prefect over Judea and Samaria, is a controversial reference to Jesus. The statement has aroused controversy because it sounds as though it had been written by a Christian. About the activity and crucifixion of Jesus under Pontius Pilate, these words appear:

> Is was during this period that a wise man named Jesus appeared, if one really ought to refer to him as a man. You see, he was able to perform incredible deeds and was a teacher of those who were friends of truth. He persuaded many among both Jews and Greeks. He was the Anointed. And when Pilate had condemned him to the cross on the testimony of our leaders, those who had embraced him at first continued to do so. To these persons he appeared alive again on the third day, God's prophets having prophesied these and many other marvelous things about him. And the clan of Christians, who take their name from him, have not ceased to exist to this day.

2. Ant 18:116–119. Within the immediate context of book 18, Josephus has been discussing a dispute between Aretas IV, king of Nabatea, and Herod Antipas, tetrarch of Galilee and Perea. The quarrel involved the daughter of Aretas IV. She had been married to Herod Antipas for many years. But Herod Antipas fell in love with his brother Herod's wife Herodias; and Herodias agreed to marriage with Antipas after he divorced his first wife, who ran home to dad. Her father Aretas IV send his army into battle against the army of Herod Antipas and won a decisive victory. In this passage, a report of how some Jews understood Herod Antipas' defeat leads to an expansive reflection on JB's ministry and execution:

> But to some of the Jews it seemed that Herod's army had been destroyed by God, who was exacting vengeance (most certainly justly) as satisfaction for John who was called Baptist. For Herod indeed put him to death, who was a good man and one who commanded the Jews to practice virtue and acts with justice toward one another and with piety toward God, and so to gather together by baptism. For ⟨John's view was that⟩ in this way baptism certainly would appear acceptable to God if they used it not for seeking pardon of certain sins but for purification of the body, because the soul had already been cleansed

before by righteousness. And when others gathered together around John (you see, they were also excited to the utmost by listening to his teachings), Herod, because he feared that his great persuasiveness with the people might lead to some kind of strife (for they seemed as if they would do everything which he counseled), thought it more preferable, before anything radically innovative happened as a result of him, to execute John, taking action first, rather than when the upheaval happened to perceive too late, having already fallen into trouble. Because of the suspicion of Herod, ⟨John⟩, after being sent bound to Machaerus (the fortress mentioned before), was executed there. But the opinion of the Jews was that the destruction of the army happened for vengeance of ⟨John⟩ because God willed to afflict Herod.

There is general recognition that the writings of Josephus owe their survival to Christian, not Jewish, circles. Much debate has centered around the question of the authenticity of these two passages about Jesus and JB. Is the reference to Jesus, in its entirety, a Christian addition to the original narrative? Or does the current wording simply reflect a Christian emendation that makes Josephus the story teller sound like the Christian he was not? In particular, the references to Jesus as the Messiah, the Christ, and to the resurrection sound like Christian additions. Similar questions have been raised about the passage referring to JB.

At least at a superficial level significant differences appear between the portrayals of JB in the Christian gospels and in this Jewish historical writing. Or to state it another way: whereas in the Christian writings JB appears only in closest association with Jesus, in Josephus the two are not linked in any way. The passages themselves occur at different points in the narrative. The passage about Jesus occurs first within the framework of passages related to Pontius Pilate. The passage about JB occurs in connection with comment on Herod Antipas. Perhaps this lack of relationship between Jesus and JB in Josephus lends support for the claim that Josephus included references to Jesus and to John, although the wording of the former text may have received tampering by Christian hands.

How does Josephus present JB? What are significant similarities and differences between the previously surveyed Christian presentations of JB and his treatment at the hands of Josephus?

Portrayal of JB in Josephus

Josephus introduces John with the same nickname accorded him in the synoptic gospels, "the Baptist," hence JB. At the outset, Josephus also describes JB as "a good man." Both this nickname and this description are supported by Josphus' presentation of JB's message.

Josephus summarizes JB's message in fourfold terms. JB requires of his hearers "to practice virtue," consisting of "justice toward one another" and "piety toward God," and invites such righteous folk "to gather together by baptism." The righteous or virtuous life, therefore, represents the prerequisite for baptism—a condition, as Josephus says, for baptism "to appear acceptable to God." So understood, baptism does not serve its recipients as a means "for seeking pardon of certain sins." Rather, baptism serves "for purification of the body, because the soul had already been cleansed before by righteousness."

According to Josephus, therefore, JB's two characteristic activities are speaking and baptizing. Although related to one another, these activities do not appear to be as integrally related here as in the synoptics. His message represents a call to the life of "virtue" (aretē)—a call to the cleansing of the "soul" (psychē). Baptism represents a consecration of the "body" (sōma) and a public declaration that the "soul" has already been cleansed. Furthermore, nowhere in his narrative does Josephus portray JB as actually baptizing anyone.

Therefore, Josephus presents JB as a moral teacher. Given the stress on virtue and the distinction between body and soul, it can even be said that Josephus presents JB as a hellenistic moral teacher.

Josephus explicitly says that JB directed his message to "the Jews." No specific groups or sects among the Jews are mentioned by name, as the gospels often do. Josephus' later reference to "others" who joined the crowds around JB, however, could be his way of suggesting that this hellenistic-like teacher had even non-Jews in his audience.

Other differences between Josephus' characterization of JB and that in the gospels, especially the synoptics, should be noted. First, Josephus makes no specific mention of the locale of JB's activity of speaking and baptizing. There is no mention of the wilderness nor of the Jordan River. Secondly, Josephus makes no attempt to describe JB's appearance nor his diet. Although asceticism was well established not only within the prophetic tradition of Judaism but within hellenistic moral tradition, Josephus does not underscore JB's own asceticism. These differences between the *Antiquities* and the gospels are understandable. Josephus' interest in JB lies elsewhere. Josephus is primarily concerned with JB's fatal clash with the tetrarch Herod Antipas.

From a historical point of view, it is precisely in their presentations of JB's fate that the greatest discrepancies appear between the *Antiquities* and the gospels. Josephus states that Herod Antipas moved against JB out of a concern that his speaking might lead to some kind of "sedition," or "strife" (stasis), among the people. The reason for JB's eventual execution, therefore, is couched in political terms. Unlike the synoptics, there is no intimation by Josephus that JB had condemned Herod Antipas on the moral grounds of marrying his brother's wife although Josephus has reported Herod Antipas' marital shenanigans. Furthermore, Josephus has identified the brother to whom Herodias was first married as Herod. The synoptics identify this brother as Philip.

Although Josephus does not identify the locale of JB's public activity, he does name the place of his execution—Machaerus. Machaerus was a fortress-palace in southern Perea east of the Dead Sea. Machaerus was second in importance only to the city Tiberias on the western shore of the Sea of Galilee in Herod's tetrarchy of Galilee and Perea. The synoptic accounts of JB's death did not name a place but implied that his death occurred in Galilee, thus probably in Tiberias. Also, Josephus does not even report the method of execution used on JB. But neither does he report the other details of JB's condemnation and execution known from the synoptics—the festival day, the banquet, the daughter of Herodias, her dancing, the oath of Herod Antipas, the request originating with Herodias, the head on a platter.

Therefore, Josephus' *Jewish Antiquities* takes its place alongside Mark, Q, John, and Thomas as an important literary source for understanding JB as a historical figure. However, Josephus approaches JB without a Christian perspective, although he certainly has his own agenda, not only in his narrative about JB but throughout his writings.

MANDAEISM

Mandaeism is the religion practiced by a small sect whose adherents live today in southern Iraq and neighboring Iran. The Mandaeans represent the oldest surviving gnostic sect. Their name comes from the word *manda*, literally "knowledge" in the Mandaean language. In characteristic gnostic fashion, their worldview represents a striking dualism between good and evil, light and darkness, spirit and matter. The predicament of the individual soul involves separation from the lightworld and entrapment in the material body.

The Mandaeans came to the notice of westerners in the 16th and 17th centuries when they were encountered by Portuguese missionaries. The missionaries referred to the Mandaeans as "Christians of St. John" because of their esteem for JB and their practice of water baptism. The ritual of baptism is not an initiation rite performed only once. Mediated by a priest, the complicated ritual of baptism is repeated as often as the believer desires. The immersion in living (running) water associates the participant with the lightworld insofar as the lightworld is reflected in the water. The act confers purification from sins and other uncleanness. In some sense, water baptism also anticipates another complicated ritual celebrated at death which transfers the soul from the earth to the lightworld beyond.

Modern scholarship has concerned itself with the question of the origins of Mandaeism and the relationship between ancient Mandaeism and early Christianity. Our interest stems from the prominence of JB in the Mandaean literature and the possibility that the literature contains independent literary evidence for the historical career of JB.

Literature and Origins

The Mandaean literature includes a monumental work called the *Ginza*, a varied collection of myths, hymns, and exhortations, and the so-called *Book of John*. Both volumes contain references to JB, and the latter bears his name.

It has been said that the Islamic conquests of the 7th and 8th centuries crystallized Mandaeism as known today. The Muslims looked with favor upon peoples whose religion involved a sacred book and a prophet. Both Judaism and Christianity already qualified for acceptance and toleration. Accordingly, the Mandaeans qualified themselves by proclaiming the *Ginza* to be their scripture and JB to be their prophet. That JB achieved prominence in response to the spread of Islam is suggested by the frequent reference to him in their literature by the Arabic form of his name, *Yahya* (or, *Jahja*), alongside the Mandaean *Yohana*. But this development itself assumes that there was already literature among the Mandaeans and knowledge of JB. What can be said about pre-Islamic Mandaeism?

The Mandaean language, written in a beautiful script, represents an east Aramaic dialect. Within the Mandaean language, however, are traces of west Syrian linguistic influence. Of interest for this discussion is the Mandaean word *yardna* which means "living water," but which also designates "the Jordan River." Such linguistic clues, as well as statements in their literature, have led to the possible conclusion that the Mandaeans did originate in the territory around the Jordan River as one of the many baptizing movements around the beginning of the common era. Subsequently, they emigrated into northern Mesopotamia and then into southern Babylonia where their descendents still live. That the Mandaeans owe their origin to JB as founder remains unlikely and speculative. The references to JB in the Mandaean literature seem to be dependent upon the references to JB in Christian literature. As a baptizing gnostic sect, the Mandaeans praise JB who becomes a spokesman for their beliefs; and they cast Jesus in the role of an apostate.

Passages from Mandaean literature selectively reproduced here do not provide additional evidence for JB as a historical figure. They do, however, illustrate how stories about JB in Christian writings were adapted even for use against Christianity by the Mandaeans.

Texts about JB

1. *Ginza*. A messenger from the lightworld reveals the coming of JB and his later interaction with Jesus.

> Then, in that time a child will be born with the name John, the son of the old father Zacharias, which came to him in old age at the summit of one-hundred years. The mother Elizabeth was pregnant with it, and as a woman in old age she brought it forth. When John has become strong and grows in that age of Jerusalem, faith will dwell in his heart, and he will take possession of the Jordan and practice baptism forty-two years before Nebo assumes a body and goes into the world. When John has become strong in that age of Jerusalem, takes possession of the Jordan, and practices baptism, Jesus Christ will come, will walk in humbleness, will be baptized with the baptism of John, and will become wise through the wisdom of John. Then he will turn from the word of John, will change the baptism of the Jordan, will twist the words of truth, and will call forth evil and deceit in the world.

2. John 30. Jesus seeks baptism by John (*Jahya*) but receives baptism only upon the command of an intermediate being named Abatur.

> Jahja [Arabic for "John"] instructs in the nights, John in the evenings of the night. Jahja instructs in the nights. Light shone forth on the worlds. Who talked to Jesus? Who spoke to Jesus Christ the son of Mary? Who spoke to Jesus so that he went to the bank of the Jordan and said to him, "Jahja, baptize me with your baptism and invoke over me the name that you invoke. If I turn out to be a disciple, I will mention you in my writing. If I do not turn out to be a disciple, expunge my name from your scroll."
>
> Jahja answered Jesus Christ by saying to him in Jerusalem, "You have deceived the Jews and have lied to the priests. You have caused the seed to stop from men and childbearing and pregnancy from women. In Jerusalem you deconsecrated the Sabbath, which Moses enjoined. You lied with horns, and you proclaimed disgrace with the trumpet."
>
> Jesus Christ answered Jahja by saying to him in Jerusalem, "If I have deceived the Jews, may the flaming fire consume me. If I have lied to the priests, may I die two deaths instead of one. If I have stopped the seed from men, may I not cross over the great eschatological ocean. If I have stopped childbearing and pregnancy from women, may the judge be set before me. If I have deconsecrated the Sabbath, may the

flaming fire consume me. If I have deceived the Jews, may I step on thistle and thorn. If I have proclaimed disgrace with the trumpet, may my eyes not fall upon Abatur [the judge of souls]. Baptize me with your baptism, and invoke over me the name that you invoke. If I turn out to be a disciple, I will mention you in my writing. If I do not turn out to be a disciple, expunge my name from your scroll."

Jahja answered Jesus Christ by saying to him in Jerusalem, "A deaf person does not become a scholar, and a blind person does not write letters. A desolate house does not rise, and a widow does not become a virgin-bride. Stinking water does not become fragrant, and a stone does not soften in oil."

Jesus Christ answered Jahja by saying to him in Jerusalem, "A deaf person does become a scholar, and a blind person does write letters. A desolate house does rise, and a widow does become a virgin-bride. Stinking water does become fragrant, and a stone does soften in oil."

Jahja answered Jesus Christ by saying to him in Jerusalem, "If you were able to explain this to me, you would be a wise Christ."

Jesus Christ answered Jahja by saying to him in Jerusalem, "A deaf person does become a scholar: The child that comes from the woman in labor grows and becomes great. Through wage and charity he is established. Established through wage and charity, he ascends to see the place of light.

"A blind person who writes letters: The adherent of evil who has become the adherent of good. He abandoned fornication, he abandoned theft, and he believed in the great life.

"A desolate house that rises: The magnate who has been humbled. He left his fortresses, he left his passions, and he built a house at the sea. He built a house at the sea, and he opened its two doors in order that he might bring the abased, open the door, and receive him. When he wanted to eat, he laid out for him the platter in good faith. When he wanted to drink, he mixed for him the vessels of wine. When he wanted to sleep, he spread him a bed in good faith. When he wanted to depart, he led him on the paths of truth. He led him on the paths of truth and faith, and he ascended to see the place of light.

"A widow who becomes a virgin-bride: The woman who became a widow in youth. She chastened herself and remained still until her children were grown. When she goes beyond, her presence shall not be removed from her husband.

"Stinking water that becomes fragrant: The daughter of a prostitute who has become a lady. She goes up the town and down the town without moving the veil from her face.

"A stone softens in oil: The heretic who has descended from the mountain. He abandoned magicians, he abandoned spells, and he believed in mighty life. He found the orphan, he satiated him, and he filled the arms of the widow.

"Jahja, baptize me with your baptism and invoke over me the name that you invoke. If I turn out to be a disciple, I will mention you in my writing. If I do not turn out to be a disciple, expunge my name from your scroll. You will be held responsible for your sins, and I will be held responsible for my sins."

When Jesus Christ said this, a letter came from the house of Abatur: "Jahja, baptize the liar in the Jordan. Go down in the Jordan, baptize him, ascend to its bank, and confirm him."

Our survey of the literary evidence for the historical JB has been completed. Neither JB nor his immediate followers left documentary testimony to his life and career. Most of the evidence comes from Christian circles. Six gospels contain potentially valuable information about JB: Mark; Q; Matthew; Mark; Luke; John; and Thomas. Four of these gospels represent independent sources: Q, Mark, John, and Thomas. Matthew and Luke-Acts contain materials peculiar to them that also may be independent traditions about JB and the movement initiated by him. And there are the Pseudo-Clementines also with traditions of possible historical worth. In addition to these Christian writings, the *Jewish Antiquities* by the Jewish historian Josephus makes comments about JB potentially of great historical significance, since he writes as a non-Christian. The fragmentary gospels of the Ebionites, the Nazoreans, and the Hebrews, the Infancy Gospel of James, and the Mandaean writings contain nothing of value for understanding JB. We now turn from the literary evidence itself to historical assessment of these materials.

III

Historical assessment of
JOHN
the
BAPTIST

Literary texts about a person become evidence for that person as a historical figure when the historian assesses those texts and draws historical conclusions. As we have noted, the texts about JB were reduced to narrative statements in order for the Seminar to evaluate them historically. Taking into account position papers previously circulated, the members of the Seminar discussed corporately and voted individually on the statements. Each participant used the appropriate color to register the degree of historical certainty appropriate in his or her judgment for that statement:

> Red   Certainty.
> Pink   Probability.
> Gray   Possibility.
> Black   Improbability.

The votes were then tabulated to establish the collective historical conclusion of the Seminar. The same weighted scale and formula adopted for the sayings phase of the Seminar were used. (For particulars, refer to Appendix A, "Voting Guidelines and Calculation.")

Here in PART THREE the narrative statements about JB are arranged in the same biographical order and arranged under the same headings as reported at the conclusion of the INTRODUCTION. Only now each heading constitutes a separate chapter about JB: his historical setting; his birth, family, and upbringing; his ministry; his relationship to Jesus; his imprisonment and death; the Baptist movement; and, finally, apocalypticism, Jesus, and JB.

Before each narrative statement stands an S or an A to indicate whether the statement is a status or an action statement. Beneath the narrative statement appears a box score. The first four numbers represent the percentage of votes cast according to colors: from red, through pink and gray, to black. The next number constitutes the weighted average for all votes cast and, therefore, the basis for the final color grade. Although the computer carried the averages to four decimal places as listed below, only two decimal places are shown in the box score:

> Red   .7501 up
> Pink   .5001 to .7500
> Gray   .2501 to .5000
> Black .0000 to .2500

Following the narrative statements, with their accompanying box scores, appears commentary. That commentary identifies the literary evidence presupposed by the statements and explains the reasoning underlying the final collective judgments of the Seminar. Within the commentary appear letters and numbers in parentheses (for example, G4). These letters and numbers refer to the rules of evidence used by the members of the Seminar in their historical assessment of the literary evidence. E.g. G4 refers the reader to General rule, number 4. (See Appendix D, "Rules of Evidence.")

11 The historical setting

The narrative statements which establish the historical setting for JB's life include status statements about the locale of his ministry and the participants in his story. The locale involves places important in Israel's founding past: the so-called wilderness and the river called Jordan. Among the participants are residents of town and country, representatives of the main religious sects, and the Roman appointed ruler of Galilee and Perea.

Locale

S: **The wilderness is the region around the Jordan River.**

R 45%   P 55%   G 0%   B 0%   avg .82   **red**

The wilderness and the Jordan River are the two places mentioned repeatedly in the gospels in association with the activity of JB. Mark appears as the source for the references in Matthew and Luke. John represents an independent source (G2).

Mark, followed by Matthew and Luke, refers to the wilderness (Mark 1:4 par) as the locale of JB's activity and as the fulfillment of the prophecy of Isaiah with its reference to the wilderness (Isa 40:3, LXX//Mark 1:3 par). Mark also points to the Jordan River as the place of JB's baptizing with water (Mark 1:5, 9). John has JB identify himself as that voice crying in the wilderness in fulfillment of the prophecy of Isaiah (Isa 40:3, LXX). Whereas Matthew has seemingly narrowed the area designated as wilderness to that region west of the Jordan, since the author speaks about the "wilderness of Judea" (Matt 3:1), Luke implies that wilderness encompassed the entire area around the Jordan (Luke 3:1). John explicitly includes as wilderness the territory east of the Jordan, that is the territory of Perea (John 1:28; 3:26).

The Fellows affirmed, with a vote colored red, that the wilderness does designate the region around the Jordan River. This would include the western and the eastern slopes of the valley as the river makes its way southward toward, and empties into, that salty sea called Dead. It was also noted that the wilderness can be used in an expanded sense to designate the desert areas around the Dead Sea as well.

Participants

S: **There were Jerusalemites and Judeans.**
R 90%   P 5%   G 0%   B 5%   avg .94   **red**

S: **There were Pharisees and Sadducees.**
R 90%   P 0%   G 10%   B 0%   avg .94   **red**

S: **There were toll collectors and soldiers.**
R 95%   P 0%   G 5%   B 0%   avg .97   **red**

The gospels associate different categories of persons with JB during his public ministry. Mark, followed by Matthew, refers in rather exaggerated terms to the inhabitants of the city of Jerusalem and the surrounding territory of Judea as coming forth to him for baptism (Mark 1:5 par). In the introduction to a Q saying of JB, Matthew has JB declare those words against the Pharisees and Sadducees, two of the main religious sects, whereas Luke has JB speak the same words to the crowds (Q 3:7–9). Mark also mentions Pharisees in conjunction with the disciples of JB regarding the practice of fasting (Mark 2:18 par). Only Luke in material peculiar to that gospel, however, specifies toll collectors and soldiers among those coming to JB for baptism (Luke 3:10–14).

The particular categories of persons mentioned in the gospels in association with JB's activity, his baptizing and his preaching, may be the redactional work of the individual gospel writers (W2). But with red votes, the Fellows declared that there were indeed Jerusalemites and Judeans, Pharisees and Sadducees, toll collectors and soldiers within the broader social setting of JB's ministry.

S: **There was a tetrarch named Herod Antipas.**
R 100%   P 0%   G 0%   B 0%   avg 100   **red**

S: **There was a woman named Herodias, who was married to Herod's brother.**
R 90%   P 10%   G 0%   B 0%   avg .97   **red**

Mark, followed by Matthew and Luke, claims that Herod Antipas arrested and eventually executed JB because JB had denounced Herod Antipas' marriage to Herodias the wife of his own brother (Mark 6:14–29 par). Josephus also mentions Herod Antipas and his marriage to Herodias the wife of his brother although he does not refer to JB's condemnation of that marriage (Ant 18:109–119). Two sources from very different circles, therefore, mention Herod Antipas as having married Herodias who had been married to his brother (G1, G2).

The formulation of the propositions based on these two sources calls for some comment.

First, Mark refers to Herod Antipas as "king" whereas Matthew, Luke, and Josephus identify him by the title of "tetrarch." There is general recognition, based on substantial evidence, that the Romans, having bestowed upon Herod the Great the title of "King of the Jews" (40–4 B.C.E.), subsequently refused this title for his three sons who succeeded him in ruling over portions of his land. Archelaus ruled over Judea and Samaria as ethnarch (4 B.C.E.–6 C.E.). Herod Antipas ruled over Galilee and Perea as tetrarch (4 B.C.E.–39 C.E.). Philip ruled over the areas to the north and northeast also as tetrarch (4 B.C.E.–34 C.E.). As formulated, the narrative statement follows Matthew and Josephus by using the title tetrarch, not king, for Herod Antipas.

Secondly, Mark and Matthew identify the husband of Herodias as Herod Antipas' brother Philip. Luke simply omits the name of the brother. Josephus identifies the brother by the name Herod. Much has been written about differences between Mark and Josephus at this point. A number of historical options have been proposed including the suggestion that Philip and Herod are simply different names for the same person: just as there was a Herod Antipas, so a Herod Philip. As formulated, however, the narrative statement takes a cue from Luke and sidesteps this particular issue by omitting the name of the brother whose wife Herod Antipas married.

The members of the Seminar were virtually unanimous in affirming, with red votes, that there was a tetrarch named Herod Antipas who married Herodias the wife of one of his brothers.

S: **There were Essenes.**
R 100%   P 0%   G 0%   B 0%   avg 100   **red**
S: **There was a Jewish Sect at Qumran.**
R 90%   P 5%   G 5%   B 0%   avg .95   **red**
S: **The Jews at Qumran were Essenes.**
R 30%   P 60%   G 10%   B 0%   avg .73   **pink**

These narrative statements differ from those considered to this point. They are *not* derived from texts that refer explicitly to JB. In fact, nowhere in early Christian literature are there references by name to Essenes or to Qumran.

The Essenes represent one of the four so-called philosophical schools described by Josephus as having been prominent among his people the Jews in the first century. The others were the Sadducees, the Pharisees, and the Zealots. Historical scholarship has established that the Essenes did constitute a Jewish sect alongside the Pharisees and Sadducees although the character of those called Zealots has been hotly debated.

Khirbet ("Ruin") Qumran is the name of a site just off the northwest shore of the Dead Sea. After the discovery of ancient scrolls—the Dead Sea Scrolls—in nearby caves beginning in 1947, this site was excavated and linked to the scrolls. The ruins were understood to include a room, with furniture, which had been used for the writing of scrolls. A pool among the ruins was said to have been the place for the ritual washings practiced by the members of the community in accordance with the regulations outlined in the scrolls. The scrolls were dated to the first century c.e., and earlier. The destruction of the settlement at Qumran was dated around 68 c.e. and credited to the Romans as their legions made their way back toward Jerusalem during the Jewish war.

Given the description of the Essenes in Josephus, the content of the scrolls, and the physical remains at Qumran, the view that the Jewish sect at Qumran was a community of Essenes became nearly universally accepted—within and without the scholarly world. Much was written about the possible relationship between the beliefs and practices of this community of Essenes and emerging Christianity. Also of particular interest was the possible relationship between this community and JB, between its ritual washings and his baptism. One suggestion—rejected by virtually all scholars—was that JB had been the leader of the Qumran community whom the scrolls called "the teacher of righteousness."

In recent years, however, the view that the Jewish sect at Qumran was Essene and the producer of the scrolls has been vigorously challenged. The community may have been Sadducean. The scrolls may have originated in Jerusalem. The settlement may have been a fortress. And so the rethinking has proceeded.

Both the phrasing of the three narrative statements above and the results of the voting reflect this renewed debate involving Qumran and the scrolls—and JB. Collectively, the Seminar affirmed with red votes that there were Essenes and that there was a Jewish sect at Qumran. Although the Seminar expressed continued support for the "Essene hypothesis," the pink vote suggests less certainty that the Jews living at Qumran were in fact a community of Essenes.

12 BIRTH, FAMILY, AND UPBRINGING

The narrative statements related to the personal background of JB focus on him and his family—a father named Zechariah and a mother named Elizabeth. Of particular interest is the possibility of his family's and, therefore his, priestly lineage.

S: **There was a person named John the Baptizer (Baptist).**

R 95%   P 0%   G 5%   B 0%   avg .96   **red**

JB appears in the two principal sources underlying the synoptic Gospels of Mark, Matthew, and Luke: Mark and Q. JB appears in materials peculiar to the Gospels of Matthew and Luke respectively: M and L, especially in the Lucan infancy traditions. JB also appears in the Gospel of John and the Gospel of Thomas which are literarily independent of the synoptics and Q. (G1, G2, G3, G4). There are narratives about JB, sayings by JB, and sayings by Jesus about JB (G5). As one standing outside Christian circles, Josephus also makes reference to JB in his history of the Jews (G1). Therefore, both the number of independent sources and the variety of literary forms offer overwhelming evidence that there was a man known by the name of John the Baptist, or Baptizer. The red vote of the Fellows, therefore, simply acknowledges the preponderance of the evidence.

The names used in the narrative statement, of course, are of different kinds. "John" represents the given name—the name given at birth. John (Greek, *Iōannēs*; and Hebrew, *Yohanan*) is a common Jewish name meaning "Yahweh is gracious." Several prominent figures bear this name at the turn of the common era. John Hyrcanus I and John Hyrcanus II were priest-kings of the Hasmonean family who ruled in Jerusalem before the rule of Herod and his sons. John son of Zebedee was one of the disciples of Jesus. John son of Zakkai—Yohanan ben Zakkai—was the Pharisaic leader of the formation, or reformation, of Judaism after the fall of Jerusalem to the

Romans. John also was the name of the prophet who received the revelation of Jesus Christ preserved in the New Testament book of that name. "The Baptizer," or "the Baptist," represents a nickname derived from the activity by which he distinguished himself (sometimes a participle, *ho Baptizōn*, usually a noun, *ho Baptistēs*, in Greek). In the gospels, the nickname appears in both narratives and discourse (for example, Mark 1:4 par; 6:14, 24, 25 par; Q 7:20, 33).

Josephus explicitly recognizes this distinction between the given name and the nickname when he introduces JB with these words: "John who was called Baptizer" (Ant 18: 116). Luke also recognizes the distinction in narratives peculiar to that gospel. The story of JB's birth and circumcision is preeminently a naming story (Luke 1:57–64). When gathered together, the neighbors and relatives would have named the newborn child "Zechariah" after his father; but the mother Elizabeth says that he will be given the name "John," the name revealed earlier to Zechariah. Later, in his introduction of the adult John to his readers, Luke refers to him in characteristically Jewish fashion as "John son of Zechariah" (Luke 3:2). Only thereafter does John begin the activity which earned for him the name "Baptizer."

S: **JB was the son of a priest named Zechariah.**
    R 14%   P 0%   G 29%   B 57%   avg .24   **black**
S: **JB's mother was a woman named Elizabeth.**
    R 14%   P 5%   G 19%   B 62%   avg .24   **black**
S: **JB was a priest.**
    R 10%   P 19%   G 52%   B 19%   avg .40   **gray**
S: **JB was circumcised.**
    R 21%   P 63%   G 11%   B 5%   avg .67   **pink**

Only Luke presents literarily independent narratives about the birth, family, and upbringing of JB, since the Infancy Gospel of James builds upon the Lucan story (G2, G4). The Fellows of the Seminar, as virtually all scholars, recognized that Luke had carefully composed the infancy accounts in Luke 1–2 about JB and Jesus as an introduction to the gospel and to the entire two volume work of Luke-Acts (W1, W2, W3).

Perhaps more importantly from a historical point of view, these parallel stories and the traditions presupposed by them have been shaped under the influence of similar stories of religious heroes in Jewish scripture (Old Testament) and later Jewish lore (O4). The annunciation stories, in particular, reflect the stereotyped pattern present in the birth-annunciation accounts of such heroes as Isaac, Samson, and Samuel. That pattern occurs here with reference to JB: problem (old age and barrenness in the case of Elizabeth); entrance of the angel (identified as Gabriel); response of fear by the recipient (Zechariah shaken while officiating in the temple); declaration of the message by the angel (Elizabeth will conceive a son to be named John); and response of puzzlement by the recipient (Zechariah wonders how given their age); and final assurance and sign by the angel (Zechariah to be struck dumb until all accomplished).

Because of the single attestation to the family background of JB, and because of the compositional and literary character of the infancy narrative described above, the Fellows collectively concluded that it was improbable that JB's father was a priest named Zechariah and that his mother was named Elizabeth. The votes colored black, however, were marginal and very close to gray, close to possibility. In fact, the Fellows did vote gray, possibility, on the statement that JB himself was a priest.

Although composed by Luke for Luke-Acts, the infancy narratives (especially Luke 1) contain detailed and accurate knowledge about the temple cultus and the priesthood: the division of the priesthood (1:5, 8), the casting of lots for the burning of incense (1:9), the limited time of service in the temple (1:8, 24), the tendency toward intermarriage among priestly families (1:5), and the rural habitation of priests (1:39, 65). In spite of their stereotypical formulation, the stories about JB's infancy contain details which "fit" the religious and social environment of first century Jerusalem (G6). Some have even used this accurancy of detail to suggest that a written source originating in Baptist circles underlies Luke 1 (See cameo essay, "Luke 1–2 and a Possible 'Baptist' Source.")

For the priestly origin of JB to be a possiblity, however, a plausible historical scenario must be constructed to explain how he came to swap a life as a priest for a ministry in the wilderness along the Jordan (G7). Based on various ancient literary sources beyond Luke 1 (including Josephus and the Dead Sea Scrolls), modern interpreters have reconstructed scenarios to explain how JB the priest's son became a prophet-like figure.

These historical reconstructions often revolve around three observations: that there was a growing division between the urban priests centered around Jerusalem and the rural priests scattered through the country side and small villages; that Qumran as an Essene settlement had a priestly foundation in opposition to the temple cultus and priesthood; and that Essenes reportedly adopted children and reared them in accordance with their own beliefs.

Therefore, JB could have been adopted by Essenes, such as the sectarians as Qumran, only later to rebel against their exclusiveness and to inaugurate his own baptizing ministry in the wilderness in the very vicinity of Qumran. The possibility, not probability nor certainty, that JB was a priest receives expression in the gray vote of the Seminar.

All texts and sources about JB from Christian circles, and the brief narrative by Josephus, present JB as a Jew with a ministry and message that reflect his Jewishness (G6). Jewishness for a male presupposes circumcision on the eighth day in accordance with the command of Yahweh to Abraham (Gen 17:9–14). Paul proudly refers to his own circumcision on the eighth day (Phil 3:5). The circumcision of Jesus is reported in Luke (Luke 2:21). Although no testimony by JB to his own circumcision exists, the Seminar voted that JB was probably circumcised. The pink vote by the Fellows of the Seminar, however, is based upon the recognition of JB's Jewishness rather than the specific reference to his circumcision in Luke 1 that prompted the narrative statement about circumcision.

13 MINISTRY OF BAPTIZING AND PREACHING

A narrative statement of locale introduces the historical assessment of JB's ministry. After statements related to JB's style of ministry, come statements about his characteristic activities, his baptizing and his preaching. The response, or responses, to his activities are gauged by the next series of propositions. This section ends with a consideration of his social role within the context of first century Palestinian Judaism and the broader hellenistic world.

Locale

S: **JB appeared in the wilderness and moved about in the region around the Jordan River.**
R 72%   P 26%   G 2%   B 0%   avg .88   **red**

We noted in our discussion of the historical setting for JB's ministry that the wilderness and the Jordan River are the two places repeatedly associated with JB in the gospels. There we reported how the Seminar affirmed with a red vote that the wilderness included the region around the Jordan River. The Seminar with similar certainty, represented by another red vote, declared that JB appeared in the wilderness and moved about in the region around the Jordan River.

Mark, the earliest narrative gospel, cites the prophet Isaiah as the source for a combined scriptural text which includes Isa 40:3 with its reference to a voice crying in the wilderness (1:2–3). Mark then introduces JB in the wilderness preaching as the fulfillment of that scriptural text (1:4). Isa 40:3 plays a formative role in the JB story in all four narrative gospels (Mark 1:3 par, John 1:23) and, no doubt, in the pre-gospel tradition (W4, 04). Nonetheless, the members of the Seminar were certain that the wilderness and the region around the Jordan River constituted, in fact, the locale of JB's activity. The evidence was there both in number of sources and variety of literary forms.

The wilderness and the Jordan River are the places repeatedly mentioned in narratives as the locale for JB's ministry. Mark (1:3, 4, 5, 9) appears as the source for the references in Matthew and Luke; and John (1:23, 28) stands as an independent source (G2, G3, G4).

Understandably, as sayings gospels neither Q nor Thomas explicitly identifies the setting for JB's ministry within a narrative, although both contain the narrative of Jesus' threefold testing in the wilderness (Q 4:1–13). There is, however, a Q saying by Jesus about JB—voted pink in its Matthean version—that associates JB with the wilderness (Q 7:24b–25; also Thom 78:1–2)(G5).

Neither does Josephus explicitly mention the place of JB's activity. He does identify the site of JB's execution, Machaerus, the fortress-palace of Herod Antipas, located in Perea, less than twenty miles southeast of the Jordan River, east of the Dead Sea. If Josephus is correct about the place of JB's execution—and the Seminar supported his claim with a red vote—then Josephus provides supporting evidence that the wilderness around the Jordan River was the locale of JB's ministry. Machaerus would be the appropriate place of imprisonment and death for someone who had called public notice to himself in the the Jordan valley and surrounding territory (G1).

Style

S: **JB was an ascetic.**
R 20%   P 76%   G 4%   B 0%   avg .72   **pink**

S: **JB lived on locusts and raw honey.**
R 4%   P 48%   G 44%   B 4%   avg .51   **pink**

S: **JB dressed in camel hair.**
R 4%   P 28%   G 60%   B 8%   avg .43   **gray**

S: **JB wore a leather belt around his waist.**
R 0%   P 28%   G 60%   B 12%   avg .39   **gray**

When Mark introduces JB, Mark describes him as living a lifestyle appropriate for one whose place of ministry is the wilderness around the Jordan River (1:2–6). JB apparently lives a life of self-denial and self-discipline. He is an ascetic. He eats locusts and raw honey. He dresses in a garment of camel hair and wears a leather belt around his waist. Matthew follows Mark in describing the diet and the attire of JB in terms of locusts and raw honey, camel hair and leather belt; but Luke omits these particulars.

With a strong pink vote, the Fellows indicated a high degree of probability that JB was ascetic. This judgment had a much broader base than just this Marcan text. There are stories and sayings, representing different sources, which suggest that JB led an austere way of life (G4, G5).

A contrast is often made between the restraint of JB and the excesses of Jesus. There is the Marcan story about fasting (Mark 2:18–20). Disciples of JB who are said to fast, ask Jesus why his disciples do not fast. Jesus' immediate retort about the groom's friends not fasting while the groom is present received a pink vote by the Seminar (Mark 2:19 par). There are Q sayings of Jesus about JB which suggest that he dressed in simple clothes and refused food and drink. The Q saying about attire received a pink vote in its Matthean version, as mentioned in the discussion above about the wilderness as the locale of JB's ministry (Q 4:24b–25; also Thom 78:1–2). The Q saying about eating and drinking received only a gray vote, for reasons to be explained; but this does not deny that beneath the saying in its present form lies a valid contrast made by Jesus between JB's lifestyle and his own (Q 7:33–34).

Beyond the specific ascetic traits associated with JB in individual stories and sayings, however, is the broader association of JB throughout the gospels with the prophets and prophetic tradition from Israel's past (e.g. Mark 6:14–15 par, 8:27–30 par). The prophetic tradition itself had been nurtured by the memory of Israel's simpler semi-nomadic past. Prophets became known for their distinctive dress in the skins of animals (Zech 13:4; Heb 11:37). This semi-nomadic tradition had found social expression not only through the great prophets, whose messages were preserved in the scriptures, but through groups committed to an ascetic way of life. Among these groups were the Nazirites and Rechabites of old who committed themselves to abstinence from wine and even to continued dwelling in tents (Judg 13, Jer 35). Israel's past, and therefore expected future, became embodied in the presumably Essene sectarians at Qumran in JB's own day.

Collectively the Fellows also considered it probable that JB lived on locusts and wild honey, although the pink vote here was by a considerably narrower margin than the pink vote on the broader issue of JB's asceticism. The gray votes on the statements about JB's dress in camel hair and his wearing a leather belt around his waist indicated possibility, but no more.

The reason for the discrepancy between the pinks and the grays lies in the relationship between the narrative details in Mark and the scriptural text of 2 Kgs 1:8 (W4, O4). This latter text contains a description of the dress of Elijah the prophet: a garment of haircloth and a leather girdle around his loins. The gray votes reflect a suspicion that the gospel writer (W4), or those transmitting the tradition (O4), had draped JB in the dress of Elijah in keeping with their theological interests. Locusts and raw honey are not mentioned in the Elijah passage; and they represent menu items available in the Jordan valley in JB's day (G6). Therefore, possibility becomes probability as indicated by the color pink.

Characteristic Activities

A: **JB baptized with water (characteristic activity).**

R 86%   P 9%   G 5%   B 0%   avg .94   **red**

A: **JB preached (characteristic activity).**

R 62%   P 19%   G 14%   B 5%   avg .79   **red**

S: **JB's characteristic activities took place in the wilderness.**

R 52%   P 43%   G 5%   B 0%   avg .83   **red**

What kinds of activities characterized JB's ministry? What was the locale of these activities? These narrative statements, two action statements and a status statement, were formulated in the broadest terms in order to elicit a collective judgment from the Seminar about the kinds of things JB did.

Even a cursory reading of the ancient literature about JB suggests that his ministry had two dimensions: water baptism and proclamation. As we noted in our survey of that literature, most portrayals of JB hold these two activities together although with varying degrees of emphasis. Mark presents the two activities as integrally related. JB's message is summarized as a baptism of repentance leading to the forgiveness of sins (Mark 1:4) and the one cited saying by JB involves a contrast between the current water baptism of JB and a future spirit baptism by one mightier than he (Mark 1:8). As a sayings gospel, Q highlights JB's preaching activity but does mention his baptizing activity as a theme of his message (Q 3:16–17). Since Matthew and Luke use both Mark and Q, their portrayals also present the two activities of water baptism and proclamation as integrally connected. John, however, by making JB into a witness to Jesus as the Christ, de-emphasizes his preaching function and subordinates his baptizing activity to his role as witness (especially John 1:31). JB does not baptize Jesus, but rather water baptism becomes an activity that JB the witness and Jesus the object of his witness undertake parallel to one another (John 1:28; 3:22–24,25–26). Josephus also recognizes that JB's activity involved both water baptism and speaking, although he presents JB as more of a moral teacher than preacher (Ant 18:116–118).

Within the literature, two titles are associated with JB: baptist and prophet. We have already commented on the former as his special nickname. We shall comment on the latter when considering his social role within the context of first century Judaism. These two names, or epithets, by which JB became known are grounded respectively in his related activities of baptizing and preaching.

The breadth and variety of the literary evidence led to the collective judgment on the general narrative statements about JB activity (G4, G5). JB baptized with water. JB preached. Both red.

The higher degree of certainty about JB's baptism with water in contradistinction to his preaching, as reflected in the final voting percentages, can probably be explained in two ways. First, some Fellows preferred to think of baptism, not preaching, as JB's most characteristic activity, as reflected in his nickname. Secondly, other Fellows preferred to describe JB's speaking activity as teaching, not preaching—as instruction, not exhortation.

Another status statement about the locale of JB's ministry had declared that JB appeared in the wilderness and moved about in the region around the Jordan River. The status statement here makes specific reference to the wilderness as the setting for JB's characteristic activities, of water baptism and proclamation. The Seminar reaffirmed the certainty of the wilderness as the locale of JB's ministry with another vote colored red.

Baptizing

The following series of narrative statements relate to the baptizing dimension of JB's ministry. Already, however, we shall be considering the preaching dimension insofar as his baptizing activity is a theme of his proclamation.

A: **JB preached baptism.**

R 62%   P 19%   G 14%   B 5%   avg .79   **red**

This statement recognizes that baptism was an integral theme of JB's message. Mark and Q, followed by Matthew and Luke, provide evidence for this both in narrative discourse (Mark 1:4 par) and in sayings by JB (Mark 1:7–8; Q 3:16–17). Josephus also implies that an explanation of the meaning of baptism was included in JB's call for a virtuous life (Ant 18:117). The Seminar concluded with some degree of certainty that JB preached baptism; thus, the color red.

A: **JB's baptism was a form of Jewish immersion rite.**

R 38%   P 38%   G 19%   B 19%   avg .70   **pink**

This statement addresses two issues: first, the issue of the cultural and religious context within which JB's baptizing should be viewed; and, secondly, the specific mode of his baptizing.

The statement addresses the issue of the cultural and religious context of JB's baptizing. Josephus has certainly worded his presentation of JB's activity in categories congenial to a hellenistic audience; but there is no evidence which would suggest that JB's baptizing activity should be considered in the light of Graeco-Roman practices, such as the rites of the mystery religions. This means that JB's baptizing activity should be viewed in relation to Jewish ablution practices—the use of water to cleanse the body for religious purposes. Jewish ablution practices are documented in a sizable body of literature. That literature includes not only the Hebrew Scriptures but the apocryphal and pseudepigraphal writings, the Dead Sea Scrolls, and the histories of Josephus.

The statement also addresses the issue of the mode of JB's baptizing. Within the Judaism of JB's day, ablutions could take the mode of sprinkling, washing, or immersion. It is generally recognized that the immersion of proselytes, often appealed to as the model of JB's practice, was not established until the reorganization of Judaism after the fall of the temple. But before 70 C.E., immersion was practiced extensively in some circles, such as among the Essenes and by the Qumran community, whether Essene or not. Bannus, the holy man with whom Josephus spent three years, seemingly also practiced immersion. The baptism of JB was baptism in the form of immersion (G6). The narrative texts about JB in the gospels and Josephus mention *that* JB baptized but are relatively silent about *how* JB baptized. The baptism of Jesus, however, is described in language that suggests immersion: ". . . he got up out of the water . . ." (Mark 1:9–11 par). Also, the Jordan River, as the site of JB's baptizing activity, would lend itself to immersion. Furthermore, the Greek words used with reference to JB's activity, both in the gospels and Josephus, are based on the stem *bapt-* which means "to dip," "to submerge." There were other Greek words, common in the New Testament itself, readily available to describe washings other than immersion. In the footwashing story about Jesus in John, for example, both *louō* and *niptō* are used in the same sentence with the former used to indicate a complete washing, the latter a washing of extremities (John 13:10). Therefore, one wag in the Seminar referred to JB as the "Big Dipper."

Even with this evidence, however, the Fellows expressed only probability about the baptism of JB's being a Jewish *immersion* rite. The lack of descriptions of his actual practice prevented greater certainty: pink.

A: JB administered baptism himself.

R 38%   P 52%   G 10%   B 0%   avg .76   **red**

This statement suggests that JB was somehow personally involved in conducting the rite of baptism in relation to those who received it. The rite was not performed by persons by themselves, independent of JB.

In narrative discourse, JB's baptism is described, in the passive voice, as being administered "by him" (Mark 1:5, 9). In a saying by JB, preserved in multiple sources, he appropriately describes his action in the active voice: "I have been baptizing . . ." (Mark 1:8; Q 3:16; also John 1:26)(G4, G5). Ablutions, including immersions, within the Judaism of JB's day were commonly self-administered. The fact that JB attracted to himself the nickname "the Baptist" implies that there was something distinctive about the baptism he advocated. That distinctiveness may have been his having performed it himself. The members of the Seminar, with a vote colored red, expressed the view that JB certainly did administer baptism himself.

The evidence, however, does not allow an informed judgment about the exact nature of JB's involvement in his administration of baptism. He could have dipped the person into the water. He could have held the hand of the person during the immersion. He could have led the person into the water and with raised hands pronounced a blessing or declared some statement. The Baptist may have practiced immersion as do his later Christian namesakes; but the *mechanics* of immersion as acted out by his namesakes should not be considered to correspond to the mechanics acted out by JB. JB's namesakes are Christians, heirs of the movement of the Reformation period that advocated the re-baptism (thus their name, Ana-baptists) of Christians as adult believers. JB himself was not a Christian, in spite of his portrayal in John and the later conferral of sainthood upon him.

A: **JB's baptism was done in flowing water.**

R 43%   P 43%   G 9%   B 5%   avg .75   **pink**

This narrative statement grows primarily out of the evidence, already surveyed, that the Jordan River served as a site, if not the only site, of JB's baptizing activity (especially Mark 1:5, 9 par). John mentions "Aenon near Salim" as a site where JB also baptized because "there was plenty of water around" (1:23). The location of Aenon has been much debated, but the term Aenon itself means "spring." Therefore, the mention of this place as a site for JB's baptizing activity lends further support to the notion that his baptizing was done in flowing water (G4). The use of flowing water, even the Jordan River, also characterizes some immersions in Hebrew Scripture and in later Jewish literature (for example, 2 Kgs 5:9–17)(G6).

In the gospels, however, the Jordan is often not qualified by the word "river." Therefore, the Jordan can function more as a regional reference rather than the specific place where baptism occurs (compare Mark 1:5 and Luke 3:3; also John 1:28, 3:26, 10:40). Furthermore, although JB apparently uses natural sources of water for his baptism, this does not necessarily mean that the water could be described as flowing. At least no source about JB describes his baptism in these terms. In fact, the water of the Jordan River, a pool in Judea or Perea, or an oasis in the wilderness would not necessarily be flowing.

The Seminar collectively affirmed with certainty (a red vote) that the wilderness around the Jordan River served as the locale of JB's characteristic activities of preaching and baptizing. But because of the limitations and ambiguity of the evidence, the Seminar took a position not of certainty, but of probability, on the declaration that JB's baptism was done in flowing water: pink.

A: **JB's baptism was understood to express repentance.**

R 52%   P 39%   G 9%   B 0%   avg .81   **red**

This and the next four narrative statements represent an attempt to establish how JB's baptism was perceived by him and those who presented themselves to him for immersion, probably in flowing water, such as the Jordan River. The first statement focuses on the notion of repentance.

It has often been observed that the Greek verb *metanoeō*, found in New Testament texts and commonly translated into English as "repentance," means "change of mind," whereas the underlying idea expressed by the Hebrew word *shub* means "reversal of direction." The Scholar's Version has adopted the translation, "change of heart."

JB's concern for repentance expresses itself explicitly in two sources, the one narrative discourse, and the other a saying by JB (Mark 1:4; Q 3:8)(G4, G5). In the prophetic traditions of the Hebrew Scripture, the motif of repentance is linked with the theme of judgment; and so it is in the Q saying (Q 3:7–9; also see Q 3:16–17). Also in later Jewish pseudepigraphical literature and the Dead Sea Scrolls, repentance is associated with immersion (G6). Although emerging Christianity certainly connected repentance with the baptism in the baptism practiced by the church (for example. read Acts), it is unlikely that this meaning was *just* read back into the baptismal practices of JB (O3). Even Josephus, although using hellenistic turns of phrase, implies that JB expected a change in the lives of those who would receive his baptism (Ant 18:117). The Fellows, therefore, declared with certainty that JB's baptism was understood to express repentance. The vote came out red. The collective judgment expressed about the next four propositions was less certain and more in the range of probability.

A: **JB's baptism was understood to mediate God's forgiveness.**

R 33%   P 38%   G 24%   B 5%   avg .67   **pink**

That JB's baptism was understood not only to express repentance but, in some sense, to mediate God's forgiveness of sins is explicitly noted only in Mark, but followed by Luke, among the gospels: "So, John the Baptizer appeared in the widerness calling for baptism and a change of heart that lead to a forgiveness of sins" (Mark 1:4; also Luke 3:3). The Marcan narrative both provides the basis for this narrative statement and serves as its principal supporting literary evidence (G4).

Several observations, however, lend credence to the statement the JB's baptism was understood to mediate God's forgiveness.

First, on this issue the relative silence of Christian sources may be supporting testimony. Early Christianity clearly connected forgiveness of sins and repentance with the baptism of the church (again, read Acts). But the church made the exclusive claim that God's forgiveness of sins was through Jesus Christ (for example, Mark 2:1–12 par; Luke 4:12). The Marcan claim that JB's baptism involved God's forgiveness of sins stands in tension even with that gospel's later presentation of Jesus, much less the general claims on behalf of Jesus within the church. Therefore, the Marcan claim may preserve historical memory precisely because it runs against the grain of later Christian teaching about forgiveness through Jesus as the Christ (N3, W4).

Secondly, Josephus even seems to deny that JB's baptism serves to mediate God's forginesss. He says that baptism must *not* be used to gain pardon for sins but for purification of the body (Ant 18:117). Nonetheless, Josephus does explicitly talk about pardon of sins *within the context* of his interpretation of JB's baptizing practice. As the silence of Christian sources about JB's baptism relative to the forgiveness of sins may be supporting testimony, so the denial of a relationship between baptism and the forgiveness of sins by Josephus—in explaining the practice to his hellenistic audience—may similarly lend support. Perhaps JB's baptism was understood to mediate God's forgiveness (W4).

Thirdly, this understanding of JB's baptism would also be consistent with similar claims on behalf of immersion in the Judaism of JB's day. Pseudepigraphal writings and the Dead Sea Scrolls sometimes link together not only immersion and repentance but immersion and God's forgiveness (G6).

Therefore, the direct testimony of literary sources on this issue was limited. The Seminar did not express certainty with a red vote. But there was enough significant circumstantial evidence to prompt the Seminar to express probability with a vote colored pink.

A: JB's baptism was understood to be a protest against the temple establishment.

R 5%   P 45%   G 55%   B 0%   avg .52   **pink**

Characters appear in the narratives about JB that connect him in some way, however tenuous, to Jerusalem and the temple. Mark, followed by Matthew, includes Jerusalemites among those who come out to be baptized by him (Mark 1:5 par). Matthew also—in the introduction to a Q saying—mentions Sadducees, representatives of the predominantly priestly sect, as being among the recipients of JB's harshest words of condemnation (Matt 3:7). John goes so far as to identify members of the temple establishment, priests and Levites, as coming from Jerusalem out into the wildeness to ask JB for his ID card: "Who are you?" (John 1:19) It is widely recognized that narrative details such as these often represent the work of the narrators themselves, whether the writers of the texts or the transmitters of the tradition (W2, O2). But the Seminar, in an action yet to be discussed, does consider it probable that Sadducees were among those coming out into the wilderness to hear JB.

The narrative statement at hand, the statement about JB's baptism as a protest against the temple establishment, is not derived directly from a specific text—not from a particular story, not from a reported saying. This statement represents an implication of the previous action discussed immediately above.

If JB's baptism was understood to mediate God's forgiveness, then his baptism provides a striking parallel to the atoning sacrifices of the temple cultus under the overall supervision of the high priest who, in JB's day, was Caiaphas (18–36 C.E.). Just as the sacrifices of the temple cultus mediated forgiveness of sins to the persons making the sacrifices, so forgiveness of sins was mediated to those receiving baptism at the hands of JB.

The supporting evidence for the statement at hand is circumstantial, but weighty. That evidence comes from the widely attested role of the temple within first century Judaism and the varying perceptions of its leadership. The temple itself was Yahweh's chosen dwelling place where the prescribed rituals of worship—centered in the varied sacrifices—had been entrusted to a hereditary priesthood. From one angle, therefore, the temple and its leadership represented the historic faith and symbolized the future hope of Israel, a hope against hope in a time of Roman domination. But from another angle, the temple and its leadership served as a reminder of collaboration with the occupying power and a growing economic disparity between the rich and the poor; and the economic and social divisions within the populace extended into the priesthood itself.

The Qumran community as depicted in the Dead Sea Scrolls, for example, had grown out of a protest movement in the second century B.C.E. and had become something of a counter-community against the temple and its unfaithful and corrupt leaders. At Qumran the sacrifices of the temple, at least for the time being, were no longer a means of atonement for sin. Immersion was required for uncleanness caused by sin both as an initiatory act by those entering the communitry and as a ongoing act by those within the community. Immersion became effective when accompanied by those God-given spiritual qualities expected of members of the community. Prayers from the elect became fit and right offerings to God.

Considering JB's baptism within this broader cultural context, the Seminar concluded that a baptism which mediated God's forgiveness also, in all probability, would have been understood as a protest against the temple establishment (G6). Thus, a pink vote. This probability, along with the possibility of JB's own priestly background, provide interesting bases for historical reflection on the dynamics operative in JB's ministry in the wilderness around the Jordan River, both his motivations and the varied responses to him.

A: **JB's baptism was understood to purify from uncleanness.**

R 19%   P 43%   G 38%   B 0%   avg .60   **pink**

Historically, washings by whatever mode—within Judaism as well as other religions—presuppose uncleanness. That uncleanness could be the result of either physical or moral contamination. In the gospels, as we noted above, JB's baptism is explicitly related to the moral sphere. There is talk therein about repentance and the forgiveness of sins. In these Christian documents, however, the language of purification, or cleansing, is not used with reference to JB's baptism (but note Q 3:17). Josephus the Jewish historian, however, does use the language of purification and cleansing with reference to the baptism of JB (Ant 18:117).

This narrative statement about the baptism of JB, therefore, hangs specifically on the testimony of Josephus (G4) and, more generally, on the widely attested understanding of ablutions, including immersions, within first century Judaism (G6).

In spite of the limited textual evidence that JB's baptism was understood to purify from uncleanness, there was strong opinion within the Seminar that the most certain feature of JB's baptism was his action as a purifier, as one who cleanses. This view rested on the broader cultural context of Judaism within which JB's baptism was conducted (G6). This view also dismissed the talk about repentance and forgiveness of sins as *just* the language of the church (O3). Therefore, the collective judgment of the Seminar fell between certainty and possibility, that is, probability. JB's baptism was probably understood to purify from uncleanness. The color pink represents that judgment.

A: **JB's baptism was understood as an initiation into a Jewish sectarian movement.**

R 19%   P 29%   G 42%   B 10%   avg .52   **pink**

This statement addresses the issue of the initiatory character of JB's rite of baptism. Several observations, based primarily on other historical conclusions, support this proposition.

First, JB preached baptism and evidently required it for those who expressed repentance and who through the mediation of his baptism received God's forgiveness of their sins (see above).

Secondly, JB's preaching and baptizing evidently created a distinction between those who accepted his message and rite and those who rejected the same: the repentant and the unrepentant, the forgiven and the unforgiven, the clean and the unclean (see above).

Thirdly, JB's activity resulted in a movement active during his lifetime, and even after his death, which apparently paralleled and rivaled the Jesus movement (to be discussed below). JB had disciples who were remembered for their practice of fasting, praying, and baptizing (Mark 2:18; Luke 11:1; also Acts 18:24–28; 19:1–7). That his ministry led to social formation supports the claim that JB initiated a Jewish sectarian movement with baptism as an initiatory rite.

Fourthly, JB's rite of baptism was evidently administered once as though it were an initiation. At least there is no indication in any of the sources or texts that JB's baptism was to be repeated as was, for example, the immersions at Qumran.

Fifthly, the use of baptism, or immersion, as a rite of initiation existed among sectarian groups in first century Judaism. Although immersions were repeated by those who were full members of the Qumran community, immersion also served an initiatory function for that community.

Sixthly, the use of baptism as an initiatory rite within early Christianity could also be invoked as evidence for a similar use by John.

Admittedly, however, the presentation of JB's baptism in the gospels as a non-repeatable act could be considered an accommodation of his baptism to the later church's understanding of its own baptism as non-repeatable (O3). Furthermore, JB's baptism could be viewed as a generic purification that distinguished it from the particular purification practices of such sects as the Sadducees, Pharisees, and Essenes.

Given the evidence in support of and the reservations about the statement, the Seminar collectively decided that JB's baptism was probably understood as an initiation into a Jewish movement. The vote turned out to be another pink.

A: **JB's baptism was understood to foreshadow an expected figure's baptism.**

R 9%   P 29%   G 33%   B 29%   avg .40   **gray**

This narrative statement is based on the saying attributed to JB in Mark 1:8, which has parallels in Luke 3:16ac and Matthew 3:11ac (Q). In this saying JB contrasts his water baptism with the spirit baptism of one who will succeed him.

The saying itself will be discussed in our consideration of those sayings in the gospels that are attributed to JB. As formulated, however, the above statement suggests that JB used his water baptism as a foreshadowing of the baptism of the church to be instituted by Jesus. Certainly the saying on which the proposition rests was so understood by the gospel writers since they incorporated it into their gospels (W4). The saying would have been understood similarly by those who transmitted it orally prior to the writing of the gospels (O3). Because the proposition reflects the church's view of the relationship between JB and Jesus, between the baptism of JB and the baptism of the church, the Seminar's collective judgment was only in the range of possibility. Therefore, a gray.

Preaching

Narrative statements related to the baptizing dimension of JB's ministry have been considered. We turn now to the preaching, or teaching, dimension. We shall consider statements related not to water but to words.

A: **JB taught repentance.**

R 59%   P 26%   G 4%   B 11%   avg .78   **red**

A: **JB taught repentance apart from baptism.**

R 0%   P 15%   G 30%   B 55%   avg .20   **black**

The review of the narrative statements about JB's characteristic activity of baptizing, as acted upon by the Seminar, disclosed two certainties: JB preached baptism; and his baptism was understood to be an expression of repentance. This review of the narrative statements about JB's characteristic activity of preaching begins with two certainties, the one stated positively and the other negatively: JB taught repentance, but he did not teach repentance apart from baptism. Such is the meaning of the red and the black votes.

JB's concern for repentance appears explicitly in two sources and there in two different literary forms (G4, G5), in the Marcan narrative and in a Q saying (Mark 1:4; Q 3:7–9). By appropriating material from Mark and Q, Matthew and Luke have incorporated the repentance theme into their presentations of JB's baptizing ministry. Luke has reinforced that theme with the further addition of L traditions which contain JB's ethical exhortations for changes of behavior by his hearers (Luke 3:10–14). Josephus also, although using language appropriate for his hellenistic audience, implies that JB expected a change in the lives of those who presented themselves for baptism (Ant 18:117).

Collectively, therefore, the Seminar strongly endorsed the one proposition, and just as strongly denied the other. JB *certainly* taught repentance, and he did *not* teach repentance apart from baptism. JB's call for repentance was inextricably related to his practice of baptism.

Some Fellows understood these propositions as a denial that JB himself was a preacher of repentance—a prophet-like preacher of repentance, an apocalyptic preacher of repentance. This position was based on the claim that only Q, with JB's fiery words of judgment (Q 3:7–9, 17), actually portrays him as a proclaimer of repentance. The other sources, including Mark, allegedly have JB simply talking about repentance. Accordingly, the Q portrayal of JB as a proclaimer of repentance was a creation of the Q community, which similarly, at a point in its history, expanded its portrayal of Jesus in an apocalyptic direction. Just as Jesus the wisdom teacher also became Jesus the apocalyptic preacher, so JB (John the Baptizer) became an apocalyptic preacher (W4, W5, O3). Other Fellows did not understand the propositions, as stated, necessarily making such claims. Subsequently, as we shall see, the Seminar reaffirmed its collective judgment that Jesus as a historical figure was non-apocalyptic but that JB during his historic ministry acted like a prophet and was an apocalyptic preacher.

A: **Mark 1:4 and Matt 3:2 summarize the message of JB.**

Mark 1:4. "So, John the Baptizer appeared in the wilderness calling for baptism and a change of heart that lead to forgiveness of sins."

Matt 3:2. [*"In due course* John the Baptist appears in the wilderness of Judea, calling out:] 'Change your ways because Heaven's imperial rule is closing in'."

R 6%   P 12%   G 35%   B 47%   avg .25   **gray**

Mark 1:4, perhaps cited more than any other single text in our study, constitutes Mark's narrative introduction of JB to his readers as the fulfillment of the prophets (Mark 1:2–3//Mal 3:1; Isa 40:3, LXX). Mark summarizes JB's message in indirect, not direct, discourse. We have already determined that Mark here has captured with varying degrees of probability important dimensions of what JB was all about: baptism, repentance, and forgiveness.

When Mark's narrative introduction is taken over by Matthew, two important shifts take place with the summary of JB's message (Matt 3:2). First, Matthew replaces indirect discourse with direct discourse. This represents a common literary technique used throughout the gospel. Secondly, Matthew makes JB into a preacher of the kingdom of heaven. The summary of JB's message corresponds exactly with the summary of Jesus' message (Matt 4:17) and resembles the summary of the message of Jesus' disciples (Matt 10:7). These summaries represent the creative work of the gospel writer (W4).

Therefore, the only overlap between the Marcan and the Matthean summaries of JB's message lies in their common emphasis on change, or repentance. This is the only point at which there is any possibility of Matthew's summary recalling the actual message of JB. This accounts for the Seminar's gray vote when these two texts were considered together.

A: **JB spoke the words in Mark 1:7, Luke 3:16b and Matt 3:11b (Q).**
[Compare John 1:26–27; also Acts 13:25.]

Mark 1:7. "Someone more powerful than I will succeed me, whose sandal straps I am not fit to bend down and untie."

Luke 3:16b(Q). ". . . but someone more powerful than I is coming, whose sandal straps I am not fit to untie."

Matt 3:11b (Q). ". . . but someone more powerful than I will succeed me. I am not fit to carry his sandals."

[**John 1:26–27.** "I baptize, yes, but only with water. Right there with you is someone you don't yet recognize; he is the one who is to be my successor. I don't even deserve to untie his sandal straps."]

[**Acts 13:25.** "But after me one is coming, the sandals of whose feet I am not fit to untie."]

R 13%   P 44%   G 26%   B 17%   avg .51   **pink**

The words of JB reported in Mark 1:7 clearly constitute a saying independent of the words of JB that follow in Mark 1:8. As evident in Luke 3:16 and Matthew 3:11, the Sayings Gospel Q had fused these two independent sayings into a single saying. Therefore, the Seminar followed Mark by considering the words attributed to JB in Mark 1:7 and the words attributed to him in Mark 1:8 as originally independent sayings. Separate votes on the sayings were requested; and separate votes were conducted.

Both in Mark and in Q, albeit with slightly different wording, this saying of JB makes two claims about a future coming one in comparison with JB himself. First, the coming one will be more powerful than JB. Secondly, the coming one is described as having sandals which JB is not worthy to unfasten, or carry. The versions of the saying reported in John and in Acts mention only the second claim: JB is unworthy to unfasten the sandals of the coming one.

The vote of the Seminar on this saying in Mark 1:7 fell in the range of probability: pink. This means that the Seminar went on record affirming these probabilities:

that JB talked about a coming figure;

that JB compared himself with that coming figure; and

that the coming figure would,

first, be more powerful than JB and

secondly, wear sandals that JB would be unworthy to untie.

Several reasons can be given for this collective judgment. First, the saying is attested in at least three sources: Mark, Q, and John (G4). If the version in Acts came to Luke from a source independent of the version he found in Q, then the saying appears in four sources. Very few of Jesus' sayings are this widely attested. Secondly, the saying, especially in the synoptic versions, does not describe the coming one in specifically Christian terms as though the saying were the creation of the church (W4, O3). Thirdly, JB's proclamation of a mighty coming one coheres with his wilderness ministry of baptizing and preaching (G6). Fourthly, the silence of Josephus about JB's eschatological message and his expectation of a future figure is understandable. Throughout his apologetic writings, Josephus indicates a dislike for the messianic expectations rife among his people because those expectations led to unrest and, ultimately, to the disasterous war against Rome. Nonetheless, Josephus implies that JB's proclamation had an eschatological, even a messianic, dimension. Josephus says that Herod Antipas so perceived JB's eloquence as a political threat that he seized and executed JB to forestall an uprising.

The endorsement of this saying as in some sense historical, still does not deal directly with matters of meaning. How did JB, or his hearers, understand the identity of this expected figure? What exactly was to be this figure's function?

Relative to the identity of this figure, some have claimed that JB was speaking of the coming of Yahweh—the coming of God. Others have tried to fit JB's view into one of the known categories of expected figures: the kingly messiah descended from David, the priestly messiah descended from Aaron, a prophet such as Elijah-returned, the apocalyptic Son of man, and so on. Based on the reference to the expected figure's sandals—however symbolic—and the explicit mention of the expected figure's power by comparison with JB himself, it does seem that JB was referring to an individual other than Yahweh. But whatever his identity, the figure certainly comes with Yahweh's sanction in order to effect Yahweh's work. Relative to the function of this figure, however, this saying in itself discloses little in particular. But the figure will have the power to effect whatever Yahweh wills.

Other sayings attributed to JB, however, provide evidence for the possible function, or functions, of the expected one. To these saying we now turn.

A: JB spoke the words in Mark 1:8, Luke 3:16a,c and Matt 3:11a,c (Q)

Mark 1:8. "I have been baptizing with water, but he will baptize you with holy spirit."

Luke 3:16a,c (Q). "I baptize you with water . . . . He'll baptize you with [holy] spirit and fire."

Matt 3:11a,c (Q). "I baptize you with water to signal a change of heart. . . . He'll baptize you with holy spirit and fire."

R 9%   P 30%   G 35%   B 26%   avg .41   **gray**

Unlike the saying of JB reported in Mark 1:7, this saying in Mark 1:8 appears only in Q—not in John, not in Acts. In terms of sources, therefore, the saying has double attestation—neither triple, nor quadruple, attestation.

Like the saying in Mark 1:7, however, this saying in Mark 1:8 has JB contrast himself with an expected figure. All three versions of the saying have JB contrast his activity of water baptism with the baptizing activity of the one yet to come.

But among the three texts in Mark, Luke, and Matthew differences in details appear. Broadly stated the issue becomes: does Mark or Q (Matthew and Luke) preserve the earlier form of the saying? Or, more narrowly stated: with what will the expected figure baptize? Only with *spirit* (as Mark reads)? With *spirit and fire* (as Luke and Matthew now read)? Or only with *fire* (as Q may have read before the incorporation of the saying into Luke and Matthew)?

The Seminar itself neither passed judgment on a reconstructed text nor differentiated among the synoptic readings. The Seminar voted on the three synoptic texts as a group. The result fell only in the range in possibility: gray. In spite of the attestation of the saying in Mark and Q, the Fellows thought that this saying too obviously reflected the church's view of the relationship between JB and Jesus, between their respective bap-

relationship between JB and Jesus, between their respective baptisms, to be considered probable (W4, 03). It might be observed, however, that if the earliest form of the saying about the coming one mentioned only a baptism by *fire* then the saying would cohere with JB's preaching of a baptism of repentance in anticipation of the coming judgment. The next saying of JB to be considered does affirm the judgmental function of this expected one.

A: JB spoke the words in Luke 3:17 and Matthew 3:12 (Q).

> **Luke 3:17.** "His pitchfork is in his hand, to make a clean sweep of his threshing floor and to gather wheat into the granary, but the chaff he'll burn in a fire that can't be put out."
>
> **Matt 3:12.** "His pitchfork is in his hand, to make a clean sweep of his threshing floor and to gather wheat into the granary, but the chaff he'll burn in a fire that can't be put out."
>
> R 8%   P 69%   G 15%   B 8%   avg .60   **pink**

This saying attributed to JB appears only in Q. In Q these identical words presuppose JB's announcement of the one coming mightier than he whose sandals he is unworthy to touch. That saying and this saying are indissolubly linked by the introductory pronoun: "His . . ." Therefore, in Q these words amplify and describe the expected one's eschatological act.

In the previous saying, that act is described parallel to JB's water baptism rather cryptically as a baptism of spirit and fire. Now an agricultural image is used that reflects farming practices characteristic of first century Palestine (G6). The one coming acts like a farmer. He seemingly throws the cut grain into the air with his pitchfork in order to separate the wheat from the chaff. Then he gathers the wheat into his granary and burns the chaff.

One interpretation sees the judgmental edge of this image in the *act of throwing* the grain into the air followed by the gathering of the wheat and the destruction of the chaff. Another intriguing interpretation suggests that the instrument in the farmer's hand is not a pitchfork for winnowing but a shovel used after the winnowing for cleaning the threshing floor. The winnowing has already occurred; and the grain lies on the floor already separated from the chaff. The judgmental edge lies in the *act of cleaning* the floor by gathering the wheat for preservation and the chaff for destruction.

According to the latter interpretation, JB implies that his baptizing ministry is the winnowing. Separation occurs as the repentant and unrepentant, the forgiven and unforgiven, the clean and the unclean identify themselves through their acceptance or non-acceptance of JB's baptism. The expected figure ratifies and completes what has been inaugurated in JB's activity of baptizing and preaching. This latter view is consistent with conclusions already established about JB and his ministry.

Although this Q saying appears in only one source (G4), the Fellows collectively decided that something similar to these words were said by JB. The pink vote signifies that decision. These words attributed to JB cohere, literarily and thematically, with the other words to which they are linked and with broader dimensions of his ministry.

Also, although no available evidence indicates that these words were intentionally omitted by Mark and John, their non-attestation in Mark and John are as understandable as their inclusion in Q and subsequently in the gospels of Matthew and Luke. The Gospel of Mark itself has been called an apocalypse in gospel form because of its intentional presentation of Jesus as a preacher of the end-times (especially Mark 13). JB is cast in the role of the baptizing forerunner, the implicit Elijah-returned, who prepares the way for Jesus as the Christ by preaching a baptism of repentance for the forgiveness of sins and by pointing to Jesus as one who will baptize with holy spirit. It is Jesus as the Christ who proclaims eschatological deliverance and destruction, respectively, for those enduring or not enduring to the end (Mark 13:13). In the Gospel of John, JB has become a witness to Jesus as the Christ; and neither JB nor Jesus preaches an apocalyptic message of the end-times.

The community that produced the Sayings Gospel Q, according to one reconstruction of its history, originally had looked to Jesus as a sage and wisdom teacher. This view was reflected in the earliest version of Q, which was a collection of wisdom teachings, including provocative parables and witty aphorisms. In a later crisis, that community came to look upon Jesus not only as sage and wisdom teacher but as an apocalyptic preacher who proclaimed judgment and the coming Son of man, the son of Adam. This view came to be reflected in later versions of Q. The apocalyptic material about JB also belongs to these later versions of Q, as we know the document through its incorporation into the narrative gospels of Matthew and Luke.

A: JB spoke the words in Luke 3:7–9 and Matt 3:7–10 (Q).

Luke 3:7–9 (Q). [So John would say to the crowds that came out to be baptized by him,] "You spawn of Satan! Who warned you to flee from the impending doom? Well then, start producing fruit suitable for a change of heart, and don't even think of saying to yourselves, 'We have Abraham as our father.' Let me tell you, God can raise up children for Abraham right out of these rocks. Even now the axe is aimed at the root of the trees. So every tree not producing fruit gets cut down and tossed into the fire."

Matt 3:7–10 (Q). [When he saw that many of the Pharisees and Sadducees were coming for baptism, John said to them,] "You spawn of Satan! Who warned you to flee from the impending doom? Well then, start producing fruit suitable for a change of heart, and don't even think of saying to yourselves, 'We have Abraham as our father.'

Let me tell you, God can raise up children for Abraham right out of these rocks. Even now the axe is aimed at the root of the trees. So every tree not producing fruit gets cut down and tossed into the fire."

R 6%   P 44%   G 25%   B 25%   avg .44   **gray**

These words attributed to JB, with identical wording in Matthew and Luke, occur only in Q. The narrative introductions to these words in Matthew and Luke probably represent the work of each gospel writer since the groups addressed reflect their individual interests (W2). Elsewhere Matthew in similar fashion refers to Pharisees and Sadducees by adding Sadducees to a passage that had reference only to Pharisees (cf. Matt 16:1 with Mark 8:11). Luke also stresses at many points the crowds and masses of people (Luke 3:21; cf. Luke 11:29 with Matt 12:29).

Both Matthew and Luke use these words to introduce the preaching of JB to their readers. What an invective! JB calls for repentance in the light of imminent doom. Appeal to Abraham, the father of Israel, will be to no avail. Again the image for judgment comes out of a natural setting characteristic of first century Palestine (G6). Here not a pitchfork, not a cleansing shovel, but an axe. But just as the chaff will be burned, so the unproductive tree will be thrown into the fire.

Although Matthew and Luke use these words to introduce JB's message, they relate them to the other sayings of JB in different ways. Matthew has joined this axe saying (Matt 3:7–10) to the saying about baptism with spirit and fire (Matt 3:11) and to the saying about the pitchfork (Matt 3:12) so as to form a continuous block of teaching material. This is characteristically Matthean insofar as Matthew has organized Jesus' teaching into five great discourses. Luke has inserted between this axe saying (Luke 3:7–10) and the sayings about baptism and the pitchfork (Luke 3:16, 17) a body of special Lucan material which consists of JB's ethical directives (3:11–15).

Fifty percent of the Fellows gave these words an endorsement in the range of certainty or probability but the weighted average indicated a final verdict in the upper range of possibility (gray). Three or four considerations led to this result. First, this JB saying was attested in only one source; and it was not linked with a saying that was multiply attested, in contrast to the pitchfork saying, which is paralleled by the link between JB's water baptism and the coming baptism of spirit and fire (G4). Secondly, this saying itself seems to be an expanded literary construction more characteristic of a written composition than a brief saying suitable for oral transmission (O2). Thirdly, this saying reflects even more explicitly than the other sayings the apocalyptic orientation of the Q community which may have composed it for incorporation into their sayings gospel (W4).

At the same time, in spite of the gray rating, the voice of JB echoes through these words. The call for repentance and the declaration of impending divine judgment are consistent with what has been established about JB and his ministry. Interestingly, the image that appears in each of the three JB sayings considered so far is that of fire: a baptism with spirit and *fire*, chaff thrown into *fire*; and the unproductive tree also cast into *fire*. Fire is a symbol for divine judgment that runs through the prophetic books of Hebrew Scripture and the later apocalyptic works in the apocrypha and pseudepigrapha (G7).

A: **JB spoke the words in Luke 3:11 and Luke 3:13 and Luke 3:14.**

Luke 3:11. [The crowds would ask him, "So what should we do?" And he would answer them,] "Whoever has two shirts should share with someone who has none; whoever has food should do the same."

R 6%   P 24%   G 35%   B 35%   avg .33   **gray**

Luke 3:13. [Toll collectors also came to be baptized, and they would ask him, "Teacher, what should we do?" He told them,] "Charge nothing above the official rates."

R 6%   P 6%   G 53%   B 35%   avg .27   **gray**

Luke 3:14. [Soldiers also asked him, "And what about us?" And he said to them,] "No more shakedowns! No more frame-ups either! And be satisfied with your pay."

R 6%   P 6%   G 53%   B 35%   avg .27   **gray**

These are the three ethical injunctions inserted by Luke into the midst of the Q material about JB's apocalyptic preaching (between Luke 3:7–9 and Luke 3:16–17). In this threefold dialogue, JB responds to questions asked first by the crowds and then respectively by particular groups among the crowds, specifically toll collectors and soldiers. JB's responses to the latter groups involve directives appropriate for these groups. The crowds are told to share their shirts with have-nots. Toll collectors are instructed not to overcharge. Soldiers are commanded not rob or blackmail, and to be content with their wages. All these directives involve economic issues.

The Fellows of the Seminar again responded to these sayings attributed to JB with a vote indicating a possibility that they, in some way, go back to JB (gray). A couple of considerations led to this judgment and counted against a higher evaluation of probability or certainty. First, the narrative framework and the sayings themselves represent material peculiar to Luke and, therefore, represent L material or L traditions (G4). Secondly, the content of the material, both the identified recipients and the economic focus of these injunctions, reflect the special interests of Luke. Throughout the Gospel of Luke, and the Book of Acts, the writer emphasizes the inclusiveness of the Christian story. The writer also underscores the economic implications of the Christian story by reporting stories and sayings which condemn the wealthy and exalt the impoverished (W4). Nonetheless, the congruence between these commands for personal ethical transformation and JB's call for repentance with its threat of judgment does allow for a possible relationship between these specific injunctions and the voice of JB.

A: JB spoke the words reported in John 1:15, 19–24, 29–34, 35–42; 3:22–30; including:

John 1:15. "This is the one I was talking about when I said, 'He who is to come after me is actually my superior, because he was there before me.'"

John 1:23. "I am the voice of someone shouting in the wilderness, 'Make the way of the Lord straight' – that's how Isaiah the prophet put it."

John 1:29. "Look, the lamb of God, who does away with the sin of the world."

John 1:32–34. "I have seen the spirit coming down like a dove out of the sky, and it hovered over him. I wouldn't have recognized him, but the one who sent me to baptize with water told me, 'When you see the spirit come down and hover over someone, that's the one who baptizes with holy spirit.' I have seen this and I have certified: This is God's son."

John 3:27–30. "You can't lay claim to anything unless it's a gift from heaven. You yourselves can confirm this: I told you I was not the anointed but had been sent on ahead of him. The bride belongs to the groom, and the best man stands with him and is happy enough just to be close at hand. So I am content. He can only grow in importance; my role can only diminish."

R 0%   P 0%   G 0%   B 100%   avg .00   **black**

By consensus, the Seminar agreed that these words attributed to JB represented the creativity of the gospel writer, not words of the historical JB (W4). Therefore, color them black.

Response to his activities

A: JB's exhortations and activities had a widespread appeal.

R 58%   P 42%   G 0%   B 0%   avg .86   **red**

This narrative statement expresses the public response to JB in the broadest, most general terms. The Fellows of the Seminar expressed their collective judgment that indeed he had a widespread appeal. The vote was a dark red with no votes for less than probability in this regard. This judgment rests upon the evidence from the gospels as well as the testimony of Josephus.

Each of the narrative gospels describes the ministry of JB, sometimes in rather exaggerated terms, as having attracted masses of people into the wilderness. Mark, for example, says that "everyone from the Judean countryside and all the residents of Jerusalem streamed out to him" (Mark 1:5 par). The Sayings Gospel Q preserves a saying of Jesus about JB which presupposes his popularity among the masses who had gone into the wilderness to see him (Q 7:24b–25; cf Thom 78:1–2). The gospel evidence, therefore, includes multiplicity of sources (G4) and variety of literary forms (G5).

Josephus' narrative account about JB's represents particularly striking testimony to the breadth of JB's appeal (Ant 18:118). That Josephus himself, writing toward the end of the first century, knew about the activity and death of JB gives a clear indication that JB was remembered outside Christian circles apart from his association with Jesus. Furthermore, the account itself claims that the arrest and execution of JB by Herod Antipas was precisely because the ruler feared that his popularity among the crowds might result in some kind of public disturbance or uprising.

A: **In response, people repented.**

R 52%   P 28%   G 10%   B 10%   avg .75   **pink**

A: **In response, people were baptized.**

R 50%   P 25%   G 20%   B 5%   avg .73   **pink**

JB's ministry involved the teaching of repentance and the practice of water baptism. These narrative statements are formulated to establish some sense of the response by the people to his characteristic activities. The Seminar voted that their response probably involved repenting and being baptized. Color the votes pink and pink.

The principal notation that people going forth to see JB actually repented and were baptized appears in the Gospel of Mark with the statement that they "were baptized by him in the Jordan river, admitting their sins" (Mark 1:5 par). This kind of summary statement in Mark and the other synoptic gospels prepares for the presentation of the most celebrated recipient, from a Christian viewpoint, of JB's baptism—Jesus of Nazareth (Mark 1:9–11 par). The Gospel of John also explicitly notes how "people kept coming to be baptized" in Aenon near Salim although the writer does not speak about repentance (John 3:23). Although there are these kinds of notations in two sources, Mark and John (G4), historical conclusions of probability about how people responded to JB by repenting and being baptized follow by inference from other established conclusions. JB taught repentance and practiced water baptism. He did not teach repentance apart from baptism. His exhortations and activities had a widespread appeal. Therefore, people in all probability repented and were baptized.

A: **JB had disciples.**

R 13%   P 60%   G 27%   B 0%   avg .62   **pink**

This narrative statement rests upon the numerous references in the gospels to disciples of JB. Just as Jesus had disciples, so JB had disciples. The same Greek word *mathētai* (plural) is used both for those special followers of Jesus, the twelve, and for the unnumbered followers of JB.

A composite profile of the followers of JB can be delineated based on these references. The disciples of JB were active during the period of his own baptizing ministry. No explicit comment indicates that his disciples assisted him in baptizing those who presented themselves (but note John 3:22–23, 25; 4:1–2). Their lives, however, were marked by such holy practices as fasting (Mark 2:18 par) and praying (Luke 11:1; also Luke 5:33). JB's disciples seem to engage in debate with their contemporaries over matters of religious practice including purification (John 3:25). They are presented as united with the Pharisees over against the disciples of Jesus (Mark 2:18 par; Luke 11:1). The imprisonment of JB did not put a halt to the activity of his disciples. Supposedly, while in prison, he sent his disciples to Jesus to ask whether Jesus was the expected one or not (Luke 7:18–19 and Matt 11:2–3). Therefore, his disciples also engaged themselves in discussion not only over matters of religious practice but eschatological speculation as well. After JB's execution at the hands of Herod Antipas, his disciples took care of his body (Mark 6:29 par). Although JB is presented as personally involving himself in baptizing others, the practice of his baptism seemingly outlasted him apart from the baptism practiced by the emerging church (Acts 18:24–28; 19:1–7).

Collectively, the members of the Seminar affirmed that JB probably had disciples. They entered a pink vote. Three different sources testify to this: Mark, Q, and John (G4). All four narrative gospels and Q (the sayings gospel) preserve and highlight this testimony (G5). Unlike the gospels, Josephus does not state that JB initiated a movement or had disciples. He stresses the general appeal of JB's ministry and the political threat posed by his oratory. There is, however, an oblique comment in Josephus to the effect that the Jews had been gathered or joined together by baptism (Ant 18:117). This at least implies a bonding of some kind among the recipients of JB's baptism.

That JB had initiated a movement during his lifetime was used as evidence in support of the proposition that his baptism was understood as an initiation into a Jewish sectarian movement. His baptism was in all likelihood so understood, in part, because JB probably had disciples.

A: **Pharisees came to hear JB.**

R 19%   P 38%   G 43%   B 0%   avg .59   **pink**

A: **Sadducees came to hear JB.**

R 37%   P 42%   G 21%   B 0%   avg .72   **pink**

A: **Toll collectors came to hear JB.**
    R 14%   P 38%   G 48%   B 0%   avg .55   **pink**

A: **Soldiers came to hear JB.**
    R 14%   P 43%   G 38%   B 5%   avg .55   **pink**

These narrative statements are based on specific references in the gospels to those categories of people who came forth to hear JB as he preached and baptized in the wilderness. The reference to the Pharisees and Sadducees stands in the Gospel of Matthew (Matt 3:7). The references to the toll collectors and soldiers appear in the Gospel of Luke (Luke 3:12, 14). It is quite possible that all these references are editorial notations created by the gospel writers to provide narrative settings for JB's sayings (W2, W4). The votes of probability, or pink, must be based on more than the specific references to these groups. If JB's exhortations and activities had widespread appeal, then in all probability among those who came to hear him were Pharisees and Sadducees, toll collectors and soldiers.

Sadducees, however, received a vote indicating a higher degree of probability than the other specified groups. Some Fellows thought that Matthew had accurately preserved the audience against whom JB's invective (from Q) was directed: "When he saw that many Pharisees and Sadducees were coming for baptism. . ." (Matt 3:7–10). According to this view, the reference to the Sadducees was part of the received Q tradition and the complementary reference to the Pharisees was an addition by Matthew. Support for this comes from a couple of observations. First, Matthew displays a special interest in Pharisees throughout the gospel and also describes Jesus' opponents in one text as "Pharisees and Sadducees" (Matt 16:1). Secondly, the content of JB's words would appropriately apply to that Jewish sect whose members represented the temple leadership in Jerusalem.

Relation to Contemporary Movements
and Social Role

S: **JB was part of a broader baptizing phenomenon or movement.**
    R 58%   P 42%   G 0%   B 0%   avg .86   **red**

This narrative statement casts a wide net around JB's baptizing ministry. The statement assumes that there was in the cultural and religious setting of Palestine and the surrounding area, such as Syria, the common practice of water baptism in the centuries before and after his appearance. The Mandaeans, for example, represent this amorphous movement, as do many groups and sects described in the writings of the church fathers. Rabbinic Judaism came to practice proselyte baptism. The statement also recognizes the prominence of ablutions, including immersions, within the more immediate geographical and temporal setting of JB's activity. We have called attention to the bathings practiced generally by the Essenes, by the Jewish sect at Qumran, which probably was Essene, and Bannus the holy man mentioned by Josephus. The statement itself was not intended to suggest any direct or causal relationship between JB and any of these groups or individuals, but simply to recognize that JB represents another expression of this widespread phenomenon. The Seminar affirmed with certainty that JB, in this sense, was part of a broader baptizing movement. This certainty is symbolized by a dark red.

S: **JB was an Essene.**
R 0%   P 5%   G 60%   B 35%   avg .23   **black**

S: **JB was a member (or former member) of the Qumran community.**
R 0%   P 5%   G 65%   B 30%   avg .25   **black**

S: **JB was a former Essene.**
R 0%   P 17%   G 78%   B 5%   avg .37   **gray**

These narrative statements were designed to elicit from the Fellows some judgment about JB's possible relationship to that sect and community about which so much has been written over the past forty or so years—the Essenes and the community of Qumran.

In this report of the Seminar's collective understanding of JB, we have often appealed to the Dead Sea Scrolls, the community of Qumran, and by implication to the Essenes, in order to cast light on JB's activity. JB appeared in the wilderness; and the sectarians of Qumran understood their community to be in the wilderness. In the scroll known as the Manual of Discipline, the Qumran community applies to itself the same text applied to JB in the gospels: "A voice cries, 'In the wilderness prepare the way of the Lord'" (Isa 40:3; cf Mark 1:3). Both JB and the Qumran community practiced immersion. Both JB and the Qumran community understood their immersions to express repentance, to mediate God's forgiveness, and to purify from uncleanness. Both JB and the Qumran community, whether implicitly or more explicitly, understood themselves to be set over against the temple establishment in Jerusalem. JB possibly and Qumran most definitely had ties to the priesthood. Also, both lived with the imminent expectation of God's eschatological act of deliverance and destruction. Finally, both saw a correlation between a present immersion in water and a future cleansing with the spirit.

In spite of repeated claims for a connection between JB and Qumran and the many identified parallels between them, however, the fact remains that *no* ancient source overtly links JB with the Essenes or with Qumran. One might have expected Josephus to mention ties between JB and the Essenes, if he had known about such ties. Josephus offers descriptions of the Essenes in his writings and, on occasion, identifies characters on the basis of their Essenic connections. If there had ever been some connection between

JB and the Essenes, it lies in the past when JB comes into public view in the gospel stories and in the narrative by Josephus. Therefore, the Seminar voted that JB was probably not an Essene: black.

The Seminar also voted the improbability that JB was a member, or former member, of the Qumran community: black. Along with the parallels between JB and the Qumran community, as known through its literature, there are some striking differences. JB appears to proclaim a call for baptism and repentance which was open to all. The Qumran community seems turned in on itself, sharply delineating between those within and those without. The cultic program of the covenanters at Qumran involved regular, repeatable immersions. The baptism of JB, administered by him, was in all probability an initiation into a Jewish sectarian movement, but a movement open to all who would repent and be baptized.

Although the Seminar considered it improbable that JB was a member (or former member) of the Qumran community and improbable that he was an Essene, the Seminar did affirm the possibility of his having been a former Essene: gray. Perhaps this shift from improbability to possibility stemmed from the Seminar's recognition that the Essenes represented a wider phenomenon than the sectarians at Qumran and the Seminar's lack of certainty that the Qumran community was in fact an Essene settlement.

A closer examination of the votes, however, leads to a couple of interesting observations. On the one hand, a majority of the Fellows did hold forth at least the possibility that JB was an Essene and that JB had some kind of ties with Qumran. On the other hand, not one Fellow expressed historical certainty about any of these propositions.

S: **JB was a lone Jewish sage and holy man (like Bannus).**

R 10%   P 10%   G 48%   B 42%   avg .24   **black**

The Essenes constituted one of the principal Jewish sects active in JB's day during the first half of the first century in Palestine. The settlement at Qumran, quite possibly an Essene community, also enjoyed a certain prominence during this period as the scrolls and the archaeological remains testify.

This narrative statement recognizes that there was more to the Judaism of the first century than just this sect or that community. There were those individuals who, in a sense, just did not belong. Josephus offers rich testimony to the diversity of Judaism in his native land. As we have noted, it is Josephus who mentions (in his *Life*) a lone Jewish sage and holy man by the name of Bannus. Josephus claims to have spent three years with Bannus in the wilderness. Bannus was evidently a vegetarian and practiced ablutions of cold water day and night for the sake of ritual purity.

This narrative statement was intended to gauge to what extent JB may have fit this mold. Although a majority of the Fellows saw some correspondence between JB and a lone sage and holy man like Bannus, the collective vote was one of improbability: black. Ironically, therefore, JB seems to have been considered by the Seminar to be too solitary to fit the group mold of the Essenes, or the community of Qumran, and too social to fit the solitary mold of a Bannus. That is, JB appears as a solitary figure in the wilderness but publicly preaching a baptism of repentance for the forgiveness of sins, which resulted in another sectarian movement.

S: **JB imitated Elijah.**
R 0%   P 15%   G 62%   B 23%   avg .31   **gray**
S: **JB acted as a prophet.**
R 31%   P 46%   G 15%   B 8%   avg .72   **pink**
S: **JB was an apocalyptic preacher.**
R 16%   P 56%   G 12%   B 16%   avg .57   **pink**

There can be little doubt about the social role into which JB has been cast when we meet him literarily for the first time in the church's gospels. Mark and Q, followed by Matthew and Luke, cast JB in *the role of a prophet*.

These four gospels portray JB as the *Elijah-returned*, or *Elijah-like, prophetic forerunner* to Jesus as the Christ, although the emphases and nuances differ from gospel to gospel. Mark and Q present JB as the fulfillment of Malachi 3:1, an Elijah text (Mark 1:2; Q 7:26). Mark even dresses JB in the garb of Elijah (Mark 1:6). The implicit presentation of JB as Elijah-returned in Mark and Q gives way to the explicit identification of JB as Elijah-returned in Matthew (especially Matt 11:14–15; 17:13). Just as explicitly, Luke identifies JB as the Elijah-like forerunner to Jesus as the Christ (Luke 1:16).

More specifically, in these four gospels the title *prophet* itself is bestowed upon JB. In the Marcan narrative, the gospel writer underscores how the people recognized JB to be a prophet (Mark 6:15 par; 11:32 par). In a Q saying Jesus himself reportedly called JB a prophet (Q 7:26; also Q 16:16). In material peculiar to Luke, Zechariah declares that his infant son JB will be called a prophet of God (Luke 1:75); and the gospel writer himself introduces the adult JB in terms reminiscent of the prophets of ancient Israel (Luke 3:2). The Gospel of Thomas also contains a passage in which the title of prophet may, by implication, apply to JB (Thom 52:1–2). Therefore, John constitutes the personal name, the Baptizer or the Baptist the nickname, and prophet the honorific title.

JB also proclaims an *apocalyptic message* of impending destruction and deliverance. Only a hint of the apocalyptic dimensions of JB's message appears in Mark with JB's announcement of an expected figure more worthy and more powerful who will baptize with holy spirit (Mark 1:7–8 par). But Q makes the apocalyptic dimension of JB's message explicit with JB's sayings about the coming judgment of fire (Q 3:7–9, 17).

These narrative statements are intended to test the historical validity of the gospels' having cast JB in these terms. Broadly expressed: is this presentation of JB the creation of the early church or does it correspond in some way with JB the historical figure? Narrowly stated: Did JB intentionally imitate Elijah? Did he actually act like a prophet? Can he rightly be called an apocalyptic preacher?

The Seminar expressed great reservations about JB's having actually imitated Elijah. The portrayal of JB as Elijah does serve the interests of the early church as the believing community tried to come to terms with the relationship between JB and Jesus (W4, O3). The portrayal also obviously represents an accommodation of JB to the themes of the Hebrew Scriptures and later Jewish lore (O4). Nonetheless, the possibility of JB's having in some sense cast himself as Elijah was not denied. This theme does appear in the two earliest sources Mark and Q (G4). Thus: a gray vote.

The Seminar also considered whether JB should be denied not only the

---

John the Baptist in Historical Research–I

Since the 18th century, historical interest in John the Baptist has expressed itself along two lines of inquiry. Scholars engaged in the quest for the historical Jesus have concerned themselves, of neccessity, with John and his relationship to Jesus. Along the way, other scholars have focused on John as their primary subject. Both approaches were included in a brief, but informative, essay published some twenty years ago by John Reumann with the appropriate title, "The Quest for the Historical Baptist" (1972).

Among the scholars mentioned by Reumann were a number of pioneering figures in life-of-Jesus research whose interest in John derived from their search for Jesus. They included: Hermann Samuel Reimarus, *Wolfenbüttel Fragments* (1774–1778); David Friedrich Strauss, *Leben Jesu* (1835–1836); Ernst Renan, *Vie de Jesus* (1863); Albert Schweitzer, *Von Reimarus zu Wrede* (1906); and Günther Bornkamm, *Jesus von Nazareth* (1956). Each is a classic; and each, at one time or another, has been translated into English. It comes as no surprise that their John the Baptists, in various ways, served their Jesuses. Reimarus presented John as a political revolutionary. Strauss discovered John beneath the layers of legend which now enshroud him. Renan viewed John as a young romantic. Schweitzer interpreted John within the context of apocalyptic expectation. Bornkamm considered John as a prophet of the coming kingdom.

Reumann also mentioned scholars whose writings centered more exclusively on John. In fact, the latter section of his essay involved a detailed comparison of ways John was viewed by Carl H. Kraeling, in his monograph *John the Baptist* (1951), and by John A. T. Robinson, in a series of articles (1957–59).

Both Kraeling and Robinson exhibit biographical interest in John. Both reconstruct, at least in broad outline, the shape of John's life without ignoring his

specific mantel of Elijah but also the mantel of prophet itself, for all the reasons stated above (W4, O3, O4). Perhaps JB should be thought about solely in terms consistent with his nickname—as a baptizer, a purifier, not as a prophet. However, the Seminar acknowledged that JB most probably did act like a prophet and was probably considered such in his own day. As we have affirmed, his ministry was marked not only by the act of baptizing but by proclamation; and that proclamation was most likely understood to be a threat to the temple establishment. As we shall establish, JB most certainly posed a threat to the political establishment. Therefore, the attribution of the prophet title to JB, attested in multiple sources and multiple literary forms, is consistent with the way JB acted during his ministry (G4, G5). Thus: a pink vote.

The Seminar also debated the appropriateness of describing JB as an apocalyptic preacher. The apocalyptic dimensions of JB's message obviously had an appeal to the community that produced the Q gospel. That

---

relationship to Jesus. Kraeling presents John as one born into a priestly family in the hill country of Judea who goes to Jerusalem to follow in the footsteps of his father by officiating in the temple; but instead, John becomes an ascetic prophet proclaiming a baptism of repentance in the wilderness. Why? Disgust with the secularized priesthood in Jerusalem made him do it! Robinson also presents John as one born into a priestly family in the hill country of Judea; but the advanced age of his parents leads to his being reared at Qumran. John later breaks with the sectarians of Qumran. Why? A difference over eschatology made him do it! John believed the coming judgment to be even more imminent than they did; and so he embarked on a wilderness ministry of his own.

Kraeling wrote before the impact of the Dead Sea Scrolls had been fully felt in scholarly circles. Consequently, he looked to the later Mandaean literature for possible influences on John. Robinson, however, exploited fully the Dead Sea Scrolls and their apparent connections with Qumran to assist him in his reconstruction of John's life and ministry.

Reumann's review of the literature on the Baptist was a tribute to Morton Enslin whose own reconstruction of the historical Baptist deviated sharply from that of most scholars.

Enslin favored the presentation of John in Josephus which makes no reference to Jesus. He saw in the gospels evidence of *Christian* attempts to remove John as a rival to Jesus and to present John as the precursor to Jesus in fulfillment of the prophecy of Malachi. Enslin represented that rare scholar who denied that John had baptized Jesus. Morever, Enslin even doubted that the two contemporaries had ever met. They were certainly not kinsmen by birth. (For bibliographical information about the Reumann essay, and about the writings of Morton Enslin therein commemorated, consult the selected bibliography in this volume.)

document incorporates into its presentation JB's reported sayings of judgment (Q 3:7–9, 17)(W4). The explicit apocalyptic notes sounded here were considered consistent with those implied in JB's multiply attested saying about the expected one (Mark 1:7–8; Q 3:16; also John 1:26–27)(G4). In all probability, JB was an apocalyptic preacher. Thus: another pink vote.

A: **JB was perceived as a hellenistic moralist.**

R 0%   P 4%   G 24%   B 72%   avg .11   **black**

This narrative statement is based on the portrayal of JB in the writings of Josephus. Writing for a hellenistic audience in the wider Graeco-Roman world, as we have observed, Josephus describes the activities of JB in the categories of a hellenistic moralist (Ant 18:116–119). The purpose of this proposition was to ascertain whether the Seminar believed this description to be simply the perspective of Josephus or whether JB's own contemporaries in the wilderness perceived him in similar fashion. The vote was for improbability: black. This means that Josephus' portrayal represents his apologetic and does not accord with the way JB was viewed by his contemporaries. Within that milieu, the categories of prophet and apocalyptic preacher more appropriately describe what he was about and how he was perceived.

14 JOHN THE BAPTIST AND JESUS

JB is remembered primarily because of his association with the man named Jesus who came to be confessed as the Messiah, the Christ, the Anointed. These narrative statements focus on the relationship between these two. (See cameo essays, "John the Baptist in Historical Research.")

S: **There was a person named Jesus.**
  R 95%   P 0%   G 5%   B 0%   avg .96   **red**

On occasion, during the two hundred years of the historical quest for Jesus, the very existence of such a person from the Galilean village of Nazareth has been denied. From the standpoint of the Jesus Seminar, however, this narrative statement was formulated within the context of its consideration of JB for the sake of completeness. The action taken by the Seminar was perfunctory. Just as there was a person named John the Baptist, or Baptizer, so there was most certainly a person named Jesus. The red vote by the Fellows simply acknowledges the overwhelming nature of the evidence.

Mention has been made of the work of the Seminar in its systematic examination of more than a thousand different versions of 503 *sayings* attributed to Jesus in early Christian literature. Both the multiplicity of sources and the variety of literary forms have been noted (G4, G5). This study of JB itself represents the first step by the Seminar in a comprehensive review of the *stories* about Jesus. The anticipated review of stories about Jesus will also reflect a multiplicity of sources and a variety of literary forms.

Furthermore, evidence for the existence of a person named Jesus also comes from non-Christian circles (G1). In conjunction with our discussion of Josphus' reference to JB, we noted the possibility that this Jewish historian also makes reference to Jesus in his *Jewish Antiquities*, although later Christian editors may have altered the original text. References to Jesus also appear in Rabbinic writings and in works by Roman historians. Both Tacitus in his *Annals* and Suetonius in his *Twelve Caesars* make passing references to Jesus and the movement which traced its origins to him.

S: **JB's mother Elizabeth was related to Jesus' mother Mary.**

R 0%   P 5%   G 0%   B 95%   avg .03   **black**

S: **JB was related to Jesus.**

R 0%   P 14%   G 0%   B 86%   avg .05   **black**

These narrative statements are based not just on a single text but on a single word. In the special Lucan material, in the infancy narratives, the angel Gabriel announces to Mary that she will conceive and bear a son to be named Jesus who would be called the son of God (Luke 1:26–38). The angel then informs Mary that Elizabeth has already conceived a son, a son later to be named John. The angel refers to Elizabeth as Mary's *sungenis*, variously translated as "kinswoman," "cousin," or "relative" (Luke 1:36).

The Seminar considered it highly improbable that JB's mother was related to Jesus' mother Mary and, therefore, improbable that JB was related to Jesus. The votes were very dark blacks. First, the claim of blood relationship is solely attested (G4); and there is no intimation anywhere else in the gospels of such a relationship (G7). Secondly, whatever the exact history of the traditions preserved in Luke 1, the notation of blood relationship appears in one of the later stages and may even be redactional by the gospel writer. The notation clearly serves his theological interest insofar as he has carefully constructed the infancy narratives to parallel the respective infancies of JB and Jesus, but with the subordination of the former to the latter (W4, W5). Thirdly, the notation of blood relation stands on the lips of the angel within a story reflecting characteristics of annunciation stories in the Old Testament and later Jewish lore. (O3, O4).

S: **JB's locale overlaps that of Jesus.**

R 85%   P 5%   G 10%   B 0%   avg .92   **red**

S: **JB's time overlaps that of Jesus.**

R 81%   P 14%   G 5%   B 0%   avg .92   **red**

S: **Jesus began his public ministry at the time JB was imprisoned.**

R 0%   P 43%   G 52%   B 5%   avg .46   **gray**

These narrative statements grow out of two very different presentations of the relationship between the ministries of JB and Jesus. The synoptics gospels, on the one hand, and the Fourth Gospel, on the other, differ significantly in their presentations of locale and time—and the beginning of Jesus' ministry.

The Gospel of Mark, followed by Matthew and Luke, suggests that JB conducted his ministry in the wilderness around the Jordan River, in Judea and Perea. His ministry precedes the ministry of Jesus. Jesus comes to JB to be baptized by him in the Jordan; and Jesus follows his baptism with a retreat of his own into the wilderness. Only after JB is imprisoned does Jesus inaugurate his own ministry in Galilee: "After John was locked up, Jesus came to Galilee proclaiming God's good news . . ." (Mark 1:14 par). Thus Jesus succeeds JB. Neither their locales nor their times overlap. In the Gospel of John, however, their locales and times overlap.

The Gospel of John does *not* report the synoptic stories of JB's baptizing Jesus and Jesus' subsequent withdrawal into the wilderness. The gospel opens with both JB and Jesus in the wilderness as JB bears witness to Jesus as the one from God. Jesus then departs for Galilee in the north to prepare for his ministry while JB continues his baptizing ministry in the south (John 1:19–51). The gospel even notes that Jesus and his disciples later had a ministry marked by baptizing in the south—in Judea and beyond the Jordan, presumably in Perea (John 3:22–24, 25–26; 4:1–4). Two parenthetical comments, perhaps by a later redactor, are of interest: "Remember, John hadn't yet been thrown in prison" (John 3:24); and "Actually, Jesus himself didn't baptize; his disciples did the baptizing" (John 4:2).

The geographical and temporal schemes in both Mark and John reflect the theological interests of the respective gospel writers (W3). Mark portrays JB as the prophetic *forerunner* who is *succeeded* by Jesus as the Christ. John portrays JB as the witness to Jesus *in the presence of* his own disciples and Jesus himself.

Nonetheless, the Fellows expressed a high degree of certainty that the scheme in John more accurately reflects historical circumstances. The ministries of JB and Jesus did overlap both in terms of locale and time. The votes were both reds. Although the Fellows have recognized Jesus' discourses in the Fourth Gospel to represent the creative work of the gospel writer and his community, collectively they join with those scholars who perceive historical reminiscences embedded in the narrative outline. The incidental details about the interaction between JB and Jesus in the Gospel of John are difficult to understand simply as the creation of the author. The details obviously caused consternation even within his own community, as evidenced by the aforementioned parenthetical comments (N3). There is also a saying of Jesus in the Gospel of Thomas which, if an allusion to JB, implies that Jesus and JB were engaged in simultaneous ministries (Thom 52:2). If an authentic saying from Jesus, this word would give independent support to the Johannine presentation (G4, G5). The Seminar, however, voted this saying black.

At the same time, however, the Fellows have not ruled out the possibility of Jesus' ministry having begun *in some sense* at the time JB was arrested, as the synoptics suggest. The color gray indicates this possibility. Perhaps this was the occasion for Jesus' having relocated the principal sphere of his activity from the south to the north. Perhaps this was when Jesus set aside baptizing as a feature of his own ministry. Or, still again, maybe Jesus began to realize the hollowness or futility of JB's apocalyptic proclamation and began to sharpen his own message of God's rule.

A: **JB baptized Jesus.**

R 77%   P 18%   G 5%   B 0%   avg .91   **red**

A: **Jesus saw the heavens open and the spirit descend on him like a dove.**

R 0%   P 12%   G 44%   B 44%   avg .23   **black**

A: **Jesus heard a voice from heaven at his baptism saying, "You are my favored son."**

R 0%   P 8%   G 36%   B 56%   avg .17   **black**

These three narrative statements are based on the Marcan story of JB's baptism of Jesus (Mark 1:9–11 par). That brief, straightforward Marcan narrative has two principal components. First, there is the simple declaration that Jesus came from Nazareth in Galilee and was baptized by JB in the Jordan River. Secondly, there is a description of Jesus' inner experience which has dimensions of both a vision and an audition, a seeing and a hearing. Jesus sees the heavens open and the spirit descends on him like a dove; and he hears a heavenly voice declare that he has received divine approval.

The Fellows are certain that this story preserves the memory of an occasion when John the so-called Baptizer baptized Jesus who would be called the Christ. Therefore, the Fellows are certain of *the fact* that JB baptized Jesus: red. But the Fellows consider it highly unlikely that the details as stated correspond to Jesus' experience on that occasion. They believe that the current story represents a symbolic account that was developed over time to identify Jesus as the Christ, the Son of God (O2, O3): black and black.

Why certainty of the baptism itself, particularly given its singular attestation in Mark?

First, the claim that JB baptized Jesus runs against the grain of the church's confession of Jesus as the Christ. Since JB's baptism was a baptism of repentance for the forgiveness of sins, Jesus' acceptance of that baptism for himself implies that his submission was an act of repentance for the forgiveness of sins. It seems improbable that the church would simply have created an account of this event (N3).

Secondly, the reported baptism of Jesus by JB became an embarrassment to the church. Both Matthew (Matt 3:13–17) and Luke (3:21–22) try to offset the embarrassment by imaginative adaptations of the Marcan story for their gospels. Matthew has inserted special M material into the Marcan story: a conversation between JB and Jesus in which JB expresses the inappropriateness of his baptizing Jesus. Jesus commands him to proceed in accordance with the divine plan. Matthew also changes the opening word of the heavenly voice from the second personal pronoun "You . . ." to the demonstrative pronoun "This . . ." What Mark has presented as Jesus' inner experience has become public in Matthew insofar as JB also hears the voice. Luke performs an intriguing sleight of hand. He reports the imprisonment of JB by Herod Antipas even before he narrates the baptism of Jesus (Luke 3:18–20). In the brief baptism account that follows, JB is not even mentioned by name. Luke uses the passive voice: " . . . after Jesus had been baptized . . ." The Gospel of the Nazoreans, cited by Jerome, also responds to the embarrassment of Jesus' baptism by JB. The mother and brothers of Jesus exhort him to go with them to be baptized by JB, but Jesus asks: "In what have I sinned that I should go and be baptized by him? Unless what I have said is ignorance." Again it seems improbable that the church would have simply created an account of this event (N3).

Thirdly, although the story of Jesus' baptism is only explicitly reported in Mark, scholars occasionally have argued that the Sayings Gospel Q contained a version of the story and that the Gospel of John reflects independent familiarity with it. As evident in Matthew and Luke, Q had a detailed account of Jesus' testing in the wilderness; and the testing account in some ways presupposes a baptism account (Q 4:1–13). Whereas Matthew intimated that JB *heard* the heavenly voice, John has JB say that he *saw* the spirit coming down like a dove and resting on Jesus; and JB—not God—*declares* Jesus to be God's son (John 1:32–34). Therefore, the baptism story may be multiply attested (G4).

An interesting observation, however, qualifies somewhat the level of certainty about JB's having baptized Jesus. The claim that JB baptized Jesus could have been created in the earliest period of the Jesus movement when JB was the one with public recognition and prestige. Instead of Jesus' baptism by JB being an embarrasment, therefore, such a baptism would have given Jesus honor and his movement legitimacy in the eyes of those who had themselves been followers of JB.

Why the Seminar's black votes for the details of what is presented as Jesus' inner experience—the vision and the audition? The answer lies close at hand. These features reflect the christological interest of the church generally and of Mark in particular (W4, O3). The vision and the audition function as an epiphany by which Mark has God validate Jesus as God's son. The epiphanic character of the baptism in Mark is repeated later in the story of the transfiguration (Mark 9:1–8). On a mountain with Jesus, his disciples experience a vision and an audition. Mark again has God validate

Jesus as God's son. Both epiphanies are cast in phraseology and motifs that recall passages in Hebrew Scripture and motifs from later Jewish lore (O4). The words of the audition, for example, echo such texts as Ps 2:7 and Isa 42:1.

The Seminar, however, did reflect on what might have happened to Jesus on the occasion of his baptism by JB. The following narrative statements were formulated in the midst of discussion and debate to address that issue.

A: **Jesus had visionary experiences.**

R 23%   P 23%   G 45%   B 9%   avg .53   **pink**

A: **Jesus had a visionary experience at the time of his baptism.**

R 9%   P 41%   G 32%   B 18%   avg .47   **gray**

A: **Jesus had a vision at his baptism.**

R 8%   P 28%   G 36%   B 28%   avg .37   **gray**

A: **Jesus had a powerful religious experience at his baptism.**

R 19%   P 39%   G 27%   B 15%   avg .54   **pink**

The specific question of what happened to Jesus on the occasion of his baptism by JB was addressed within the framework of a broader question: Was Jesus subject to what might be called paranormal experiences? Did he have what might be classified as visions? Or, using the language of the narrative statement, did he have visionary experiences? The Seminar decided that in all probability Jesus had visionary experiences. The vote was colored pink.

It was recognized that explicit textual evidence for visionary experiences by Jesus is weak. The Marcan baptismal and transfiguration accounts (Mar 1:9–11; 9:1–8) and perhaps the Q story of the testing in the wilderness (Q 4:1–11) are virtually the only gospel passages that can be understood as vision narratives. But there is also the brief statement of Jesus, only in Luke, in response to the seventy who return exclaiming that even demons have submitted to them: "I was watching Satan fall like lightning from heaven" (Luke 10:18). This declaration, however, may simply be symbolic talk instead of a vision report.

The Seminar based its vote of probability on themes and similar content that cut across literary forms and represent different literary sources (G5). First, there are texts in which Jesus speaks of the spirit's being on him or operating through him (Q 11:20: Luke 4:16–30). Secondly, there is abundant evidence that Jesus functioned as a healer and exorcist. Thirdly, there is language suggesting intimacy between Jesus and God, such as Jesus' address of God as Abba, Father (Mark 14:36 par; Q 11:2–4). Fourthly, there is an emphasis upon the authority of Jesus in sayings and stories, often in contrast to tradition. Fifthly, there are periodic notations that Jesus practiced withdrawal and long hours of prayer.

Therefore, although the Seminar had denied with black votes that the Marcan story of Jesus' baptism preserves an accurate description of his baptismal experience, the participants acknowledged the possibility that his experience involved some kind of visionary experience or vision. The votes were gray and gray. The Seminar was comfortable describing what happened to Jesus at his baptism by JB as a powerful religious experience. That this occurred to him, making his baptism a pivotal moment in his life, was considered quite probable. The pink vote signals this probability.

A: **Jesus was a disciple of JB.**
R 36%   P 23%   G 36%   B 5%   avg .64   **pink**

A: **Jesus deliberately separated from JB's movement.**
R 18%   P 45%   G 27%   B 9%   avg .58   **pink**

A: **Some of JB's disciples became followers of Jesus.**
R 22%   P 60%   G 18%   B 0%   avg .68   **pink**

These three narrative statements explore the possible origins of the Jesus movement in the movement initiated by JB. In order, the statements consider the relationship between Jesus and JB, between Jesus and the movement initiated by JB, and between members of the JB movement and Jesus. As formulated, the first two statements represent inferences from texts rather than statements directly based on texts. The third statement does rest, in part, upon a specific text.

No text openly states that Jesus was a disciple of JB. The principal passage from which the statement is derived, of course, is the Marcan account JB's baptism of Jesus (Mark 1:9–11 par). That Jesus submitted to JB's baptism clearly indicates that he accepted and approved of JB's activity. Some Fellows questioned the appropriateness of using the term "disciple" if this meant that Jesus was a student and itinerant follower of JB. But here the term "disciple" is used more broadly to mean simply that Jesus accepted what JB was up to and in some broad sense belonged to the movement initiated by him. The Marcan story of Jesus' dispute with the authorities in the temple about his own authority contains words of Jesus which affirm what was implied by Jesus' submission to baptism: that JB had God-given authority (Mark 11:27–33 par). Also, according to the Gospel of John, Jesus—for a season—seems to have undertaken a baptizing ministry of his own, thereby implying that Jesus, through the mediation of JB, participated in his broader baptizing movement (John 3:25–26; 4:1–2). Circumstantial evidence in multiple sources and different literary forms, therefore, led to a collective judgment of probability by the Seminar (G4, G5). In all likelihood, Jesus was a disciple of JB in the broadest sense: pink.

Also, no text explicitly declares that Jesus deliberately separated from the JB movement. What one encounters in the synoptic gospels generally, however, is the recognition that the Jesus who was baptized by JB suddenly appears as an independent operative. The Fourth Gospel also, although retaining hints of parallel and competing ministries by JB and Jesus, shows Jesus suddenly working exclusively on his own. But more specifically, the so-called eulogy of JB by Jesus, preserved in Q and Thomas, strongly suggests a deliberate separation by Jesus from the JB movement. Jesus talks about the greatness of JB, but then elevates even the least in God's kingdom above him (Q 7:28; Thomas 46:2). Once again circumstantial evidence in multiple sources and different literary forms resulted in a judgment of probability (G4, G5). Jesus probably did deliberately separate from the JB movement: pink. As formulated, however, the narrative statement does not identify *when* that separation occurred nor *what* might have brought it about, whether it be JB's imprisonment, his death, or some other factor.

There is a passage in the Gospel of John that tells how disciples of JB became followers of Jesus (John 1:35–50). These verses represent the Johannine account of how Jesus first called disciples. At the direction of JB himself, two of his own disciples begin following Jesus. Jesus turns and beckons them to continue on with him. One of these disciples is unnamed, the other happens to be Andrew, Simon Peter's brother. Jesus later also enjoins Simon Peter, Philip, and Nathaniel to come with him. These events apparently occur in the south, in the wilderness region; and Jesus then travels with his followers to Galilee. This entire tableau, with its emphasis upon JB as witness, reflects the theological agenda of the gospel writer (W3, W4). The setting and the details in the story also stand at odds with the account of Jesus' first call of disciples in the synoptics. In Mark, at least, Jesus calls Andrew and Peter, and James and John—pairs of brother and fisher folk—away from their labors by the Sea of Galilee (Mark 1:16–20). This call scene certainly accords with the theological agenda of Mark, which centers Jesus' ministry in Gailee and later gives a list of precisely twelve disciples, including these four (W3, W4). Scholars have sometimes harmonized the divergent accounts in the Gospels of John and Mark. Accordingly, Jesus makes initial contact with his future disciples in the south and calls or recalls them after their return to Galilee. Whatever the historicity of the particular story in John, however, the Fellows agreed on the probability that some of JB's disciples became disciples of Jesus in spite of only one explicit passage about such an occurrence (G4): pink. Supporting evidence for this transfer of disciples from JB to Jesus also comes from a general motif often detected in the gospel narratives (G5). The authors, and their inherited traditions, seem to presuppose that disciples of JB became integral to the Jesus movement and later to the emerging church. For example, see the Lucan infancy narrative (Luke 1).

Therefore, the actions of the Seminar on these three narrative statements affirm that the JB movement served as the social and religious context for the birth of the Jesus movement while their leaders were still alive and active. The movements not only overlapped in time and place but intersected one another.

A: **JB wondered whether Jesus were his successor (Q 7:18–19).**
    R 0%   P 14%   G 63%   B 23%   avg .30   **gray**

A: **Jesus considered himself to be JB's successor.**
    R 0%   P 9%   G 77%   B 14%   avg .32   **gray**

A: **The public considered Jesus to be JB's successor.**
    R 0%   P 14%   G 72%   B 14%   avg .33   **gray**

A: **Jesus' disciples considered Jesus to be JB's successor.**
    R 5%   P 55%   G 40%   B 0%   avg .55   **pink**

These four narrative propositions are aimed at trying to identify *who* wondered whether Jesus was, or considered Jesus to be, the *successor* of JB. As we have seen, three different sources report a saying of JB in which he talks about a future coming one who would be more worthy and mightier than he (Mark 1:7; Q 3:16b; John 1:27). With a pink vote, the Seminar collectively ruled that in all probability JB said something like this.

There is also a Q story which claims that while in prison JB sent his own disciples to Jesus asking him whether or not he were the coming one (Q 7:18–29). Jesus replies by telling JB's disciples to go report what they had seen and heard about Jesus' ministry. A list of Jesus' activities follows, including the specific kinds of healings he performed. Jesus' reply to JB, taken in its entirety, was voted black by the Seminar in its earlier sayings phase. The dependence of Jesus' answer at many points corresponds too closely to passages in Hebrew Scripture (04), which means that the the answer represents an expression of the church's apologetic (W6).

All four of these narrative statements take their point of departure from the saying of JB: "Are you the one who is to come or are we to wait for another?" (Q 7:18–19). In these statements, therefore, the word "successor" means more than simply continuity between JB and Jesus. Rather "successor" specifically means Jesus' fulfillment of JB's proclamation of an expected figure. In the SV translation of John 1:26–27, JB refers to the expected one as his "successor."

Because JB talked about a coming one and because there exists some continuity between JB and Jesus, the JB movement and the Jesus movement, the Fellows postulated a series of possibilities. It is possible that JB wondered whether Jesus were his successor: gray. It is possible that Jesus' considered himself JB's successor: gray. It is also possible that even the public considered Jesus to be JB's successor: gray.

It is not until we turn to Jesus' disciples, however, that we can think in terms of probability. JB's disciples turned and followed Jesus not just initially during their historical ministries but during the early years of the church. They must have considered Jesus to be JB's successor. The Fellows collectively ruled that in all probability they did: pink.

A: **JB's supporters identified JB as Elijah.**

R 8%   P 42%   G 35%   B 15%   avg .47   **gray**

A: **Jesus identified JB as Elijah.**

R 8%   P 16%   G 64%   B 12%   avg .40   **gray**

A: **Jesus' disciples identified JB as Elijah.**

R 4%   P 20%   G 36%   B 40%   avg .29   **gray**

A: **Mark or Q identified JB as Elijah.**

R 25%   P 58%   G 4%   B 13%   avg .65   **pink**

In considering JB's relationship to contemporary movements and his own social role, we recalled how both Mark—followed by Matthew and Luke—and Q portray JB as the *Elijah-returned, or Elijah-like, prophetic forerunner* of Jesus as the Christ. We began an attempt to discover at what level this correlation between JB and Elijah began. The Seminar collectively decided with a vote colored gray that JB himself possibly could have imitated Elijah. The motif does appear in the two earliest Christian sources that bear witness to JB: Mark and Q.

The four narrative propositions presented here continue the effort to discover at which points historically and literarily the Elijah theme entered the traditions about JB.

The argument was presented that the Elijah theme must have originated in a pre-Christian, Jewish setting even before the death of JB. After his beheading, according to this view, the creation of a public reputation for JB as Elijah would have been impossible. The claim that JB was in some sense Elijah would have been contradicted by the fact of his demise. If JB himself did not imitate Elijah, therefore, his reputation as Elijah must have originated with one or more of three parties mentioned above: JB's own followers, Jesus himself, or Jesus' followers. The series of gray votes indicates that the Seminar considered all of the options as historically possible. JB's own supporters could have identified him as Elijah. Even Jesus could have identified JB as Elijah. And Jesus' disciples could have identified JB as Elijah. Both Mark and Q, however, do associate JB with the Elijah text from Malachi 3:1 (Mark 1:2; Q 7:27)(O4). Consequently, a substantial majority of the Fellows considered it more probable that the identification of JB as Elijah originated with the early church and collectively gave a pink vote to the statement that Mark or Q identified JB as Elijah.

A trajectory of this motif runs through the varying layers of the tradition as written. In Mark and Q, the identification of JB as Elijah is only implicit on the lips of Jesus (Mark 9:9–13; Q 7:27). Matthew and Luke, in individualistic ways, make the identification explicit. In Matthew, this identification appears on the lips of Jesus (Matt 11:14–15; also 17:13). In Luke, the angel Gabriel associates JB with the prophet Elijah (Luke 1:17). Over against this tendency, the Gospel of John—with its definition of JB as witness to revelation and Jesus as the revelation—has JB himself deny to the inquisitive authorities that he is Elijah (John 1:21).

A: Jesus identified JB as a great figure.

R 54%   P 46%   G 0%   B 0%   avg .85   **red**

If Jesus were not the origin of the identification of JB as Elijah, how did Jesus himself retrospectively look upon the one who had baptized him? Within the context of Jesus' so-called eulogy of JB in Q 7:24–28, Jesus reportedly declares to the crowds: "Come on, what did you go out to see? A prophet? Yes, that's what you went out to see, yet someone more than a prophet." (Q 7:26) Therefore, did Jesus talk about JB as a prophet, even more than a prophet?

The above narrative statement was originally formulated on the basis of this specific saying and read: Jesus identified JB as a great prophet. Some Fellows observed that a formulation using the word "prophet" would require them to vote black. First, the word or category of prophet is characteristic of the Q community (W4). Secondly, a related saying in the Gospel of Thomas does not mention JB as a prophet (Thom 78:1–2)(G4). Thirdly, the question about JB as a prophet is linked to the quotation from Mal 3:1 to demonstrate that JB was the prophetic forerunner to Jesus, hence more than a prophet (O4).

By common agreement the word prophet was replaced with a more general or generic phrase. The Seminar was certain that Jesus had identified JB as a great figure; and no member expressed less than probability in this regard: red. The textual support for this strong judgment lies in another saying also preserved in Jesus' eulogy of JB: "I tell you, among those born of women none is greater than John" (Q 7:28a). The Fellows were convinced that Jesus said something like this since probably only he in Christian sources could have called JB the greatest among all human beings. The Gospel of Thomas also preserves an independent version of this Q saying (Thom 46:1)(G4). This exaggerated claim for JB by the historical Jesus prompted the development of the saying attributed to Jesus which then put JB in his place: " . . . yet the least in God's domain is greater than he" (Q7:28b; also Thom 46:2)(O3).

A: Jesus contrasted his behavior with that of JB (Q 7:33–35; 16:16).

R 27%   P 59%   G 14%   B 0%   avg .71   **pink**

The Q community incorporated sayings of Jesus into its gospel which contrasted him and his movement with JB and his movement. The above mentioned saying of Jesus about JB's greatness among all those born of women has been linked to a statement in which Jesus then says: " . . . yet the least in God's domain is greater than he" (Q 7:28b; also Thom 46:2). As noted above, the Fellows considered this to be an expansion of Jesus' original words about JB's greatness by Jesus' followers or the church. These words seem to reflect the subsequent rivalry between the followers of Jesus and the followers of JB (O3). Even the least under God's rule through Jesus is greater than the greatest figure to appear before Jesus.

The narrative statement considered here, however, finds its basis in two other Q sayings in which Jesus in varying ways contrasts his ministry with the ministry of JB.

The first saying: "Just remember, John appeared on the scene, eating no bread and drinking no wine, and you say, 'He is demented.' The son of Adam appeared on the scene both eating and drinking, and you say, 'There is a glutton and a drunk, a crony of toll collectors and sinners!' Indeed, wisdom is vindicated by all her children" (Q 7:33–35).

The second saying appears with very different wording in its Lucan and Matthean versions. In Luke: "Right up to John's time you have the Law and the Prophets; since then God's imperial rule has been proclaimed as good news and everyone is breaking into it violently" (Luke 16:16). In Matthew: "From the time of John the Baptist until now Heaven's imperial rule has been breaking in violently and violent men are attempting to gain it by force. You see, the Prophets and even the Law predicted everything that was to happen prior to John's time" (Matt 11:12–13).

As words of Jesus, the Seminar in its sayings phase voted both these Q sayings in their entirety as gray. The initial saying includes the phrase "son of Adam" which many Fellows consider to refer to the apocalyptic figure at the end of history and, therefore, a formulation of the early church (O3). The second saying in each version reflects the theological interests of their respective authors (W4). The Lucan version separates salvation history into distict periods. The Matthean version clearly relates JB to Jesus' theme of the kingdom of heaven.

The Sayings Gospel Q, reports sayings by Jesus in which Jesus contrasts himself with JB. Does this contrast go back to the historical Jesus? In what areas does Jesus contrast himself and his movement with JB and his movement? The Seminar voted that in all probability Jesus did contrast his behavior with JB: pink.

This contrast certainly has to do, first, with a difference in styles of ministry. The contrast between the ascetic JB and the libertine Jesus in Q 7:33–35 includes slander against Jesus that would scarcely have been created by the church (N3). Jesus did compare his style of eating and drinking with JB's style of abstinence. This Q saying was supporting evidence for the Seminar's determination that JB was in all likelihood an ascetic.

This contrast may also have to do with a difference in their relationship to the kingdom of God. Both the Lucan and the Matthean versions of Q

16:16, a saying considered by some to be unrecoverable in its original form, does involve the theme of the kingdom of God. Our survey of JB's message—however limited the evidence—showed that his apocalyptic message of a coming judgment did not utilize the theme of "the kingdom of God." It was Matthew that made JB into a kingdom preacher (W4). As generally recognized by historical research and confirmed by the Jesus Seminar in its sayings phase, the phrase "kingdom of God" in many gospel sayings reflects the very *voice* of Jesus. The Jesus Seminar has collectively expressed the view that Jesus understood "kingdom of God" non-apocalyptically as a present possibility and reality.

Out of the work of the Jesus Seminar (and now the Jesus Seminar as John Seminar) has emerged this kind of contrast between the historical JB and the historical Jesus. JB was an ascetic apocalyptic preacher of a coming judgment to be actualized by an expected figure. His baptism prepared for that judgment all who accepted his baptism of repentance for the forgiveness of sins. The wilderness was the primary setting for his activities of preaching and baptizing. Jesus was a sage whose pithy aphorisms and profound parables challenged his hearers in non-apocalyptic terms to a new visioning of reality with corresponding actions that could be described as "the kingdom of God," or "God's domain." He celebrated life with eating and drinking. The primary setting of his ministry included the smaller towns and villages of Galilee.

Perhaps the different behaviors between JB and Jesus with respect to fasting and non-fasting are consistent with the different orientations of their ministries. JB's ministry was one of preparation for God's coming judgment. Fast! Jesus' ministry was one that held forth God's rule as present possibility. Eat and drink! The Seminar gave a pink evaluation to Jesus' saying about the bridegroom: "The groom's friends can't fast while the groom is with them, can they? So long as the groom is around, you can't expect them to fast" (Mark 2:19 par). In characteristic fashion, the Gospel of John has JB himself bear witness to Jesus as bridegroom: "The bride belongs to the groom, and the best man stands with him as is happy enough just to be close at hand. So I am content. He can only grow in importance; my role can only diminish" (John 3:29–30). These words may have been judged as black in terms of their not having been actually uttered by JB. But these words are faithful to the historical reality of Jesus' ministry as one of celebration.

15 IMPRISONMENT AND DEATH

The narrative statements considered here relate to the events of the end of JB's life. Herod Antipas, his ill-gotten wife Herodias, and her daughter are the key players in the drama that allegedly begins not with a wedding but a birthday celebration and ends with a head on a platter.

A: **Herod Antipas had JB imprisoned.**
    R 88%   P 12%   G 0%   B 0%   avg .96   **red**

A: **Herod Antipas had JB executed.**
    R 92%   P 8%   G 0%   B 0%   avg .92   **red**

A: **JB denounced Herod Antipas.**
    R 92%   P 8%   G 0%   B 0%   avg .97   **red**

A: **JB criticized Herod Antipas' marriage to Herodias.**
    R 44%   P 56%   G 0%   B 0%   avg .81   **red**

A: **JB's activities posed a threat to Herod Antipas' ability to maintain peace and stability.**
    R 72%   P 24%   G 4%   B 0%   avg .89   **red**

A: **Herod Antipas had JB executed for political expediency.**
    R 76%   P 24%   G 0%   B 0%   avg .92   **red**

The Fellows of the Seminar expressed their greatest historical certainty about JB in their assessment of those events related to the end of his life. Here are six narrative statements related to his imprisonment and death. Notice not only the series of red votes but the very, very few votes less than pink in color.

The reasons for such high degrees of certainty are clear. First, not only are there two independent sources bearing witness to these events, but these sources stem from very different circles. There is the Christian Gospel of Mark (Mark 6:14–29 par) and the testimony of the Jewish historian Josephus (Ant 18:118–119)(G1, G4). Secondly, although these two sources are written from very different perspectives, they appear to complement rather than to contradict each other (G7).

The first two narrative statements are based upon and supported by the accounts in Mark and Josephus. Both agree at two crucial points. Herod Antipas had JB imprisoned. Herod Antipas had JB executed. Therefore, red and red.

Mark and Josephus, however, appear to differ in their presentations of what prompted Herod Antipas to move against JB. Each presentation is consistent with the aims of the document in which it appears. The Gospel of Mark is a theological confession centered around the theme of religious martyrdom. The *Antiquities* is an apology which documents the political unrest of first century Palestine.

Mark states that JB had openly denounced Herod. More specifically, Mark says that JB had criticized Herod Antipas' marriage to Herodias: "It is not right for you to have your brother's wife!" (Mark 6:18) Consequently, Herod responds to what seems to be JB's meddling in his domestic affairs, apparently with the encouragement of Herodias. Therefore, the second pair of narrative statements are based primarily on the Marcan story, but they receive tacit support from Josephus. Josephus does not explicitly mention JB's condemnation of Herod Antipas; but, within the broader context, he does discuss Antipas' marriage to Herodias the wife of his brother (Ant 18:109–115). Josephus emphasizes the foreign policy problem thereby created. Antipas' promise of marriage to Herodias involved his agreement, apparently at her behest, to set aside his wife of long standing, the daughter of Aretas IV, the king of Nabatea. The circumstances that prompted JB to condemn Herod Antipas according to Mark are mentioned by Josephus. Again, red and red. JB denounced Herod Antipas. He criticized Herod Antipas' marriage to Herodias.

Josephus suggests that JB's activities posed a threat to Antipas' ability to maintain peace and stability. Josephus claims Herod feared that JB's eloquence before the masses might result in some kind of *stasis*, "revolt" or "sedition" (Ant 18:118). So Herod Antipas had JB executed for political expediency. Therefore, the third pair of narrative statements are based primarily on the story in the *Antiquities*. But the statements receive tacit support from the presentation of JB in Mark and in Q. Mark makes no explicit mention of the political repercussions related to JB's condemnation of Herod Antipas for his marriage to Herodias. Such a condemnation, however, obviously would have had political dimensions. First, Herod Antipas was a political figure and a condemnation of his marriage could

become an affair of state. Secondly, JB's message of a baptism in anticipation of a coming judgment was an indictment of the present order; and
his talk of a coming figure mightier than he could threaten those in power.
Thirdly, JB's activities had a widespread appeal within a social setting
politically charged beneath the layers of Roman rule. Once again, red and
red. JB's activities posed a threat to Antipas' ability to maintain peace and
stability. Herod had JB executed for political expediency.

S: **Machaerus was the site of JB's execution.**

    R 44%   P 56%   G 0%   B 0%   avg .81   **red**

Machaerus was one of the fortress palaces, including Herodium and
Masada, built or rebuilt by Herod the Great (37–4 B.C.E.). Located in southern Perea five miles east of the Dead Sea, Machaerus was under the control
of his son Herod Antipas throughout most of the latter's long rule (4 B.C.E.–
39 C.E.). When Herod Antipas' wife, the daughter of Aretas IV, discovered
her husband's intention to divorce her in order to marry Herodias, she fled
to Machaerus which was near the border of her father's kingdom (Ant
18:111).

This narrative statement is based on the account of Josephus. He matter
of factly reports that JB was brought in chains to Machareus and there
killed (Ant 18:119). The story of JB's imprisonment in Mark in itself makes
no reference to the place of JB's execution (Mark 6:14–29 par). In this
passage, however, Mark mentions that leading citizens of Galilee had been
invited to the birthday party on which occasion Herodias used her dancing
daughter to manipulate JB's execution. This notation, however, is consistent with Mark's placement of the story within the literary setting of his
gospel. Mark's has placed the story within the context of his narration of
Jesus' early ministry centered in Galilee (W2). Neither does the Q story of
JB's inquiry of Jesus from prison through his disciples mention the locale of
his imprisonment, but Matthew and Luke have placed the story within the
broader narrative context of Jesus' activities in Galilee (Luke 7:18–23//Matt
11:2–6). Matthew and Luke have followed Mark in their general outline of
Jesus' ministry with its early center in Galilee (W2). Therefore, whereas
Josephus claims Machaerus to be the place of JB's execution, the gospels
imply a site in Galilee. Tiberias, Herod's capital on the western shore of the
Sea of Galilee, was in Galilee and could have served as the execution site.
Nonetheless, the Seminar collectively expressed certainty that Josephus
was accurate in placing the imprisonment and execution of JB at Ma-
chaerus: red.

Several observations contributed to this acceptance of Machaerus as the
site of JB's execution. First, the Fellows recognized the general silence of the
gospels about locale along with the motivation of their authors in placing
the story in a Galilean literary context (W2). Secondly, the Fellows con-

sidered Machaerus to be the likely site given its geographical proximity to the known locale of JB's ministry—the Jordan valley and the surrounding wilderness (G6). Thirdly, the Fellows reviewed the archaeological data which establishes that Machaerus had the facilities to accommodate the kind of birthday bash reported in Mark (G4).

A: **Herodias requested the execution of JB.**

R 0%   P 23%   G 73%   B 4%   avg .40   **gray**

A: **Herodias used her daughter to get JB executed.**

R 0%   P 12%   G 76%   B 12%   avg .33   **gray**

A: **Herodias' daughter danced for Herod Antipas and his court.**

R 0%   P 12%   G 76%   B 12%   avg .33   **gray**

These three narrative statements are based exclusively on the Marcan account of the death of JB (Mark 6:14–29 par). Only in Mark, followed by Matthew but not Luke, is Herodias the chief instigator of JB's death. She uses her daughter to force the execution of JB whom she resented for having condemned her marriage to Antipas. After her daughter had danced on the occasion of Antipas' birthday banquet, the appreciative host himself had agreed to grant the daughter whatever she might request.

The observation was made that Herodias' manipulation here appears consistent with her portrayal by Josephus. There her apparent conniving had resulted in wresting from Antipas his promise to set aside his marriage to the daughter of Aretas IV (Ant 18:110). Nonetheless, the Fellows were unwilling to rank the events identified by these propositions any higher than possible; but still, they considered them possible. Herodias may have requested the execution of JB. She may have used her daughter to get JB executed. Her daughter may have danced for Herod Antipas and his court. The objection that a young aristocratic woman would not have danced in this fashion was met with the response that the suggestion of lewdness about the dance comes not from the text but from salacious Hollywood adaptations of the text. (See cameo essay, "John the Baptist in Film.") Therefore, the votes were colored gray, and gray, and another gray. Three reasons for these assessments might be mentioned. First, the events are only singly attested, in Mark (G4). Secondly, the story as narrated bears the marks of a good folk tale in a patron-client and patriarchal society in which responsibility is shifted from those in power to their underlings, from males to females (O3, O4). Thirdly, the events take place at a private party; and their general accuracy would require persons present to have made them public. The story itself, however, mentions that disciples of JB were allowed to claim the body. Servants present at the banquet could have related to JB's followers the gist of what had occurred on that occasion (O2).

In conclusion, it should be noted that the narrative statements do not identify the daughter of Herodias by name because neither Mark nor Matthew identifies the daughter of Herodias by name. Salome, the name by which she becomes known, appears only in Josephus; but Josephus makes no reference to her dancing as the occasion for JB's sentence unto death (Ant 18:137).

A: Herodias' daughter asked for the head of JB on a platter.
R 0%   P 4%   G 65%   B 31%   avg .24   **black**

This narrative statement also rests exclusively on Mark (G4). Although a majority of the Fellows considered this detail as likely as the other motifs related to Herodias and her daughter, the weighted vote resulted in a collective judgment of improbability. Black. The claim that Antipas not only immediately ordered the execution by beheading but had the head served to the daughter even in the midst of the festivities does stretch credulity, even though—according to the popular adage—truth may be stranger than fiction. Surely this grotesque detail bears the mark of oral story telling (O2).

16 THE BAPTIST MOVEMENT AFTER JOHN'S DEATH

Evidence that JB initiated a movement that outlived him serves as the basis for these narrative statements. The propositions here involve not Jesus and JB, but JB's followers and their relation to Jesus and the Jesus movement.

A: **Disciples of JB continued to honor him after his death.**

  R 63%   P 37%   G 0%   B 0%   avg .88   **red**

A: **The movements of JB and Jesus were rivals during Jesus' lifetime.**

  R 31%   P 43%   G 22%   B 4%   avg .67   **pink**

A: **The movements of JB and Jesus were rivals after Jesus' death.**

  R 35%   P 45%   G 15%   B 5%   avg .70   **pink**

A: **JB's movement included hellenistic Jews (like Apollos).**

  R 5%   P 43%   G 52%   B 0%   avg .51   **pink**

During his lifetime, JB in all probability had disciples, one of whom was the man named Jesus from Nazareth who had accepted his call for baptism. At some unspecified time, Jesus seems to have separated from the JB movement; and some of JB's disciples apparently became followers of Jesus himself. Such are the conclusions of the Seminar to this point.

The first stage of the JB movement, therefore, extends from the active ministry of JB until his death at the hands of the tetrarch Herod Antipas. The narrative statements here—based on the gospels—address the issue of the history of the JB movement through a second stage and then into a third: from the death of JB to the death of Jesus; and then after the death of Jesus.

The difficulty of establishing historically a chronology or a sequence of events based on the gospels should be noted up front. As we have seen, the gospel writers exercise great freedom in their arrangement of the sayings and stories inherited from oral tradition and even from written sources (W3). Some of the references in the gospels to interaction between the followers of JB, on the one hand, and Jesus or his followers, on the other, could allude to events that occurred either before or after the death of JB.

The Seminar expressed certainty, with a red vote, that the disciples of JB continued to honor him after death. This certainty rests on the abundant evidence—not to be repeated here—that his death did not end his movement. As we just noted, Mark even observes that his disciples took charge of his body after his execution and placed it in a tomb (Mark 6:29 par).

The Seminar was less certain, more in the range of probability and thus pink votes, that the movements JB and Jesus spawned were rivals both during Jesus' lifetime and after Jesus' death. That the movements of JB and

---

John the Baptist in Historical Research–II

Since John Reumann's survey article on "The Quest for the Historical Baptist" (1972), scholars have continued to express historical interest in John along two lines of inquiry. Those engaged in life-of-Jesus research have continued to write about John as Jesus' predecessor. Others have focused their attention more exclusively on John as their principal subject.

Among those who have written significant monographs on Jesus in recent years are: E. P. Sanders, *Jesus and Judaism* (1985); Marcus Borg, *Jesus: A New Vision* (1987); and John Dominic Crossan, *The Historical Jesus: The Life of a Mediterranean Jewish Peasant* (1991). Sanders considers John's baptism of Jesus as one of eight virtually certain facts about Jesus. He views John as an eschatological prophet of repentance, and Jesus as an eschatological prophet of the restoration of Israel. Borg situates John within Jewish charismatic tradition. During his baptism by John, Jesus experienced a vision and—according to Borg—was a spirit person throughout his own ministry. Crossan, in a work noted for its methodological rigor, concludes that John's baptism of Jesus does represent one of the most certain things we know about each of them. To Crossan, however, the arrest and death of John prompted Jesus to develop his own distinctive ministry. Whereas John had proclaimed a message of God's imminent apocalyptic act of judgment and practiced a baptism which mediated God's forgiveness of sins in anticipation of that act, Jesus became a sage whose kingdom ministry involved both a vision and a program of social egalitarianism.

John the Baptist has, however, attracted attention in his own right, although here too Jesus lies close at hand. Paul Hollenbach, in a provocative study (1979), imputed to John himself—and to those who responded positively to his preaching and baptizing—a vision of social justice. In a related study (1982), Hollenbach considered how Jesus, who was baptized by John and became a baptizer himself, later abandoned his baptizing ministry for a ministry of healing when he discovered that he possessed the power to exorcise. Like Hollenbach, Jerome Murphy-O'Connor in a journal article (1990) argues for parallel and cooperative ministries between John and Jesus before the arrest of John. He even

Jesus *paralleled* each other in some sense both during and after Jesus' death seems certain. The gospels show disciples of JB interacting with Jesus and his disciples over such issues as fasting and prayer (Mark 2:18 par; Luke 11:1; also Luke 5:33). Reporting events that occurred after Jesus' death, the book of Acts preserves traditions which refer to followers of JB in the wider Mediterranean world who have contact with Christian missionaries and Christian communities (Acts 18:24–28; 19:1–7). Some Fellows were reluctant to speak about this interaction and contact in terms of *rivalry*. Such a description relies primarily on the Gospel of John. There, even during the lifetimes of JB and Jesus, their respective movements are described in terms suggesting rivalry (John 3:25–26; 4:1). Furthermore, the presentation of JB

suggests that they agreed for Jesus to work in Judea and for John to work in Samaria—and later in Galilee. Recently, Otto Betz, also in a journal article (1990), has again argued for the longstanding view that John was probably reared as an Essene, possibly in the settlement at Qumran.

Of special note are two rather monumental works which devote themselves to the study of John, the one in German and the other in English: Josef Ernst's *Johannes der Täufer: Interpretation-Geschichte-Wirkungsgeschichte* (1989); and Robert L. Webb's *John the Baptizer and Prophet: A Socio-Historical Study* (1991). (The importance of Webb's work has already been acknowledged.) Both volumes are models of meticulous literary analysis and reasoned historical reconstruction. Both volumes encompass over four hundred pages. Both represent vast reservoirs of John scholarship. Life-of-John research from the previous generation flows *into* these works; and John research for the next generation must flow *from* them.

These two works, however, complement rather than duplicate one other, as their respective titles suggest. Ernst spends well over half of his writing space analyzing the different ways John has been interpreted in the New Testament writings and other early Christian and Jewish literature. Then he presents his own historical conclusions about John in a relatively brief central section; and there are no great surprises reflected here. Webb begins his study with a brief survey of sources which—like the survey by Ernst—recognizes the varying ways John has been treated, particularly by Josephus and in the canonical and non-canonical gospels. Most of Webb's monograph, however, represents a judicious quest for John as a historical figure which revolves around John's public roles of baptizer and prophet.

Both Ernst and Webb deny that the judgment anticipated by John involved cosmic destruction. God's judgment will occur within history, not at the end of history. Therefore, both are more comfortable ascribing to John the social role of a prophet instead of speaking about him as an apocalyptist. (For bibliographical information about the works cited here, consult the selected bibliography in this volume.)

in the Fourth Gospel in which JB openly denies himself to be the Christ, the Anointed, or to be Elijah, or to be the prophet has sometimes been taken as evidence of continuing rivalry beteween the JB and the Jesus movements toward the end of the first century (John 1:19ff). Other Fellows view such between-the-lines evidence in the gospels not supportive of rivalry but of *assimilation* of JB's onetime disciples into the Jesus movement. This kind of assimilation—if not rivalry—apparently did occur around the middle of the first century when the Q community expanded its emerging collection of Jesus' sayings to include sayings by and about JB. Assimilation of JB's followers into the emerging church may also be presupposed by the juxtaposition of the JB infancy traditions to the account of Jesus' in Luke 1–2. The varying interpretations of the evidence about the relationship between the JB and the Jesus movements, both before and after the death of Jesus, accounts for the less than certain pink vote on the *rivalry* between the movements.

Similar ambiguity of the evidence in the Book of Acts and differences of interpretation of that evidence also led to the vote of probability not certainty, pink not red, on the proposition that JB's movement included hellenistic Jews such as Apollos (Acts 18:24–28; cf 1 Cor 1–4). There is uncertainty about the nature and extent of the traditions underlying the story about Apollos and the subsequent story about those twelve so-called disciples encountered by Paul at Ephesus (Acts 19:1–7). There is also uncertainty whether their knowing only "the baptism of John" means they belonged to what might be called a JB movement.

17 APOCALYPTICISM, JESUS, AND JOHN

These two narrative statements conclude our historical assessment of JB, although they do not mention him by name. The common themes are apocalypticism and Jesus.

A: **Apocalypticism was introduced into the Christian tradition after Jesus' death.**
   R 25%   P 29%   G 33%   B 13%   avg .55   **pink**

A: **Apocalypticism was introduced into the Jesus tradition by some of his followers.**
   R 50%   P 25%   G 21%   B 4%   avg .74   **pink**

During its sayings phase, the Jesus Seminar assessed all the literary evidence for the words of Jesus and concluded that Jesus the historical figure was more of a sage or wise man than an apocalyptic preacher. The Jesus Seminar began its deeds phase by becoming the JB Seminar. The literary evidence bearing witness to Jesus' contemporary and predecessor, John called the Baptist or Baptizer, has been evaluated. The conclusion was that the historical JB, in all probability, was an apocalyptic preacher.

These narrative statements were intended to test once again the views of the Fellows relative to apocalypticism and Christian origins. The Fellows again affirmed the likelihood that apocalypticism was introduced into the Christian tradition after Jesus' death. The vote was colored pink. Certainly, the apocalypticizing of Jesus had already occurred by the time Paul wrote his letters in the 50s C.E., by the time Mark was written ca 70 C.E., and by the time Q reached its present form perhaps also by the year 70 C.E. The Fellows, by an even darker pink vote, declared that apocalypticism was introduced into the Jesus tradition by some of his followers. Perhaps some of these followers had at one time been participants in the JB movement whose founder was the Baptist, a prophet, and an apocalyptic preacher.

The Book of Revelation as a "Baptist" Apocalypse

The notion that the Book of Revelation represents a writing that originated with JB and his followers initially strikes one as a strange claim since the "John" mentioned in the book as the source of these visions has traditionally been identified as John the son of Zebedee, one of the twelve. But "John" was a common name. Nowhere does the John named in the book claim for himself the designation "disciple" nor does he intimate any association with Jesus during his earthly ministry. Although the suggestion that this John may have also—in some sense—been JB has not found widespread acceptance in scholarly circles, the arguments for some connection between Revelation and JB are stronger than might be expected.

The view that Revelation represents a writing originating in Baptist circles has been argued by J. Massyngberde Ford in her commentary in "The Anchor Bible" series. Foundational to this view is the recognition that nine features characteristic of JB and his apocalyptic message in the gospels also appear in the Book of Revelation. These themes or images are: (1) the lamb; (2) the expectation of "the coming one"; (3) baptism by fire; (4) the bridegroom; (5) divine wrath; (6) adultery; (7) corruptness of Jerusalem (8) trees; and (9) knowledge appropriate for a priest.

With this point of departure, the Book of Revelation is said to have developed in three stages:

1. Chapters 4–11, the apocalyptic visions which do not mention Jesus by name, contain the original revelations that came to JB before and during the period when he recognized that Jesus was in fact "the coming one." This material was probably first written down by his followers.

2. Chapters 12–22, which do refer to Jesus by name, represent an expansion of the earlier visions by a follower of JB who had knowledge of Jesus and the Jesus movement much like Apollos and the disciples at Ephesus (Acts 18 and 19).

3. Chapters 1–3, actually letters to seven churches in the Roman province of Asia, come from the time when the earlier visions and their amplifications were becoming fully "Christianized." The local churches mentioned may have been themselves Christian churches with (former) followers of JB in them. Therefore, the Revelation is a composite work that finds its ultimate origin in the apocalyptic visions made to JB. The date for the completed work, as we know it, would be in the 60s C.E..

If this book did contain authentic JB traditions, then the evidence for his message would be expanded a hundredfold. Any doubt about the apocalyptic nature of his message would be clearly answered. JB was indeed an apocalyptic preacher! The Jesus Seminar affirmed that JB was an apocalyptic preacher; but the seminar based its judgment exclusively on the evidence in the gospels.

A   VOTING GUIDELINES AND CALCULATION

For its sayings phase, the Jesus Seminar adopted two official interpretations of the four colors of red, pink, gray, and black. Participants could select either for their own guidance.

Words Option 1

red   I *would* include this item unequivocally in the data base for determining who Jesus was.

pink   I *would* include this item with reservations (or modifications) in the data base for determining who Jesus was.

gray   I *would not* include this item in the primary data base for determining who Jesus was, *but* I might make use of some of the content in determining who Jesus was.

black   I *would not* include this item in the primary data base for determining who Jesus was.

Words Option 2

red   Jesus *undoubtedly* said this or something very like it.

pink   Jesus *probably* said something like this.

gray   Jesus *did not* say this, *but* the ideas contained in it are close to his own.

black   Jesus *did not* say this; it represents the perspective or content of a later or different tradition.

The shift of the Jesus Seminar from a consideration of sayings to a consideration of deeds required a revised set of definitions. Consistent with the previous approach, two sets of interpretations were put forth:

Deeds Option 1

red   This information is virtually *certain*. It is supported by a preponderance of the evidence.

pink   This information is not certain but *probably* reliable. It fits well with evidence that is verifiable.

gray   This information is *possible* but unreliable. It is not a clear fabrication but lacks supporting evidence.

black   This information is *improbable*. It does not fit verifiable evidence, or it seems to be a fabrication.

Deeds Option 2

red   I *would certainly* put this information in the database for determining who Jesus was.

pink   I *would* accept this statement with modification in the database for determining who Jesus was.

gray   I *would not* include this statement in the primary database, *but* I might use some of its details in determining who Jesus would.

black   I *would not* include this information in the primary database for determining who Jesus was.

Both pairs of guidelines are expressed in terms of the Seminar's concern for Jesus, not JB. The interpretation of the colors in this volume on the Seminar's historical assessment of the literary evidence about JB follows most closely *Deeds Option 1*.

Once the individual members have voted on an agenda item, whether a word or a deed, the votes must be tabulated to establish the collective historical judgment of the Seminar. Throughout the life of the Seminar, the same method of calculation has been employed. In order to tabulate the vote, the colors were assigned numerical values:

red   = 3
pink = 2
gray = 1
black = 0

The total points for each ballot are added up and divided by the total number of votes cast in order to determine the overall weighted average. The scale is from three to zero. Thus far, the method of calculation resembles the method generally used in American higher education where the A, B, C, D, F grading scale is converted into a grade point average. Only the Seminar adopted not the four point scale many of its members regularly use in the classroom, but a three point scale. So far, so good. But it was decided to go one step further and to convert the weighted averages to percentages—to employ a scale of 100 rather than a scale of 3.00.

On a particular ballot, the overall weighted average on the 3 point scale is then divided by 3 in order to convert that average to a percentage using a 100 point scale. With the 100 point scale divided into quadrants and correlated with the four colors, a collective vote can be assigned a color as follows:

.7501 and up   red
.5001 to .7500   pink
.2501 to .5000   gray
.0000 to .2500   black

Although the computer is programmed to carry the averages to four decimal places, the numbers are customarily rounded off to two decimal places for public reporting.

B SEMINAR PAPERS ON JB/ ROSTER OF FELLOWS

Integral to the format of the Jesus Seminar is the development of position papers by individual members of the Seminar, or by invited participants. These papers address the issues placed on the agenda for discussion and voting at the next plenary meeting. The papers are circulated among the participants before the meeting in order to allow maximum time for a discussion of the issues. The papers prepared for the two Seminar meetings which focused on JB are listed here by author and title. These meetings were held at Edmonton, Alberta, October 24–27, 1991, and at Santa Rosa, California, February 27-March 1, 1992.

Arnal, William. "Did John Preach Repentance? Q 3:7–9, 16–17 and Some Related Texts." Edmonton.

Bjorndahl, Sterling. "Jesus and John in Q." Edmonton.

Borg, Marcus. "Jesus and Visions? The Account of His Baptismal Experience (Mark 1:10–11)." Santa Rosa.

Chilton, Bruce. "John the Purifier." Santa Rosa.

Dewey, Arthur J. "Two Heads are Better Than One: The Death of John the Baptizer." Santa Rosa.

Rousseau, John J. "Machaerus (Hebrew *Makhwar*)." Santa Rosa.

Jones, F. Stanley. "John the Baptist and His Disciples in the Pseudo-Clementines: A Historical Appraisal." Santa Rosa.

———. "Mandaean Baptismal Rites (brief visual presentation)." Santa Rosa.

Smith, Mahlon. "Jesus' Relation to John the Baptist: Q 7:18–35." Edmonton.

———. "Who Said John is Elijah?" Edmonton.

———. "Casting John as Prophet." Santa Rosa.

Tatum, W. Barnes. "The Family of John the Baptist, or Did JB, as a relative of Jesus, really swap a priest's linen coat for camel's hair?" Edmonton.

Webb, Robert L. "John as Baptizer: His Activity of Immersing in the Context of First-Century Judaism." Edmonton.

_____. "Josephus on John the Baptist (AJ 18:116–119)." Santa Rosa.

Wink, Walter. "The Baptism of Jesus: What Really Happened?" Edmonton.

ROSTER OF FELLOWS

Robert W. Funk, Westar Institute, Co-chair of the Jesus Seminar
Ph.D., Vanderbilt University

John Dominic Crossan, DePaul University, Co-chair of the Jesus Seminar
D.D., Maynooth College, Ireland

Andries G. van Aarde, University of Pretoria
D.D., University of Pretoria

Harold W. Attridge, University of Notre Dame
Ph.D., Harvard University

Robert Bater, Queen's Theological College
Ph.D., Union Theological Seminary, New York

William Beardslee, Center for Process Studies
Ph.D., University of Chicago

Edward F. Beutner, Westar Institute
Ph.D., Graduate Theological Union

Sterling Bjorndahl, Augustana University College
Ph.D., Claremont Graduate School (candidate)

Marcus Borg, Oregon State University
D.Phil., Oxford University

Willi Braun, Centre for the Study of Religion, University of Toronto
Ph.D., University of Toronto

James R. Butts
Ph.D., Claremont Graduate School

Ron Cameron, Wesleyan University
Ph.D., Harvard University

Bruce D. Chilton, Bard College
Ph.D., Cambridge University

Kathleen E. Corley, University of Wisconsin—Oshkosh
Ph.D., Claremont Graduate School

Wendy J. Cotter C.S.J., Loyola University, Chicago
Ph.D., University of St. Michael's College

Jon Daniels, Defiance College
Ph.D., Claremont Graduate School

Stevan L. Davies, College Misericordia
Ph.D., Temple University

Jon F. Dechow, Westar Institute
Ph.D., University of Pennsylvania

Arthur J. Dewey, Xavier University, Cincinnati
Th.D., Harvard University

Dennis C. Duling, Canisius College
Ph.D., University of Chicago

Karl Eklund, Berkley, Massachusetts
Ph.D., Columbia University

Robert T. Fortna, Vassar College
Th.D., Union Theological Seminary, New York

James Goss, California State University, Northridge
Ph.D., Claremont Graduate School

Heinz Guenther, Emmanuel College of Victoria University
Th.D., University of Toronto

Walter Harrelson, Vanderbilt
University
Th.D., Union Theological Seminary,
New York

Stephen L. Harris, California State
University, Sacramento
Ph.D., Cornell University

Charles W. Hedrick, Southwest
Missouri State University
Ph.D., Claremont Graduate School

James D. Hester, University of
Redlands
D.Theol., University of Basel

C. M. Kempton Hewitt, Methodist
Theological School in Ohio
Ph.D., University of Durham, England

Julian V. Hills, Marquette University
Th.D., Harvard University

Roy W. Hoover, Whitman College
Th.D., Harvard University

Michael L. Humphries, Southern
Illinois University, Carbondale
Ph.D., Claremont Graduate School

Arland D. Jacobson, Concordia
College
Ph.D., Claremont Graduate School

Clayton N. Jefford, St. Meinrad
Seminary
Ph.D., Claremont Graduate School

F. Stanley Jones, California State
University, Long Beach
Ph.D., Vanderbilt University

Perry Kea, University of Indianapolis
Ph.D., University of Virginia

Chan-Hie Kim, School of Theology at
Claremont
Ph.D., Vanderbilt University

Karen L. King, Occidental College
Ph.D., Brown University

John S. Kloppenborg, University of St.
Michael's College
Ph.D., University of St. Michael's
College

Davidson Loehr, People's Church
Ph.D., University of Chicago

Sanford Lowe, Santa Rosa Junior
College, California
D.D., Hebrew Union College

John Lown, Francis Parker School,
San Diego
Ph.D., Vanderbilt University

Loren Mack-Fisher, the Double Bar A
Ranch
Ph.D., Brandeis University

Lane C. McGaughy, Willamette
University
Ph.D., Vanderbilt University

Edward J. McMahon II, Texas
Christian University
Ph.D., Vanderbilt University

Marvin W. Meyer, Chapman
University
Ph.D., Claremont Graduate School

J. Ramsey Michaels, Southwest
Missouri State University
Th.D., Harvard University

L. Bruce Miller, University of Alberta,
Edmonton
Ph.D., University of Chicago

Robert J. Miller, Midway College
Ph.D., Claremont Graduate School

Winsome Munro, St. Olaf College
Ed.D., Teachers College, Columbia
University and Union Theological
Seminary

Culver H. Nelson, Western
International University
L.H.D., D.D., D.D.

Rod Parrott, Disciples Seminary
Foundation
Ph.D., Claremont Graduate School

Stephen J. Patterson, Eden
Theological Seminary
Ph.D., Claremont Graduate School

Vernon K. Robbins, Emory University
Ph.D., University of Chicago

James M. Robinson
Ph.D., Princeton Theological
Seminary

John J. Rousseau, University of
California, Berkeley
Ph.D., University of Paris

Daryl D. Schmidt, Texas Christian
University
Ph.D., Graduate Theological Union

Bernard Brandon Scott, Phillips
Graduate Seminary, Tulsa Center
Ph.D., Vanderbilt University

Philip Sellew, University of
Minnesota
Th.D., Harvard University

Chris Shea, Ball State University
Ph.D., University of Illinois, Urbana–
Champaign

Lou H. Silberman, University of
Arizona, Tucson
D.H.L., Hebrew Union College,
Cincinnati

Dennis Smith, Phillips Graduate
Seminary
Th.D., Harvard University

Mahlon H. Smith, Rutgers University
M.S.L., Pontifical Institute of Medieval
Studies, Toronto

Michael G. Steinhauser, Toronto
School of Theology
Th.D., University of Würzburg

Robert F. Stoops, Jr., Western
Washington University
Ph.D., Harvard University

Johann Strijdom, University of South
Africa
D.Litt. et Phil., University of South
Africa (candidate)

W. Barnes Tatum, Greensboro College
Ph.D., Duke University

Hal Taussig, Chestnut Hill College,
Albright College
Ph.D., The Union Institute

Leif E. Vaage, Emmanuel College,
Toronto
Ph.D., Claremont Graduate School

Paul Verhoeven, Brooksfilms
Ph.D., University of Leiden

Wesley Hiram Wachob, Emory
University
Ph.D., Emory University

William O. Walker, Jr., Trinity
University
Ph.D., Duke University

Robert L. Webb, Canadian
Theological Seminary
Ph.D., University of Sheffield

John L. White, Loyola University of
Chicago
Ph.D., Vanderbilt University

Walter Wink, Auburn Theological
Seminary
Th.D., Union Theological Seminary,
New York

Sara C. Winter, Eugene Lang College,
New School for Social Research
Ph.D., Union Theological Seminary,
New York

C   RULES OF PROCEDURE

General Procedures

P1   Reduce each narrative segment to narrative statements.

P2   Determine the action or complex of actions that constitutes the event—the change in status—narrated in that segment.

P3   Assess for fact or fiction the action or complex of actions that constitutes the event.

Action Statements

P4   Arrange action statements in order of their generality.

P5   Assess for fact or fiction action statements at the highest level of generality.

Status Statements

P6   Arrange status statements in order of their generality.

P7   Assess status statements for fact or fiction at the highest level of generality.

P8   Assess status statements for fact or fiction at the highest level of generality specific to particular segments.

Nuclei

P9   Distinguish introductions and and conclusions from nuclei in narrative segments and sequences of segments.

P10   Assess the nuclei of segments for fact or fiction.

P11   Isolate data derived from the order of segments and sequences in the gospel narratives and evaluate such data circumspectly: the connectives provided by the gospel writers between and among segments are largely fictive and vary frequently from performance to performance, from source to source.

Narrator and Narrative

P12   Identify the role of the narrator by determining voice and perspective and by noting marks of the narrator's presence. In assessing
the historical basis of particular segments, the Seminar should calculate the effect of limiting factors factors based on voice, perspective, and presence—on what is narrated.

P13   Distinguish showing from telling in each narrative segment.

P14   In assessing the narrative reports [of what Jesus did and said]
isolate the gist of the reports and compare the gist with the typifications regnant in the community transmitting the materials out
of which the gospels were created.

"Debris"

P15   Identify the "debris" in the Jesus tradition—elements that have not
been assimilated to the typifications characteristic of the transmitting communities.

P16   Assess the "debris" in the tradition for fact or fiction.

Repetition and Restrictions

P17   Be especially cautious in the use of traditions that are often repeated in the gospels: their repetition may owe to domestication in
emerging Christian communities, and they may thus not reflect
earlier tradition.

P18   Assess for fact or fiction only those events open to neutral
observers.

P19   Assess for fact or fiction only those events open to two or more
observers.

P20   Assess for fact or fiction only those events whose agency is open to
public verification.

P21   Assess for fact or fiction only those reports that do not require
privileged knowledge.

D Rules of evidence

In assessing literary texts as evidence about past events, historians follow certain rules. As historians, biographers follow rules of evidence is determining what an individual may have said or done. These so-called rules of evidence have variously been called standards, principles, or criteria.

During the nineteenth century and into the twentieth century, biblical scholars as historians have used and refined many rules of evidence for assessing the historical reliability of the information about Jesus preserved, especially, within the canonical gospels. The Fellows of the Jesus Seminar, as individual scholars engaged in a corporate scholarly project, have similarly used rules in arriving at a collective judgment about what Jesus may have said and done. These rules of evidence have been reviewed and discussed at some length in other written reports of the Seminar's work. For example, Robert W. Funk, with Mahlon Smith, *The Gospel of Mark: Red Letter Edition* (Sonoma: Polebridge Press, 1991), 29–52.

The study of John the Baptist by the Jesus Seminar marked the transition from the Words phase of the Seminar to the Deeds phase. This volume presents the results of that study. Both sayings attributed to JB and reports of deeds by JB, that is both his words and deeds, were put to a historical test. The rules of evidence listed here are intended to illustrate the principles of historical assessment invoked by Fellows, explicitly or implicitly, in their evaluation of the literary evidence about JB.

General Rules

G1   Canonical boundaries are irrelevant in assessing literary evidence insofar as *Scriptural texts* in themselves have no greater claim to historical accurancy than *non-Scriptural texts*.

G2 A distinction must be made between the number of *written texts* and the number of independent *sources* because some written texts are literarily dependent upon other texts as sources for their information.

G3 A text written later may be more accurate historically than a text written earlier particularly if the *later text* represents an *independent source* based on independent tradition.

G4 Sayings or actions reported in two or more *sources*, not two or more texts, have greater claim to some level of historical credibility than words or deeds singly attested.

G5 Similar content and themes in two or more *literary forms* have greater claims to some level of historical credibility than content and themes expressed only in one form.

G6 Sayings and actions, content and themes, must "fit" the *language and environment* in which they allegedly occurred to be considered historically credible.

G7 Data established as historically credible, including words and deeds, should be coherent and contribute to an *internally consistent* reconstruction of events.

G8 Beware of historical conclusions which are *congenial* to one's own theological, ideological, scholarly or personal interests!

Rules of Narration

N1 The narrator provides information unknown to the characters in the narrative but known to the reader.

N2 The narrator presupposes details given earlier in that narrative.

N3 Details that conflict with the overall narrative cannot have been invented by the narrator.

N4 Only words reported as directly quoted speech are eligible to be considered as the actual words of the speaker.

N5 Quoted speech that is entirely bound to its immediate narrative context is probably the product of the narrator, or some earlier storyteller.

Rules of Written Texts

W1 Sayings and stories are often clustered together to serve the purpose of the author.

W2 Narrative contexts for sayings and actions are often determined or created by the author.

W3 Chronology, or the sequence of events, is often revised or created by the author.

W4   Sayings and stories are often revised or created to fit the language, style, or viewpoint of the author.

W5   Sayings and stories often reflect, anachronistically, the struggle of the author and the early Christian community to interpret or adapt them to their own situation.

W6   Reports of events are sometimes revised, apologetically, to defend Jesus and his followers.

Rules of Oral Tradition

O1   Sayings and stories circulate independent of one another.

O2   The core or gist of sayings, not the exact words, and the action of stories, not the details of setting, are remembered and transmitted.

O3   Sayings and stories are interpreted and adapted to serve the interests of the teller and the early Christian community.

O4   Sayings are adapted to the phraseology and stories are accommodated to the themes of the Old Testament and common Jewish and hellenistic lore.

Selected bibliography

Aland, Kurt, Matthew Black, Carlo M. Martini, Bruce M. Metzger, and Allen Wikgren (eds.). *The Greek New Testament.* 3rd ed.; London-New York: United Bible Societies, 1975.

Betz, Otto. "Was John the Baptist an Essene?" *Bible Review* (Dec 1990): 18–25.

Borg, Marcus J. *Jesus A New Vision: Spirit, Culture, and the Life of Discipleship.* San Francisco: Harper & Row, 1987.

Bornkamm, Günther. *Jesus of Nazareth.* Translated by Irene and Fraser McLuskey with James M. Robinson. New York: Harper & Row, 1960.

Brown, Raymond E. *The Birth of the Messiah: A Commentary on the Infancy Narratives in Matthew and Luke.* Garden City, NY: Doubleday, 1977.

Crossan, Dominic. *The Historical Jesus: The Life of a Mediterranean Jewish Peasant.* HarperSan Francisco, 1991.

_____. *Sayings Parallel: A Workbook for the Jesus Tradition.* Philadelphia: Fortress, 1985.

Enslin, Morton S. *Christian Beginnings.* New York: Harper & Row, 1938.

_____."Once Again, John the Baptist," *Religion in Life* 27 (1957–58): 557–66.

_____. *The Prophet from Nazareth.* New York: McGraw-Hill, 1961.

Ernst, Josef. *Johannes der Täufer: Interpretation-Geschichte–Wirkungsgeschichte.* Berlin-New York: Walter de Gruyter, 1989.

Fitzmyer, Joseph A. *The Gospel According to Luke.* 2 vols. Garden City, NY: Doubleday, 1981, 1985.

Ford, J. Massyngberde. *Revelation.* Anchor Bible; Garden City, NY: Doubleday, 1975.

Funk, Robert W., with Mahlon H. Smith. *The Gospel of Mark: Red Letter Edition.* Sonoma, CA: Polebridge, 1991.

Funk, Robert W., Roy W. Hoover, and the Jesus Seminar. *The Five Gospels. The Search for the Authentic Words of Jesus.* New York: Macmillan, 1993.

Funk, Robert, Bernard Brandon Scott, and James R. Butts. *The Parables of Jesus: Red Letter Edition.* Sonoma, CA: Polebridge, 1988.

Hollenbach, Paul. "Social Aspects of John the Baptist's Preaching Mission in the Context of Palestinian Judaism," In *Aufstieg und Niedergang der römischen*

Welt 2.19.1. Ed. H. Temporini and W. Haase. Berlin: Walter de Gruyter, 1979: 850–75.

———. "The Conversion of Jesus: From Jesus the Baptizer to Jesus the Healer." In *Aufstieg und Niedergang der römischen Welt*. 2.25.1. Ed. H. Temporini and W. Haase. Berlin: Walter de Gruyter, 1982: 196–219.

Hutchens, Charles Lee. "John the Baptist and the Elijah Motif in the Synoptic Gospels." Th.M. thesis. Southeastern Baptist Theological Seminary. Wake Forest, NC, 1980.

Kraeling, Carl H. *John the Baptist*. New York-London: Charles Scribner's Sons, 1951.

Metzger, Bruce M. *A Textual Commentary on the Greek New Testament*. London-New York: United Bible Societies, 1971.

Metzger, Bruce M., Robert C. Dentan, and Walter Harrelson. *The Making of the New Revised Standard Version*. William B. Eerdmans: Grand Rapids, 1991.

Miller, Robert J. (ed.). *The Complete Gospels: Annotated Scholars Version*. Sonoma, CA: Polebridge, 1992.

Murphy-O'Connor, Jerome. "John the Baptist and Jesus: History and Hypothesis," *New Testament Studies* 36 (1990): 359–374.

Reimarus, Hermann Samuel. *Fragments*. Lives of Jesus Series. Edited by Charles H. Talbert and translated by Ralph S. Fraser. Philadelphia: Fortress, 1972.

Renan, Ernst, *The Life of Jesus*. Modern Library. New York: Random House, 1927, 1955.

Reumann, John. "The Quest for the Historical Baptist." In *Understanding the Sacred Text: Essays in Honor of Morton S. Enslin*. Edited by John Reumann. Valley Forge, PA: Judson Press, 1972: 181–99.

Robinson, J.A.T. "The Baptism of Jesus and the Qumran Community: Testing a Hypothesis," *Harvard Theological Review* 50 (1957): 175–191.

———. "Elijah, John, and Jesus: An Essay in Detection," *New Testament Studies* 4 (1957–58): 263–281.

Sanders, E. P. *Jesus and Judaism*. Philadelphia: Fortress, 1985.

Schweitzer, Albert. *The Quest of the Historical Jesus*. Translated by W. Montgomery. New York: Macmillan, 1968.

Scobie, Charles H. H. *John the Baptist*. Philadelphia: Fortress, 1964.

Strauss, David Friedrich. *Life of Jesus Critically Examined*. Lives of Jesus Series. Edited by Peter C. Hodgson and translated by George Eliot. Philadelphia: Fortress, 1972.

Webb, Robert L. *John the Baptizer and Prophet: A Socio-Historical Study*. JSNT SS 62; Sheffield: JSOT Press, 1991.

Wink, Walter. *John the Baptist in the Gospel Tradition*. SNTS MS 7; Cambridge: University Press, 1968.

Winter, Paul. "The Cultural Background for the Narratives in Luke I-II," *Jewish Quarterly Review* 45 (1954): 159–67, 230–42, 287.

———. "The Proto-Source of Luke 1," *Novum Testamentum* 1 (1956): 184–99.